Cross-Cultural Encounters in Joseph Conrad's
Malay Fiction

Cross-Cultural Encounters in Joseph Conrad's Malay Fiction

Robert Hampson
Professor of Modern Literature
Royal Holloway
University of London

palgrave

First published 2000 by
PALGRAVE
Houndmills, Basingstoke, Hampshire RG21 6XS and
175 Fifth Avenue, New York, N.Y. 10010
Companies and representatives throughout the world

PALGRAVE is the new global academic imprint of
St. Martin's Press LLC Scholarly and Reference Division and
Palgrave Publishers Ltd (formerly Macmillan Press Ltd).

Outside North America
ISBN 0–333–71405–9

In North America
ISBN 0–312–23528–3

This book is printed on paper suitable for recycling and made from fully managed and sustained forest sources.

A catalogue record for this book is available from the British Library.

Library of Congress Cataloging-in-Publication Data
Hampson, R. G.
    Cross-cultural encounters in Joseph Conrad's Malay fiction / Robert Hampson.
        p. cm.
    Includes bibliographical references and index.
    ISBN 0–312–23528–3
    1. Conrad, Joseph, 1857–1924—Knowledge—Malaysia. 2. Literature and anthropology—Malaysia—History—20th century. 3. Culture shock in literature. 4. Multiculturalism in literature. 5. Ethnicity in literature. 6. Malaysia—In literature. I. Title.
    PR6005.O4 Z74185 2000
    823'.912—dc21

                                                                    00–031119

10   9   8   7   6   5   4   3   2   1
09 08 07 06 05 04 03 02 01 00

Printed and bound in Great Britain by
Antony Row██████████████████

For Cedric Watts
with respect and gratitude

Contents

After some time there arrived a Frangi vessel from Goa, to trade at Malaca, and observed that Malaca was a very fine and beautiful country, and well regulated. All the people of Malaca came crowding to see the appearance of the Frangis, and they were greatly surprised as they had not been accustomed to see the Frangi figure; and they said, 'Why these are white Bengalis;' and about every one of the Frangis the Malaca men were crowding by tens to view them, twisting their beards, and clapping their heads, and taking off their hats, and laying hold of their hands. The capitan then went to the bandahara Sri Maha Raja, and the bandahara adopted him as his son; and the capitan presented the bandahara with two hundred chains of gold set with gems of extreme beauty, and Manilla workmanship, and he threw it over the neck of the bandahara. The people present were going to be in a passion with that Frangi, but the bandahara would not let them, saying 'Do not mal-treat people who are ignorant of the language;' so kind was he to them, and the capitan adopted the bandahara as his father.

Sejarah Melayu

Acknowledgements

I owe a special debt of thanks to Dr Douglas Kerr and Dr Elaine Ho of the University of Hong Kong, since this project was initiated by their kind invitation to take part in a panel on 'Literature and Colonialism' at the 34th International Congress of Asian and North African Studies in Hong Kong in 1993. I am also indebted to Dr Zawiah Yahya and Dr Fedillah Merican of the Universiti Kebangsaan Malaysia, whose response to my Hong Kong paper encouraged me to proceed and whose invitation to take part in the 'Ethnocentric Perspectives in Literature' Conference in Kuala Lumpur in 1994 prompted further thoughts on Malaysia. I am particularly indebted to my colleague, Professor Andrew Gibson, who first introduced me to the South China Seas, for his consistent encouragement in this project.

I am grateful to the Academia Sinica and the Taiwanese Society for English and American Literature, who sponsored my 1997 visit to Taiwan. Early versions of some chapters gained from exposure to seminar discussion at the Institute of European and American Studies, Academia Sinica, and at the National Sun Yat-sen University, Kaohsiung. I am particularly grateful to Professor Lee Yu-Cheng of Academia Sinica, who arranged a return visit to Taiwan in 1998, when further versions of chapters were tried out at the Chung-Hsing University in Taichung and at the conference, 'Arts, Literature and the Ocean', at the National Sun Yat-sen University. I am also grateful to Dr Hsin-fa Wu at the Chung-Hsing University and Dr Chung Ling at the National Sun Yat-sen University. Other parts of this book have been aired at research seminars at the University of Birmingham; the University of Hong Kong; the University of London Institute for English Studies; the University of Oxford; the Interdisciplinary Research Seminar in the Drama Department at Royal Holloway; and the Asia and Middle East Seminar organised by the History Department at Royal Holloway; as well as at the conference 'Islands: Histories and Representations' at the University of Kent at Canterbury. I am indebted to the organisers of these seminars and conferences for their invitations and to the participants for their observations. I am particularly grateful to Dr Andrzej Gasiorek (Birmingham); Dr Geoff Gilbert (Cambridge); Dr Rachel Potter (Queen Mary and Westfield); Dr Trudi

Tate (Cambridge); Dr Kate Flint (Oxford); Dr Susan Jones (Oxford); Professor Robert Young (Oxford); Professor Jacky Bratton (Royal Holloway); Professor Tony Stockwell (Royal Holloway); Dr Rod Edmond (Kent); Dr Vanessa Smith (University of Sydney) and Dr Bill Watson (Kent).

I am deeply indebted to Professor Tony Stockwell (Royal Holloway) and Dr Philip Holden (Nanyang Technological University, Singapore) for their generous advice on material and resources relating to Sir Hugh Clifford; to Dr Sara Salih (Oxford) and Eliane Glaser (Birkbeck) for their advice and encouragement in relation to the early chapters; and to my research students, Sobhana Kumaran (Universiti Sains Malaysia) and Dr Teng Hong-shu (Feng Chia University), for their years of intellectual companionship and stimulation – this project has grown in dialogue with theirs.

I have also benefited greatly from the generosity of numerous individual members of the international Conrad community: in particular, Dr Linda Dryden (Napier University), Dr Anthony Fothergill (University of Exeter), and Dr Andrew Michael Roberts (University of Dundee), who have all drawn my attention to relevant materials during the course of my research; Dr Keith Carabine (University of Kent); Dr Owen Knowles (University of Hull); and Professor Cedric Watts (University of Sussex).

The project would have been impossible without the kindness and patience of the librarians at the British Library; the University of London Library; the Royal Holloway College Library; the National University of Singapore; the Universiti Malaysia Library; and the Arkib Negara in Kuala Lumpur. I am grateful to the British Academy who funded my research trip to Malaysia and Singapore; to Royal Holloway College who provided the generous research leave which made the writing of this book possible; to my colleagues Dr Jerry Brotton, Professor Denis Cosgrove, Dr Robert Eaglestone, and Professor Kiernan Ryan, who offered advice at various stages; and to Dr Martin Dzelzainis, Professor Andrew Gibson, Dr Judith Hawley, and Hans van Marle, who read and commented on particular chapters. Finally, I am beyond measure grateful to Dr Gerlinde Roder-Bolton (University of Surrey) who read and commented on the entire manuscript.

All errors, misunderstandings, and resistance to good advice remain my own responsibility.

Abbreviations

Except where otherwise noted, citations from the works of Joseph Conrad are from Dent's Uniform Edition (London: J. M. Dent & Sons, 1923–28). This has the same pagination as the Dent Collected Edition (London: J. M. Dent & Sons, 1946–55) and the World's Classics edition (Oxford: Oxford University Press, 1983–). The following abbreviations are used to refer to the volumes published in the Dent Uniform Edition:

AF	*Almayer's Folly*
TU	*Tales of Unrest*
OI	*An Outcast of the Islands*
NN	*The Nigger of the 'Narcissus'*
Ty	*Typhoon*
LJ	*Lord Jim*
Y	*Youth, and two other stories*
No	*Nostromo*
SA	*The Secret Agent*
MS	*The Mirror of the Sea*
PR	*A Personal Record*
TLS	*'Twixt Land and Sea*
SL	*The Shadow-Line*
WT	*Within the Tides*
V	*Victory*
Re	*The Rescue*
NLL	*Notes on Life and Letters*
Ro	*The Rover*
TH	*Tales of Hearsay*

In addition, the following abbreviations are used for frequently-cited works related to Conrad:

LE	Joseph Conrad, *Last Essays* (London: J. M. Dent, 1926).
LL	G. Jean-Aubry (ed.), *Joseph Conrad: Life and Letters*, 2 vols (London: Heinemann, 1927).
LRBCG	C. T. Watts (ed.), *Joseph Conrad's Letters to R. B. Cunninghame Graham* (Cambridge: Cambridge University Press, 1969).

CL Frederick R. Karl and Laurence Davies (eds), *The Collected Letters of Joseph Conrad* (Cambridge: Cambridge University Press): Volume 1, 1861–1897 (1983); Volume 2, 1898–1902 (1986); Volume 3, 1903–1907 (1988); Volume 4, 1908–1911 (1991); Volume 5, 1912–1916 (1996).

Introduction

From his first novel, *Almayer's Folly*, through to *The Rescue* near the end of his career, Malaysia had an important place in Conrad's fiction. Indeed, Conrad's writing career sprang directly from his experiences of the region as a sailor and the stories he heard there. However, in this career-long writing of Malaysia, Conrad also drew on a textual tradition that included the scientific work of A. R. Wallace as well as writings by and about the White Rajah of Sarawak, Sir James Brooke. Conrad enters into this textual tradition when both the scientific project and the imperialist project had become problematic. Furthermore, in his own writing, Conrad repeatedly confronts the issue that was to become so important in twentieth-century anthropology: how to describe another culture. As the book that follows shows, Conrad's writing of Malaysia from the start engaged consciously with this problem of representation, and, from 'Karain' onwards, this problem becomes a self-conscious part of his fiction: this is not just a matter of the self-reflexive use of the traditions of adventure romance as in *Lord Jim*, but it also manifests itself in the fiction's foregrounding of writing, reading, and the production of narrative in its presentation of cross-cultural encounters.

This introductory chapter will begin with the critical reception of *Almayer's Folly* and some indications of the context, both literary and political, in which Conrad's Borneo fiction appeared. When Conrad sets his first novel in Borneo, Borneo already had certain associations in contemporary culture. Similarly, when Conrad draws on material relating to Sir James Brooke, he is not using an esoteric figure, but rather someone who, like Captain Cook, already had a place in the popular imagination. Indeed, both men were mythicised as imperial heroes. Conrad's fictional appropriation of Borneo also coincides with important developments in England's relations with Borneo and other parts of Malaysia. This chapter then recounts Conrad's own experience of different parts of Malaysia. It considers the implications of the terms 'Malaysia', 'Malaya', and 'Malay' and maps out the 'Malaysia' of Conrad's fiction. This mapping of 'Malaysia' will lead in turn to a brief consideration of navigation and cartography. The development of a universal system of latitude and longitude (and the means of determining both) was vital for the European exploration of Malaysia. This universal system also provides a paradigm for the Enlightenment project of knowledge. Chapter 2 traces the textual tradition of 'writing Malaysia' back through an eighteenth-century nexus of learned societies and East India Company officers to Francis Bacon and Renaissance voyages in an attempt to delineate the discursive formation which produced this tradition. When Conrad joined the British Merchant Navy, this was the culture into which he was initiated: a culture with specific writing practices and a particular privileging of observation ('the clear vision of a seaman able to master quickly the aspects of a strange land').[1] The book that follows represents a post-colonial project focused on the 'writing of Malaysia' as well as an exploration of Conrad's Malay fiction, with its concerns with 'race', gender, and identity, that opens onto post-modern theory.

The Annexation of Borneo

Arthur Waugh began his review of Conrad's first novel, *Almayer's Folly*, by noting that 'Borneo, a tract hitherto untouched by the novelist' had now been 'annexed by Mr. Joseph Conrad'.[2] In an earlier essay, Waugh had already associated 'new ideas' in literature with 'the discovery of new countries' and 'the acquisition of territory and knowledge'.[3] Waugh's repetition of this trope might have been prompted by Fisher Unwin's pre-publication publicity. The *Daily News* (25 April 1895) announced: 'No novelist has yet annexed the island of Borneo – in itself almost a continent. But Mr Joseph Conrad, a new writer, is about to make the attempt in a novel entitled *Almayer's Folly*'.[4] Other reviews also emphasised, either in praise or criticism, Conrad's choice of location: the *Spectator*, for example, hailed Conrad as 'the Kipling of the Malay Archipelago'; the *Nation*, by contrast, complained that 'Borneo is a fine field for the study of monkeys, not men'.[5] Generally, Conrad was seen as providing 'pictures of Malay life': one reviewer asks that Conrad might now produce 'a sketch of the Straits Settlements'; another suggested that Nina was 'a fine illustration of what may happen to the Malay in the transition which Mr Swettenham sees is imminent'.[6] For all these reviewers fiction was clearly a form of knowledge aligned with the imperialist project of occupation and exploitation. Indeed, Conrad himself was later to assert that writing a novel was 'an enterprise as much as the conquest of a colony'.[7]

As the last reviewer's comment suggests, Frank Swettenham (in the same year as *Almayer's Folly*) had also made an approach to the literary annexation of Malaysia. In his Preface to *Malay Sketches* (1895), he describes his book as 'an attempt to awaken an interest in an almost undescribed but deeply interesting people' (vii). His Introduction invokes 'a land of eternal summer' and recalls 'that Golden Peninsula, 'twixt Hindustan and Far Cathay, from whence the early navigators brought back such wondrous stories of adventure' (ix). The Malays of the Peninsula might be an 'undescribed' people, but Malaysia itself was far from being an 'undescribed' land. Swettenham's own words bear the trace of a European textual tradition that begins with Ptolemy's reference to the 'Golden Khersones' in his *Geography* and continues through those 'wondrous stories of adventure'. If Swettenham's Introduction invokes this textual tradition in relation to Malaysia, it ends, however, with a very different prospect:

> Soon the irresistible Juggernaut of Progress will have penetrated to your remotest fortress, slain your beasts, cut down your forests, 'civilised' your people, clothed them in strange garments, and stamped them with the seal of a higher morality. (x)

In this temporal perspective, the present becomes 'the moment of transition', and these 'sketches' present themselves as recording 'the Malay as he is' (xi), before he must either 'disappear or conform to the views of a stronger will and a higher intelligence'.[8]

As D. J. M. Tate has shown, Borneo itself had already been annexed for the popular imagination long before the publication of *Almayer's Folly*.[9] The *Illustrated London News*, for example, had put into circulation a very specific image of Borneo.[10] Thus, as Tate puts it, while Singapore was the 'fulcrum of British imperial power in the region' in the nineteenth century, Borneo 'with its headhunters, pirates, ... and *orang utan*, and above all the romantic figure of James Brooke' was granted 'much more space in the columns of the *Illustrated London News*' (RBB, 1).[11] The founding of the *Illustrated London News* in 1842 coincided with the start of Brooke's 'war against the pirates'. ILN (29 November 1845) carried an article 'Gallant Defeat of Malay Pirates on the Coast of Borneo', which provided a detailed and uncritical account of the attack on Sherif Osman, 'a well known daring Arab pirate', whose 'terrible piracies have paralysed the commerce of the seas around the northern portion of Borneo'. The report ended with a piece of advice which no doubt reflected the deepest wishes of Brooke's supporters:

> Nothing short of a European settlement, with a garrison and one or two small steam-vessels of war *permanently on the coast*, will effectually drive the pirates from their present haunts.

ILN (10 November 1849) carried a lengthy report on the Battle of Beting Marau, the last of four campaigns by Brooke and the Navy, responding to a resurgence of Iban and Malay activity in the Batang Lupar basin. B. Urban Vigors's report and illustrations provided a triumphalist, partisan account of how the Navy had inflicted 'a lesson which will be remembered on the coast for ages': 'we destroyed the fortified towns and crippled the resources of several other tribes'.[12] 'Lanun and Suloo pirates' (ILN, 17 January 1852), a report of the attack on the *Dolphin* and the beheading of Robert Burns, the namesake and grandson of the poet, although it made no reference to Brooke, clearly fell into the same pattern: the death was presented as an instance of unmotivated savagery and re-inforced the association of Borneo with piracy.[13]

The establishment of the new colony of Labuan off the north-west coast of Borneo in 1846 led to reflections on Brooke's achievements. An article in ILN (9 October 1847), on Brooke's arrival in Southampton, celebrated the establishment of the new colony 'destined soon to become the site of a great commercial emporium' which would rival Singapore. It praised Brooke as 'the most distinguished' of a group of Englishmen, who, 'sharing the views and inheriting the enterprising spirit of Sir Stamford Raffles', had settled in the archipelago 'and begun to instruct the natives in the means of developing the resources of their country'. 'Bruni' (ILN, 27 June 1857) similarly recalled how Brooke was 'necessitated to interfere in certain differences at Sarawak':

> The Rajahs who preceded Sir James Brooke, perceiving the wealth which [antimony] would produce, compelled the Dyaks to become their slaves in working the mines. This cruel policy led first to a dispute, and then to an insurrection. Rajah Brooke interceded and defended their cause.[14]

The ILN obituary for Brooke (4 July 1868) took a similar line: it noted how 'the new English rajah' began his reign in 1841 'with the good will of all his native subjects, whose welfare he carefully studied to promote'. The ILN helped give currency to the image of Brooke as a Victorian hero.[15] This was helped by the books by Keppel and Mundy, and particularly by the much reproduced portrait of Brooke by Grant.[16] Brooke's role as a 'White Rajah' carried the easily-decoded message of white superiority.[17] It satisfied fantasies of power (as in Kipling's 'The Man Who Would be King' or Haggard's *King Solomon's Mines*), while the myth created about him in reports like the above also disguised that fantasy of power with the reassurance that the English imperialist was not only working for the welfare of the people he annexed but also with their good will.

Conrad's annexation of Borneo for fiction, in other words, can be seen to replicate Brooke's literal annexation of Sarawak and the later annexation of Labuan. It also coincided with renewed British interest in extending its control over Malaysia. The British colonial period begins in 1786 with the acquisition of Penang. Malacca, Penang and Singapore were subsequently united under Crown control as the Straits Settlements. In 1896, Perak, Selangor, Negri Sembilan and Pahang became the Federation of Malay States. Subsequently, Perlis, Keddah, Kelantan, Terengganu and Johore became the Unfederated Malay States.[18] At the same time, Conrad's annexation of this territory was not uncontested. In September 1898, the *Singapore Free Press* published a pseudonymous article by its regular book reviewer, Hugh Clifford, 'Mr Joseph Conrad at Home and Abroad'. The article very forcefully asserted the strengths and limitations of metropolitan criticism:

> With all that the English critics said in praise of Mr Conrad's system, of his power of description, of his knowledge of the aspects of the land in which he set his characters moving, everyone who has the gift of appreciation must agree cordially. It is when the critics leave their own province, and begin to discuss the truth of Mr Conrad's personages that we dwellers in Malayan lands find reason to differ from them.

Metropolitan 'truth' is challenged by this voice from the periphery. The article then uses this distinction as the basis for a devastating attack on Conrad for his 'complete ignorance of Malays and their habits and customs'. It concludes: 'Mr Conrad's Malays are only creatures of Mr Conrad, very vividly described, very powerfully drawn, but not Malays'. In a letter to William Blackwood (13 Dec 1898), Conrad commented defensively on this article: 'Well I never did set up as an authority on Malaysia'.[19]

Conrad and the Malay Archipelago

Although Conrad's experience of Malaysia was very limited, his Malay fiction spans almost his entire writing career from *Almayer's Folly* (1895) to *The Rescue* (1920). Lloyd Fernando notes that Conrad did not have 'an intimate knowledge of Malaysian life':

> He certainly had no intimate Malay friends, and his acquaintance-ship with other Malaysians does not appear to have extended significantly beyond shipping clerks, waiters in colonial-style hotels, and other persons whom a visitor or seaman will encounter of necessity during his travels.[20]

Accordingly, the eastern world of Conrad's fiction 'falls within the expatriate round of hotels, other expatriate acquaintances, shore gossip, books by other expatriates, some of them distinguished in colonial history, and a skillful seaman's knowledge of certain harbours, bays, rivers, creeks, and shores' (LF,53). Nevertheless, 'what he lacked in intimate knowledge', he made up for 'by way of prodigiously sensitive understanding' (LF54). Fernando, in other words, represents a variation on Hugh Clifford's early criticism of Conrad's Malay fictions: that they are of interest, not for what they reveal about 'Asiatics', but because 'they represent the impression scored by Asiatics upon a sensitive, imaginative, European mind'.[21] More importantly, Fernando also suggests that the Malay archipelago provided Conrad with a means of expressing his own expatriate experience.

Conrad's first contact with the archipelago came in 1883. In September 1881, he signed on as second mate of the barque *Palestine* bound for Bangkok with a cargo of coal. After extensive delays, the *Palestine* reached Bankga Strait, off Sumatra, in March 1883, where the coal spontaneously combusted and the crew had to abandon ship. They took to the boats and rowed to Muntok on Bangka Island. The officers and crew were taken on to Singapore (on 21 March) for a Marine Court of Inquiry, and Conrad stayed on in Singapore until mid-April before returning to London.

Conrad subsequently used this experience for his short story 'Youth', which records the narrator's first encounter with 'the East'. Immediately after the explosion on the *Judea*, the narrator recounts his first experience of Malay seamen, the crew of a boat from a passing steamer: 'I've known them since, but what struck me then was their unconcern ... I thought people who had been blown up deserved more attention'.[22] This encounter of the experiencing, verbalising European and the impassive Malay sets the tone for the narrator's first experience of an 'Eastern'port. This 'arrival scene' is very carefully staged.[23] Part of that staging is through the tropes of seeing and speaking, where what is important, of course, is who sees and who speaks. The narrator's triumphant 'And this is how I see the East' (Y, 37) foregrounds the imperial gaze and the homogenised 'East' as spectacle. However, what he actually experiences in this arrival by night is only 'the scented obscurity of the shore' (Y, 37): 'There was not a light, not a stir, not a sound' (Y, 38). Despite the East's withholding of itself from his gaze, the narrator nevertheless describes his younger self as 'exulting like a conqueror' (Y, 38). This sense of triumph is challenged and problematised as the narrative proceeds. His first encounter in the port is with another European: as he approaches a steamer anchored there, he registers that 'the East spoke to me, but it was in a Western voice' (Y, 39). In fact, the voice 'raged aloud in two languages', directing its fury at what it takes to be 'a shore-boat' (Y, 39). The conqueror's silent triumph over an unseen landscape is replaced by this vituperative assertion of Western power over a still-unseen people, in a locutionary act which, through mistaken identity, interpellates the narrator as the colonial subject produced by the European colonial presence. At the same time, this 'Western voice' is itself divided, hybrid-ised. Indeed, as GoGwilt argues, this dual utterance figures an always already divided and hybridised 'Western' identity, constructed as it is through a foundational identification with an 'Eastern' religion.[24] The young man is momentarily silenced in the face of this aggressive address. His escape is marked by a shift back from the voice (and the problematics of the 'Western voice') to vision (and the security of the scopic regime). The episode ends with the narrator awakening from sleep to find himself the object of the Malay gaze:

> And then I saw the men of the East – they were looking at me. The whole length of the jetty was full of people. I saw brown, bronze, yellow faces, the black eyes, the glitter, the colour of an Eastern crowd. ... This was the East of the ancient navigators, so old, so mysterious, resplendent and sombre, living and unchanged, full of danger and promise. And these were the men. (Y, 40–1.)

The East continues to withhold its voice, so the opposition of language-producing European and impassive Malay is maintained. However, the direction of the gaze has been reversed: instead of the imperial 'how I see the East', this paragraph begins by noting that the 'men of the East' were 'looking at me' and goes on to describe the sleeping forms of his companions as the objects of this gaze.[25] More accurately, if his sleeping companions are the objects of the Malay gaze, the narrator himself, of course, sees this seeing. The paragraph begins with an interactive moment that briefly glimpses Asian agency and the possibility of reciprocity. However, the narrator's gaze immediately reduces these 'men of the East' to the trope of 'the Eastern crowd'.[26] His gaze now scopes the hitherto invisible landscape, and reads 'the fronds of palms' and 'the brown roofs of hidden houses' as constituting 'the East of the ancient navigators'. The East now becomes a 'mysterious' location which he knows on first glance to be, paradoxically, both 'living and unchanged'. The anxious moment of anti-conquest is countered by a sequence of mastering manoeuvres: the de-individualising trope of the crowd; the invocation of heroic European enterprise; the de-historicising of the location and its simultaneous appropriation for European fantasy and desire.[27] Marlow's final reflection significantly reasserts the implicit opposition between 'the brown nations' and 'the conquering race' (Y, 41–2). Nevertheless, the passage as a whole, alongside this enactment of European evasive manoeuvres, also briefly registers the fact of Asian agency and contains possibilities of critical self-questioning, both of which remain important features of Conrad's writing of Malaysia.

In February 1887, Conrad signed on as first mate of the *Highland Forest* in Amsterdam bound for Java.[28] Apparently because of a back injury caused by a falling spar, he signed off in Samarang on 1 July and went on to the European Hospital in Singapore. Conrad clearly drew on this experience for the hospitalisation of Jim, which precedes Jim's taking a post on the *Patna*. G. J. Resink also suggests that Conrad might have used his time in Singapore, 'either in the hospital or in the Raffles Library', to 'read or re-read' books by 'those other authors before him' who had 'come to look upon the Indonesian Archipelago with different if also Western eyes'.[29] In August 1887, after a brief period in the Singapore Hospital, Conrad signed on as mate with the *Vidar*, a steamship based in Singapore, which made a regular three-week circuit through the Malay Archipelago to Celebes and Borneo. Jerry Allen describes the *Vidar*'s round trip as follows:

> Leaving Singapore, she sailed through Carimata Strait, called at Bandjermasin on the south coast of Borneo, cruised up Pulo Laut Strait, stopping at the coaling station of Kota Baru on the island of Pulo Laut, crossed Macassar Strait to Donggala on Celebes, recrossed

the Strait to Samarinda in the Kutai or Coti district of Borneo, rounded Point Mangkalihat as she moved along Borneo's east coast to the Berau River, steamed slowly up that unpredictable stream to the settlement of Berau ... came down the river, passed Tandjung Batu on the Bornean coast as she headed north for her last outward call, the Bulungan River and its upstream settlement of Bulungan or Tandjung Selor. The return to Singapore was over the same route, though the ship's calls ... varied ... [30]

This resembles Captain Whalley's 'monotonous huckster's round, up and down the Straits' in 'The End of the Tether':

> Malacca to begin with, in at daylight and out at dusk ... At noon the three palms of the next place of call, up a sluggish river ... And so on, in and out, picking up coastwise cargo here and there, and finishing with a hundred miles' steady steaming through the maze of an archipelago of small islands up to a large native town at the end of the beat. (Y, 166–7)

Conrad himself made four trips and signed off in January 1888. After signing off the *Vidar*, Conrad lodged at the Sailors' Home in Singapore, and during this period he gained his only permanent command: the *Otago*, which was waiting in Bangkok, after the death of its captain. His fourteen-month captaincy of the *Otago* provided the basis for later short stories such as *The Shadow-Line*, 'A Smile of Fortune' and 'The Secret Sharer'.

Singapore was probably the place in the region best known to Conrad. The quayside area features in *Lord Jim*, 'The End of the Tether', *The Shadow-Line*, 'A Smile of Fortune' and 'The Secret Sharer'. Indeed, as Norman Sherry has demonstrated, 'The End of the Tether' makes extended reference to the topography of 'the Singapore of the 1880s'.[31] Captain Whalley's walk through the quayside area of Singapore covers the area from the Harbour Office towards the Officers' Sailors' Home, which recurs in Conrad's fiction. It takes in the Post Office ('the most important post-office in the East') on Collyer Quay; the Chinese shops on the west side of the river; the tramway (introduced in 1885); the Cavenagh Bridge (built 1868) across the Singapore river; the government offices and the Esplanade on the east bank; and St Andrew's Cathedral at the end of the Esplanade. 'The End of the Tether' also contains a picture of the hybrid crews with which Conrad would have been familiar: the European captain, mate and engineer; the Chinese carpenter, firemen and stewards; the Malay crewmen. The most important of the Malays is the Serang, with whom Captain Whalley has a symbiotic relationship: he is the 'pilot fish' to Captain Whalley's whale; he is, in effect, Captain Whalley's eyes. 'The End of the Tether', however, offers more than just the topography of the Singapore quayside and this microcosm of the ship; it also shows how Conrad constantly works to provide temporal depth to his representation. Conrad's representation of the Malay world is almost always historically situated.[32] Thus, for example, the Serang is traced back fifty years to the 'jungle village' of his birth (Y, 228), while Whalley's long career at sea permits an extended temporal perspective. As Sherry notes, Whalley's reverie, as he walks through Singapore, takes him back to his first memories of the colony, when there were just 'muddy shores, a harbour without quays' and 'the one solitary wooden pier' (Y, 194). His sight of the Governor's carriage passing along the Esplanade prompts him to a comparison of the present Governor, 'Sir Frederick' (i.e. Sir Frederick Weld), with the first Governor Whalley had known there, 'Denham' (i.e. Samuel George Bonham).[33] Whalley's temporal perspective takes in Denham despatching the *Dido*, the ship commanded by Keppel in the 1840s' 'war against the pirates', to look in on a new trading enterprise Whalley had proposed 'with a distant part of the Archipelago' (Y, 193) through to the opening of the Suez Canal in 1871 and its impact on the region ('new ships, new men, new methods of trade' (Y, 168) – including, in particular, competition from German steamers (Y, 205). His career runs from the days when he had 'been the pioneer of new routes and new trades', steering across 'the unsurveyed tracts of the South Seas' (Y, 167) through to the modern world of the 'cable tramway' (Y, 182) and the 'telegraph cable' (Y, 212). The narrative supplements this temporal range: on the one hand, the 'reef-infested region' around Pangu is used to recall 'that day, four hundred years ago, when first beheld by Western eyes from the deck of a high-pooped caravel' (Y, 242); on the other, it looks forward to the time when Van Wyck's Rajah, who hoped he would die before the white men were ready to take his country from him', has been displaced by 'a first-class Resident' and Batu Beru has become 'the centre of a prosperous tobacco-growing district' (Y, 277).

It was during his voyages on board the steamship *Vidar* that Conrad acquired the impressions and experiences upon which he was to draw in a large number of his novels and stories. He started work on the first of these, *Almayer's Folly*, when he returned to London in 1889. In *A Personal Record*, he describes how he started to write the novel and his memories of Charles Olmeijer:

I had seen him for the first time some four years before from the bridge of a steamer moored to a rickety little wharf forty miles up, more or less, a Bornean river. ... He stepped upon the jetty. He was clad simply in flapping pyjamas of cretonne pattern (enormous flowers with yellow petal on a disagreeable blue ground) and a thin cotton singlet with short sleeves. ... I had heard of him at Singapore; I had heard of him on board ... I had heard of him in a place called Pulo Laut ... I had heard of him in a place called Dongala, in the Island of Celebes, when the Rajah of that little-known sea-port ... came on board in a friendly way with only two attendants, and drank bottle after bottle of soda-water on the after-skylight with my good friend and commander Captain C–. (PR, 74–5)

Almayer's Folly was published in April 1895. His second novel, *An Outcast of the Islands*, was begun in August 1894 and published in March 1896. *The Rescue* (in effect, the third volume of a Malay trilogy) was started in March 1896, although it was not published in book form until May 1920.[34] As Hans van Marle has noted, the nucleus of *The Rescue* is present as a rumour in the earlier novel:

After his first – and successful – fight with the sea robbers, when he rescued, as rumour had it, the yacht of some big wig from home, somewhere down Carimata way, his great popularity began. (OI, 14)[35]

The basis for the story of the stranded yacht was the stranding of the French brig *Amitie* in 1866 and the attack made upon it by 'some vagabonds belonging to a certain Haji Saman'.[36] This was a story Conrad claimed to have heard 'from the captain of the brig' (CLI, 382). The basis for the story of Lingard's involvement with Hassim and Immada was 'an Englishman called Wyndham', who (according to Conrad) 'financed a very lively row in Celebes' in 1850 or 1851. *The Rescue* thus has its roots in rumour and hearsay, the storytelling of the archipelago. Conrad stopped work on the novel in 1899 and did not complete it until some twenty years later.

The Rescue is part of the two (otherwise distinct) phases of Conrad's fictional engagement with Malaysia: the early Malay fiction and the imaginative return to the archipelago after the refreshing of Conrad's Malayan memories by the visit of Carlos Marris in September 1909. Marris was the master and owner of the *Araby Maid*, an island trader. He had been living in Malaysia for over twenty years, and had sailed with Lingard's nephew, Joshua Lingard, on the *Rajah Laut*. He had also been captain of the *Vidar* long after Conrad's time. Marris had come to England in June 1909 for medical treatment after a stroke. He wrote to Conrad on 18 July 1909 to thank him, on behalf of 'the few surviving old hands', for 'giving us such a book as the "Mirror of the Sea"'.[37] The letter records the circulation of Conrad's fiction in the archipelago; the changes in the sea-life of the archipelago since Conrad's time; and Marris's own career (including gun-running to the Achinese).[38] Marris wrote again on 6 September 1909 to announce his departure on 14 September.[39] Conrad invited him to spend the day before his departure with him.[40] He described the effect of Marris's visit in a letter to his agent Pinker:

> It was like the raising of a lot of dead – dead to me, because most of them live out there and even read my books and wonder who [the] devil has been around taking notes ... the best of it is that all these men of 22 years ago feel kindly to the Chronicler of their lives and adventures. They shall have some more of the stories they like.[41]

The first fruits of the visit were 'The Secret Sharer' and 'Freya of the Seven Isles'.[42] *Victory*, 'The Planter of Malata' and 'Because of the Dollars' are clearly derived from the same imaginative vein.[43] For *The Rescue*, however, imagination was supplemented with further reading.[44] In particular, Conrad's 1914 reading of *My Life in Sarawak*, the autobiography written by Margaret Brooke, the Ranee of Sarawak, enabled him to return to the manuscript of *The Rescue*: if Brooke was a prototype for Lingard, the confrontation of '"a proud and cultivated young Englishwoman and the alien, exotic and primitive world of the Malay Archipelago," the subject of the ranee's autobiography, was also at the heart of Conrad's fictional depiction of Mrs Travers in *The Rescue*.'[45]

Conrad's Malaysia

At this point it would be useful to say something about the terms 'Malay', 'Malaya' and 'Malaysia'.[46] Paul Wheatley, in the Prologomena to his *Impressions of the Malay Peninsula in Ancient Times*, suggested that the uniformity of terrain, soil, and climate across the region of Southeast Asia meant that the 'onus for regional differentiation' was thrown onto 'external factors' such as the chances of colonisation.[47] He opted for the term 'Malaysia' used 'in the traditional sense' to indicate 'the Malay world' – that is, the Indonesian archipelago, the southern half of the Malay peninsula, and perhaps at least the southern Philippines. This, however, raises the question: what is meant by 'Malay'? Turnbull begins her *Short History* by asserting that the 'Malays' are of 'mixed ethnic background': 'some having lived in the peninsula and on the northern Borneo coast for more than a millenium, others migrating in more recent times from Sumatra, Java, Sulawesi and other Indonesian islands, but they have accepted the Malay language, have assimilated to similar customs and subscribe to the Muslim faith'.[48] This resembles the modern constitutional definition of Malay, which involves speaking Malay, subscribing to Islam and identifying oneself as Malay. Bellwood suggests that both Malay language and Malay culture have 'decidedly assimilatory characteristics'.[49] Turnbull similarly asserts that most 'Borneo Malays' were actually 'indigenous Kedayans or Melanus', who were 'converted to the Muslim religion and had adopted the Malay language and way of life' (SH, 155–6). As Milner puts it, 'Malay' is a category 'subject to redefinition':

> For centuries, people of foreign origin had been accepted into particular Malay communities. By changing oneself in such areas as language, dress, customs and religion, it was possible to 'become Malay'.[50]

In the early nineteenth century inhabitants of the peninsula apparently did not think of themselves as belonging to a single political unit or a single ethnic group. Some of the Malay histories traced back their rulers' genealogies to the Malacca sultanate (Johore, Perak, and Penang), but the Kelantan and Keddah sultanates had no such connection (IP, 14). The notion of a 'Malay race' (*bangsa Melayu*) developed in the nineteenth century through contact with European categorisation. This brings in a further complication: as well as self-identity, there is also the matter of European perceptions of the peoples of the region.

'Malaya' is, for various reasons, a problematic term. Malayu was the east Sumatran state (based near Jambi) which gave the Malay peninsula its name and language. In one version of events, it was migrants from east Sumatra to the peninsula who founded Malacca. Certainly, between the eighth and thirteenth centuries CE, there seems to have been closer contact between east Sumatra and the western Malay peninsula than between the east and west coasts of the peninsula: the Straits of Malacca operated as an interior sea, linking rather than separating. The rise of Malacca in the fifteenth century formed the basis for the subsequent development of the Malay Sultanate. Between 1824 and 1914, English involvement in the peninsula led to the gradual unification of Malaya. In 1867, the Straits Settlements (Penang, Malacca, Singapore) were transferred from the Government of India to become a Crown Colony directly under the control of the Colonial Office in London. Elsewhere in the peninsula, indirect rather than direct rule remained the policy. In 1873, Sir Andrew Clarke took over as Governor of the Straits Settlements (and High Commissioner) and began the 'residential system' of indirect rule. In 1896, Negri Sembilan, Pahang, Perak, and Selangor became the Federated Malay States. In 1909, Keddah, Kelantan, Perlis, and Trengganu were transferred from Siam to England and became the Unfederated Malay States. In 1914, Johore, which had avoided formal protectorate status by cooperating with the English, was forced to accept an English Adviser. In 1948, the Federation of Malaya was formed: it was given independence in 1957. In 1963, Borneo, Malaya and Singapore joined to form Malaysia. After Singapore left in 1965, Malaysia was re-named Malaya.

In using the term 'Malaysia', I am thinking less of this complicated political history than of the earlier currency of the term. 'Malaysia' seems to have been coined in the 1830s and was in general usage in England by the end of the nineteenth century to describe 'a geographic-zoological-botanical region comprising the Malay Peninsula, Singapore, Borneo, Sumatra, and Java' (SH, 1). This ties the project 'writing Malaysia' closely to the scientific project which features in the early chapters of this book. The term is particularly appropriate since the writings of Marsden and Raffles were part of the process that produced this 'geographic-zoological-botanical region'.

The 'Malaysia' of Conrad's Malayan fiction stretches from Singapore to Bali, from Achin to New Guinea, from Sourabaya to Manila. However, its centre is the island of Borneo. *Almayer's Folly* and *An Outcast of the Islands* take place in 'Sambir' (Tanjung Redeb) in Berau in north-east Borneo. *The Rescue* concentrates on the Carimata Straits and the south-west coast of Borneo. Patusan in *Lord Jim* takes its name from the fortified village in west Borneo near the confluence of the Sakarran River with the Batang Lupar, which was destroyed by James Brooke in 1844 during his campaign to suppress piracy. However its Conradian location is clearly in north-west Sumatra: Gentleman Brown travels from Manila towards Zamboanga (LJ, 354); then down the Straits of Macassar (LJ, 356) and across the Java Sea (LJ, 356). En route to the Indian Ocean, he clears the Sunda Straits and, less than a week later, anchors 'off the Batu Kring mouth' (LJ, 357). He and his men then take a long-boat up the Batu Kring river to Patusan Reach. The population and social formation of Patusan, however, seem to derive (in part at least) from Conrad's memories of Berau in East Borneo and Dongala in Celebes.

The wanderings of Jim and Heyst serve to mark some of the boundaries of Conrad's Malaysia. Jim's experience of 'the East' begins with his hospitalisation in Singapore and his subsequent employment on the *Patna* with its route through the Strait of Malacca to the Red Sea. After the *Patna* Inquiry in 'an Eastern port' (LJ, 28), which reads as a composite of Bombay and Singapore, Jim progresses steadily eastwards: he is seen successively 'in Bombay, in Calcutta, in Rangoon, in Penang, in Batavia' (LJ, 5). Finally, from Bangkok, Marlow takes him (via employment with de Jongh) to Stein in Sourabaya, who places him in Patusan, 'a remote district of a native-ruled state' (LJ, 220). The 'magic circle' of islands that holds Heyst enchanted is 'a circle with a radius of eight hundred miles drawn round a point in North Borneo': 'It just touched Manila .... It just touched Saigon' (V, 7).[51] It takes in Sourabaya, where Heyst transacts his business, and extends as far in the east as New Guinea.

Conrad's experience of the archipelago and his fiction about the archipelago are both largely within the historical and political frame of what Christopher GoGwilt calls 'the scramble for Southeast Asia, which brought the Malayan peninsula and parts of Borneo under formal British rule between 1874 and 1896, which saw the consolidation of Dutch rule in the Dutch East Indies ... and which witnessed the emergence of the new imperialism of the United States in the Philippines'.[52] This contemporary (or near-contemporary) experiential and fictional world is consistently placed by Conrad in a longer perspective of a history of European encounters with the area and its peoples. The fiction is haunted by the ghosts of the adventurers who represent what Conrad called 'geography militant'.[53] It is haunted, in particular, by the figure and example of Sir James Brooke of Sarawak, as well as by the ghosts of more recent adventurers, the European traders of the archipelago. At the same time, within this frame, Conrad's fiction also attends to the Arab trading and political presence within the archipelago, the political and trading activities of the Bugis, the marine activities of the Sulus and the Ilanun, and – to a lesser extent – the varied roles of the Chinese.[54]

Conrad's first novel, *Almayer's Folly*, derives from his encounter with Charles Olmeijer in Tanjung Redeb, an isolated settlement in Eastern

Borneo, on one of the *Vidar's* stops in 1887.[55] Olmeijer had for seventeen years been the representative of William Lingard, a famous trader
and adventurer with special interests on the eastern coast of Borneo,
who had set up the trading post there. In 1862 Lingard had been
rewarded with the title Rajah Laut (literally, 'Sea King') for his assistance to the Sultan of Gunung Tabor, across the river from his trading
post in Berau. This was a strategy designed to evade the terms of a
Dutch contract which banned foreigners from settling in the Sultan's
territory without permission from Batavia, but, in Batavia, Dutch East
Indies officials became apprehensive that Lingard might follow
Brooke's example and establish himself as an independent ruler.[56]
However, Lingard's monopoly of trade in Berau was broken, and, in
the 1880s, his trade diminished; his last ship, the *Rajah Laut*, was put
up for sale in 1884; he had returned to England in 1883, and he died
there in 1888.[57] The events of the novel take place after the time of
Lingard's disappearance to raise further capital in Europe, but look
back to Lingard's 'discovery' of the river twenty years earlier. The
context for the novel's actions are the early 1880s rivalry between
Dutch and British in the archipelago – more specifically in Borneo. The
British Borneo Company was granted a Royal Charter in 1881 to
govern and administer North Borneo as a way of extending British territorial claims. As a result, there were disputes with the Dutch during
1881–3, ending in 1884 with a joint British-Dutch commission to look
into boundaries.[58]

A further significant context for the early fiction is the conflict
between the European colonisers and local peoples. Perhaps the most
important of these is the on-going conflict between the Dutch and the
Achinese. In May 1873, the Dutch colonial government at Batavia
declared war on the Sumatra Sultanate of Achin. Achin fell to the Dutch
in January 1874, but the 'dispute' lingered on. Knowles notes that the
continued Achin 'unrest' contributed to a tighter official Dutch policy
on piracy and on the sale of gunpowder in eastern Borneo from the
mid-1870s, a policy which impacts on Sambir in the form of Dutch
'exaction, severity, and general tyranny, as exemplified in the total
stoppage of gunpowder trade and the rigorous visiting of all suspicious
craft trading in the straits of Macassar' (AF, 48). Through Mrs Almayer's
history, the novel registers also the maritime conflicts between Sulus and
Europeans at the other end of the archipelago, while, through
Babalatchi, with his memories of sailing 'with Lanun men' and boarding
'in the night silent ships with white sails' (AF, 206), the novel also evokes
the 'war with the pirates'. Babalatchi's reference to a time 'before an

English Rajah ruled in Kuching' (AF, 206) briefly and precisely sets the events of *Almayer's Folly* in the context of Brooke's role in Sarawak.[59] Similarly, in *An Outcast of the Islands*, Babalatchi recalls a time when 'there were not so many fireships with guns' and Lakamba was 'a great fighter' attacking 'ships with high masts' (OI, 46). Babalatchi was 'a true Orang Laut, living by rapine and plunder of coasts and ships' until 'that long career of murder, robbery, and violence' was checked 'at the hands of white men' (OI, 52).

The Rescue, which is the earliest in time of this trilogy, is set in 1859–60.[60] It is also the work which most explicitly engages with the politics of the region. The events that provide its historical basis are the struggle for succession in Wajo (beginning around 1839), which is mentioned in Mundy's narrative of Brooke. However, the novel is also located, economically and allusively, in a larger context of English and Dutch activity in the region. The main location is southern Borneo, and this draws in references to a range of English actions in relation to Borneo – in particular, Sir Thomas Cochrane's 1845 expedition against 'the pirates' (Re, 23). Lingard's involvement with the Ilanun is thus to be seen, from an English perspective, in relation to Brooke and the campaigns against the 'pirates' of the 1850s. The more important context, however, is Dutch colonisation. Mr Travers has come out 'to study the Dutch colonial system' (Re, 34) – that is, the system of forced labour – and he invokes the 1820 Treaty (Re, 147), which divided the region between the Dutch and the English. The introduction of Hassim and Immada in Part II brings in a geo-political map of Bugis activity ('every spot where European trade had not penetrated – from Aru to Atjeh, from Sumbawa to Palawan' [Re, 68]) and a summary of Bugis action ('all those national risings, religious disturbances, and ... the organised piratical movements on a large scale' [Re, 68]). This map of resistance to Dutch colonisation is alluded to in more detail later. Through Jörgensen, for example, Lingard's involvement in the Wajo war of succession is placed in the perspective of the earlier Padri War (1821–38), 'when the white-clad Padris preached and fought all over Sumatra till the Dutch shook in their shoes' (Re, 92).[61] Jörgensen's account of his own involvement in local political struggles also presents a résumé of struggles against the Dutch:

'I knew Sentot when he was King of the South Shore of Java ... the old regent who lost heart and went over to the Dutch ... I was at the taking of Singal ... I was the white man who advised the chiefs of Manangkabo ...' (Re, 102)

This brings into the novel a history of the archipelago presented from the perspective of resistance to European domination. Belarab's father fought with 'the Padris of Sumatra' (Re, 102), and Belarab himself in his youth had been involved in war against the Dutch (Re, 111). Tengga has been dispossessed of his country by the Dutch: 'Six years ago I was ruler of a country and the Dutch drove me out .... They pretended to give it back to my nephew' (Re, 173). In this context, it is perhaps no surprise that the Ilanun recognise the status (and colonial role) of Travers and d'Alcacer:

> They were such men as are sent by rulers to examine the aspects of far-off countries and talk of peace and make treaties. Such is the beginning of great sorrow. (Re, 223)

Travers was a Member of Parliament; d'Alcacer is the Spanish cultural attaché in London and nephew of the Governor-General in the Philippines. The kidnapping of Travers and d'Alcacer is thus not merely 'savagery'; it has a clear political dimension.

Geography and some explorers

In *Under Imperial Eyes*, Mary Louise Pratt describes how European 'planetary consciousness' began in the eighteenth century. She chooses 1735 as her starting-point: the date of the publication of Carl Linné's *Systema Naturae* (*The System of Nature*) and of Europe's first major international scientific expedition. Pratt argues that the descriptive apparatuses of natural history produced the European construction of global-scale measuring. In particular, she suggests, Linnaeus's descriptive system, 'designed to classify all the plants on the earth, known and unknown' (Pratt, 24), set in motion 'a project to be realised in the world' (Pratt, 25). Conrad's essay, 'Geography and Some Explorers', suggests an alternative approach.

In this essay, Conrad offers a definition of geography ('the problems of our earth's shape, its size, its character, its products, its inhabitants' [LE, 2]) and a history of geography that divides it into three phases: fabulous, militant, and scientific. The fabulous phase, the 'phase of circumstantially extravagant speculation', was when 'the medieval mind ... crowded its maps with pictures of strange pageants, strange trees, strange beasts ... imaginary kingdoms ... inhabited by men with reversed feet, or eyes in the middle of their heads' (LE, 2). Conrad refers here to the maps of medieval Christendom, what Daniel Boorstin calls the 'Great Interruption', when Christian dogma displaced classical knowledge with geographic ignorance. 'Fabulous geography' ends with 'the discovery of the New World'(LE, 4). Columbus is followed by the Conquistadores – Cortes, Pizarro, Cabeza de Vaca – 'pertinacious searchers for El Dorado who climbed mountains, pushed through forests, swam rivers, floundered in bogs, without giving a single thought to the science of geography' (LE, 4). This leads Conrad into an appraisal of Abel Tasman, 'the best seaman of them all before James Cook' (LE, 6). Conrad emphasises the difficulties the early navigators faced – in particular, the fact that they had 'no means of ascertaining their exact position on the globe':

> they could calculate their latitude, but the problem of longitude was a matter which bewildered their minds and often falsified their judgement. (LE, 7)

Tasman's skills, however, were not appreciated by his employers, 'the honourable governor-general and the council in Batavia' (LE, 7). Cook, on the other hand, 'medallist of the Royal Society, and a captain in the Royal Navy' (LE, 8) 'added New Zealand to the scientific domain of the geography triumphant of our day' (LE, 9).

Peter Hulme and Ludmilla Jordanova have suggested that the Enlightenment's self-consciousness 'was to some extent a geographical consciousness'.[62] The 'discovery' of 'new worlds' also provided a metaphor for 'the nature of scientific advance': 'marching into new territories, taming what one found there, and giving a coherent account of fresh terrain'.[63] For Bacon, there was more than just an homology between the new world of voyages and the new world of learning. Neil Rennie suggests that 'Bacon imagined science as a ship on a voyage to a new world of fact based on experience'.[64] But *The Advancement of Learning* goes further than this: 'this proficience in navigation and discoveries may plant also an expectation of the further proficience and augmentation of all sciences'.[65] The global consciousness produced by the circumnavigation of the world prompted this anticipation of a panoptical view of the whole field of knowledge.

Developments in navigation and cartography were, then, perhaps more important parts of the process than the Linnaean system. In classical Greece, Hipparchus of Nicaea (*c*.165–*c*.127 BC) had developed a map with a regular east-west/north-south grid together with the idea that each place on the map should be located by exact astronomical observation.[66] This world-wide web of latitude and longitude potentially produced a set of co-ordinates for every place on earth in a universal and uniform system, while the use of astronomical observation provided the basis for cartographic mastery of the planet. Hipparchus's work was developed and popularised by Ptolemy, who provided the basis for modern cartography.[67] However, from the 4th to the 14th century, western Europe experienced 'the Great Interruption', the period of medieval Christian cartography. This period of 'fabulous geography' ended (in Conrad's narrative) with 'the discovery of the New World'. More precisely, the new period began with Prince Henry the Navigator and Portuguese exploration of the African coast, which led to both 'the discovery of the New World and the opening of the Indian Ocean'.[68] This return to empirical mapping, based on the daily experience of sailors, rather than dogmatic and fabulous geography, was accompanied by the re-discovery of Ptolemy's universal and uniform system of latitude and longitude for world-mapping. Like Linnaeus's schema, this was not just a descriptive system, a system of representation, but was, in effect, prescriptive. Boorstin suggests that 'the greatest act of self-control' of these early Renaissance cartographers was 'to leave parts of the earth blank' (151). The unknown now became the not-yet-known, and the blank spaces on the maps called out for completion.[69]

Latitude began to appear on sea-charts from the 16th century. Longitude posed more of a problem. For example, there was no common prime meridian until 1871, when Greenwich was proposed as the common zero for passage charts. Until then, different nations had different prime meridians. Thus, the French official sea-atlas, *Neptune François*, used multiple longitude scales. Thirteen years after the fixing of the prime meridian, in 1884, Greenwich was proposed as the start of the Universal Day, thus unifying longitude and time as part of a world-wide system.[70] The background to this global unification, however, is the nexus of Royal Society, East India Company, and the experience of mariners that is discussed in Chapter 2 as part of the discursive formation that produces 'writing Malaysia'.

The main problem with longitude was actually finding it. In 'Geography and Some Explorers', Conrad draws attention to the difficulty the early navigators faced – in particular, the fact that they had 'no means of ascertaining their exact position on the globe': 'they could calculate their latitude, but the problem of longitude was a matter which bewildered their minds and often falsified their judgement' (LE, 7). Latitude was quite straightforward; it was measured by the altitude of the sun above the horizon, originally using the Jacob's Staff and later (after 1595) using the quadrant. From the 1514 translation of Book 1 of

Ptolemy's *Geography* was developed the lunar-distance method of finding longitude, but the mathematical calculations were complex – this was one of the reasons for the establishment of the Mathematical School at Christ's Hospital and for Pepys setting up the naval officers' examination with its navigational component. Conrad, of course, took the equivalent examinations (as he recounts in *A Personal Record*).[71]

The project of finding longitude was associated with the Royal Society from its early days. In 1674 the Royal Society began plans for an observatory to help ship-owners and sailors with the problem of finding longitude at sea: by providing observational data, lunar distances could be predicted more accurately. As a result the Greenwich Observatory was opened in 1676. In 1714 there was a petition to Parliament by 'several Captains of Her Majesty's Ships, Merchants of *London*, and Commanders of Merchantmen' , which prompted a Bill offering £20 000 for 'discovering the longitude'. Over the next fifty years, the components of a solution to the problem came together. In 1731, John Hadley (1682–1744), then vice-president of the Royal Society, invented the double-reflection quadrant, which became the basis for the sextant. For measuring longitude by lunar distance, there was now a catalogue of star-positions provided by the Greenwich Observatory and an appropriate measuring instrument, the double-reflection quadrant. All that lacked was a theory of lunar motion, and this was provided by Tobias Mayer in 1755. In 1761, Neville Maskelyne (1732–1811), the Astronomer Royal, was sent by the Royal Society on a voyage to and from St Helena to observe the transit of Venus and to test Mayer's tables. Subsequently, Maskelyne published *The Nautical Almanac and Astronomical Ephemeris for the year 1767*, which provided tables of the motions of the heavens in a form suitable for navigators. Since the tables were based on the Greenwich meridian, navigators using the *Almanac* were also calculating longitude on this basis. As a result, map and chart publishers began to provide longitude gradations based on Greenwich – and, eventually, Greenwich became the prime meridian. As far as longitude and cartography were concerned, Pratt's 'seeing man' was more and more situated at Greenwich.

Meanwhile, the alternative method of determining longitude, by timekeepers, was also developing. The clockmaker, John Harrison (1693–1776) was financed by the East India Company to make his first sea-clock (H1). Between 1735 and 1761, with support from the Board of Longitude and the Royal Society, Harrison developed the sea-clock through three further versions (H2, H3, H4). H4 was copied by the London watchmaker, Larcum Kendall, and his copy (K1) was used by

Cook on his second voyage (1772–75). Indeed, a secondary aim of the *Resolution* voyage was the testing of K1 and of three chronometers by John Arnold (1736–99). Subsequently, the East India Company insisted that all their ships should carry chronometers to determine longitude. These chronometers, of course, were set to Greenwich time by anyone who also wanted to use Maskelyne's *Nautical Almanac*.

It is interesting that Marsden begins his cartographic account of Sumatra with the observation that:

> The only point of the island where longitude has been settled by actual observation, is Fort Marlborough, near Bencoolen. ... From eclipses of Jupiter's satellites observed in June 1769, preparatory to an observation of the transit of the planet Venus over the sun's disc ... (HS, 2)

Subsequently, he notes how, by 'the general use of chronometers in latter times, the means has been afforded of determining the positions of many prominent points both on the eastern and the western coasts, by which the map of the island has been considerably improved' (HS, 2). Keppel records how Brook, similarly, was very concerned to chart the regions through which he sailed using chronometers. When the narrator of 'Karain' attends to 'the firm, pulsating beat of the two ship's chronometer's ticking off steadily the seconds of Greenwich Time' as 'a protection and a relief' from the 'noiseless phantoms' (TU, 40) that Karain's telling of his tale seems to have summoned up in the ship's cabin, he is not merely asserting a European scientific and rational order against Karain's very different reality; he is also very precisely attending to the fetish which confirms his identity by always allowing him to know exactly where he is.

By the early twentieth century, however, this comprehensive mapping of the globe had produced a different problem. As Conrad puts it, in his 1923 essay 'Travel', once the 'basic facts of geography' had been 'ascertained by the observations of heavenly bodies', the 'glance of the modern traveller' was confronted by 'the much-surveyed earth' (LE, 130).[72] The triumph of exploration has produced what Conrad calls 'the vanishing mysteries of the earth' (LE, 132): 'Presently there will be no back-yard left in the heart of Central Africa that has not been peeped into by some person more or less commissioned for the purpose' (LE, 129). Bacon's excited anticipation of a panoptical view of the whole field of knowledge ends in this nightmare of surveillance.

Writing Malaysia

The book that follows began as a study of Conrad's Malay fiction, exploring cross-cultural encounters, cultural identity, and cultural dislocation, and paying particular attention to issues of 'race' and gender. It focused on Conrad's first two novels, *Almayer's Folly* and *An Outcast of the Islands*; on two early short stories, 'The Lagoon' and 'Karain'; on *Lord Jim*, which represents the culmination of the first phase of Conrad's fictional engagement with Malaysia; and the two later novels, *Victory* and *The Rescue*; since these are the Malayan fictions in which encounters between Europeans and non-Europeans are most prominent.[73] As it developed, however, it had to confront, as Conrad had done, the question how to represent another culture. Accordingly, it now begins with an exploration of the textual tradition of 'writing Malaysia' in which Conrad's work situates itself.[74]

The most interesting early work on Conrad's Malayan fiction was Florence Clemens's 1939 article on Conrad's use of Wallace.[75] John D. Gordan's *Joseph Conrad: the Making of a Novelist* (1941) was the first full-length scholarly study of *Almayer's Folly*, *An Outcast of the Islands* and *Lord Jim*.[76] Gordan identified textual sources and real-life models, and explored the development of the text from manuscript through to the first collected edition. Norman Sherry's *Conrad's Eastern World* (1966), with its careful biographical research and meticuluous exploration of models and sources, provides an essential starting point for most research into the whole range of Conrad's Malay fiction. More recently, Heliéna Krenn's *Conrad's Lingard Trilogy: Empire, Race, and Women in the Malay Novels* (1990) usefully explores the three Malayan novels (*Almayer's Folly*, *An Outcast of the Islands*, *The Rescue*) as a trilogy, in which the figure of Lingard moves from the periphery to centre stage.[77] Two other works on Conrad and colonialism were relevant to this project on Conrad's Malay fiction: Benita Parry's *Conrad and Imperialism: Ideological Boundaries and Visionary Frontiers* (1983) and, in particular, Andrea White's *Joseph Conrad and the Adventure Tradition: Constructing and Deconstructing the Imperial Subject* (1993).[78] Parry attends to how Conrad transformed the characteristic genres of colonial fiction 'into vehicles for reflecting on the precepts, values and habits of thought native to these categories', undercutting ideological categories 'by illuminations of the misrecognitions and limitations' in their form of cognition. For Parry, Conrad's fictions are 'battlegrounds' for 'political doctrines and cultural systems, epistemological suppositions and ontological goals'.[79] White shows how, 'from within the genre that had constructed the imperial subject', Conrad 'wrote a fiction at odds with the traditional assumptions of the genre' (JCAT, 5). Instead of the unqualified celebration of heroism, for example, Conrad brought 'the modernist's double vision' (JCAT, 7). White is concerned with adventure fiction and travel writing as 'shaping discourses' for Conrad's fiction. She argues that nineteenth-century adventure fiction 'reinscribed the imperial subject already constructed by the currently popular travel writing' (JCAT, 7). Accordingly, she touches on some of the figures discussed at greater length in the present work – most notably James Brooke and A. R. Wallace. Her main concern, however, is to show how writers of adventure fiction were 'intent both on revealing strange worlds to their readers' and on 'shaping particular attitudes' – in particular, 'promoting an ideology of patriotic heroism and Christian dutifulness' (JCAT, 54). These fictions set up an opposition between 'the heroic Englishman and the "primitive" Other', asserting 'the essential difference between "us" and "them" in order to promote, celebrate and justify the imperial project' (JCAT, 64). Conrad, in contrast, presents unheroic protagonists; stresses the common ground between 'us' and 'them'; and, where 'the story of the Other was always told from the European point of view', in Conrad's fiction, the Other is given a voice: 'through Conrad's multiple tellings, the story of the Other and the white man in the outposts of empire became theirs as well as ours' (JCAT, 119). The white man's account is contested by other viewpoints, and 'the dialogic possibilities permitted by the discrepancies of multiple viewpoints begin to dislodge the authority of the white man's telling' (JCAT, 127).

James Clifford also provided an early point of reference for this project. In his Introduction to *Writing Culture*, he addressed some of the problems involved in representing another culture. After observing that anthropology 'no longer speaks with automatic authority for others defined as unable to speak for themselves' (WC, 10), he explores some of the attempted solutions such as the 'self-reflexive "field-work account"' (WC, 14) or 'dialogical modes' (WC, 15):

> the principle of dialogical textual production goes well beyond the more or less artful presentation of 'actual' encounters. It locates cultural interpretations in many sorts of reciprocal contexts, and it obliges writers to find diverse ways of rendering negotiated realities as multisubjective, power-laden, and incongruent. In this view, 'culture' is always relational, an inscription of communicative processes that exist, historically, *between* subjects in relations of power ... (WC, 15)

Clifford notes how 'the ground from which persons and groups securely represent others' has been dislodged: there is no longer a mountain-top 'from which to map human ways of life'; cultural analysis 'is always enmeshed in global movements of difference and power' (WC, 22). As Chapters 4 to 9 will argue, Conrad's Malayan fiction confronts this lack of secure 'ground'; it attempts to find ways to negotiate realities that are 'multisubjective, power-laden, and incongruent'; and it attends to global movements, while mapping the local. In particular, Conrad's exploitation of the 'dialogic possibilities' of multiple viewpoints and competing narratives anticipates the 'dialogic modes' of modern anthropology.

Any work discussing the imperial archive cannot avoid the influence of Said's *Orientalism* and the theoretical and critical work that has developed in response to it. Thus Rod Edmond begins *Representing the South Pacific* by engaging with colonial discourse theory and post-colonial theory, criticising both for their failure to acknowledge the historical specificity of colonial discourses and cross-cultural encounters. Edmond's attention to colonial discourses of the Pacific from Cook to Gauguin is clearly analogous to the present work's attention to the textual tradition of 'writing Malaysia' from Marsden to Conrad. Both insist on the historical specificities of cross-cultural encounters and the resulting cultural productions. Edmond also criticises colonial discourse theory and post-colonial theory for continuing to see indigenous cultures in essentially passive or reactive terms. Where Said's *Orientalism* has been criticised for denying autonomy or agency to the colonised, Edmond suggests that Bhabha's assertion of agency (in the form of mimicry) serves to define the indigenous culture reactively. He cites Henry Louis Gates's description of the dilemma facing theory in this area:

> You can empower discursively the native, and open yourself to charges of downplaying the epistemic (and literal) violence of colonialism; or play up the absolute nature of colonial domination, and be open to charges of negating the subjectivity and agency of the colonised, thus textually replicating the repressive operations of colonialism.[80]

Edmond's main strategy is to emphasise specific historical and colonial situations. As he notes, 'colonialism was never a unitary formation' (RSP, 12). Neither colonialism nor 'Europe' nor Pacific cultures were homogeneous. As regards colonialism, the position in Malaysia in the nineteenth-century was analogous to that in the Pacific: resistance in

England to the acquisition of colonies was countered by pressure from particular interest groups and unauthorised actions by individuals. But Malaysian culture is, of course, very different from Pacific culture, and neither was homogenous. Edmond engages in a 'reading back' of colonial discourses into metropolitan centres, relating European representations to 'sponsoring institutions, publishing history and other cultural contexts in which, and for which, they were produced' (RSP, 20) but without suggesting that all representations of other cultures are only self-representations. At the same time, he recognises the danger involved in concentrating on 'the conventions through which a culture was textualised' while ignoring 'the actuality of what was represented': this risks 'a second-order repetition of the images, typologies and projections under scrutiny' and a replication of the original silencing of indigenous voices. On the other hand, registering of those indigenous voices in this context also runs the risk of implying that colonisation constitutes the whole of colonised culture.[81] The present work runs the same risk of second-order repetition, silencing of indigenous voices, and privileging of colonisation as the primary experience of colonised peoples. However, as Laura Chrisman has argued, the present cannot be analysed 'in isolation from the imperialism which formally produced it'.[82]

Chapter 1 outlines the history of Malaysia up to the nineteenth century (and indicates some of the problems involved in supplying such a history). Chapters 2 and 3 attempt to trace the development of a textual tradition of 'writing Malaysia' from Marsden to Brooke. The first comprehensive account of any part of the region was William Marsden's *History of Sumatra*. This was read by Sir Thomas Raffles and provided the model for his *History of Java*. These two works by Marsden and Raffles were read by James Brooke before he set out for the archipelago. Chapter 2 offers a genealogy of this textual tradition by exploring Marsden's antecedents and his connection with the Enlightenment project of Sir Joseph Banks and the Royal Society. It also attempts to provide an analysis of the particular discursive formation within which 'writing Malaysia' was produced. Marsden, Raffles, and Brooke were, in different ways, involved in the production of texts that offered a mapping of the archipelago. But this is more than just a form of knowledge; this is a knowledge quite consciously designed to bring the area and its people under colonial control. The project of knowledge is a project of mastery. The commercial imperatives that permeate Marsden's work are finally unmasked in his praise of the 'peace' that the East India Company has brought to Sumatra, protecting the people from their chiefs and the chiefs from each other. What is intimated here, in this project of Pax Britannica, is how knowledge of local social forms is the prelude to the breaking up of those social forms and the imposition of a different cultural and social pattern. With Raffles the learning of languages, the collecting of manuscripts and information, the meticulous mapping of the region was always the prelude to the replacement of that culture with the culture of free trade and 'economic man'. Raffles's writing of Malaysia was always accompanied by actions that wrote the start of another history onto the archipelago. While Raffles sought to know and describe the original local culture, he was simultaneously putting in place a new imperial culture. Brooke was one of the performers of the new script.

Chapter 3 shows the direction which this version of 'writing Malaysia' had taken in the mid-to-late-nineteenth century. In the words of Andrea White: 'as the maps filled up, the dreams gave way to facts, often unpalatable ones, and the adventure turned inward' (JCAT, 7). The chapter focuses on the work of A. R. Wallace and Sir Hugh Clifford. Wallace's *Malay Archipelago* completes one aspect of the scientific project, initiated by Bacon and re-interpreted by the Royal Society, with his comprehensive mapping of flora, fauna and inhabitants of the archipelago. With Wallace, the Enlightenment project of knowledge might be said to have reached its peak as far as the archipelago was concerned. However, the completion of the mapping of the archipelago, its geology, flora and fauna, also produced a problematising of the 'civilisation' that initiated the mapping. Clifford's writings show the development of another aspect of that project: Clifford is in the tradition of the colonial administrator who is also an amateur scholar. Like Raffles and Brooke, he gathers information about Malaysia in order to make himself a more efficient colonist. Clifford's work also shows, however, how, by the end of the century, instead of maintaining the distance and mastery of observation, the European observer is affected by what he observes. Thus, where Wallace is troubled to square his experience of the archipelago with notions of progress and civilisation, Clifford came to be particularly concerned with what he termed 'denationalisation' – the danger of the European coming too close to the Malay and losing his own cultural identity. At the same time, Clifford's own account is a form of power-knowledge that barely cloaks the erotic basis of its discriminating gaze. Indeed, Clifford's fiction is often concerned with masculinity, sexuality, and transgressive sexual relations. Thus Chapter 3, through the very different figures of Wallace and Clifford, explores how Wallace's scientific project encounters, fails to encounter, and is disrupted by the culture of the archipelago, and how Clifford's administrative encounter with Malaysia similarly both resists and is affected by Malay culture. As Young observes:

> A culture never repeats itself perfectly away from home. Any exported culture will in some way run amok ... as it dissolves in the heterogeneity of the elsewhere (CD, 174)

Young's choice of metaphor shows that there is more than one way in which the colonised culture can survive. As Homi Bhabha puts it, 'the effect of colonial power is seen to be the *production* of hybridisation rather than the noisy command of colonialist authority or the silent repression of native traditions'.[83]

Chapters 1, 2, and 3 thus have two functions. First, they provide a mapping of the history and early English historiography of the region. They thus attempt to suggest some of the historical and material conditions of Conrad's experience of the area. Secondly, they attempt to present the discursive formation within which and against which Conrad's fiction was written. Thirdly, they show how, by the time Conrad began to write, the Enlightenment project of mapping and describing was subverted by uncertainties and self-questioning: ideas of civilisation and progress, Self and Other, which had been taken for granted, were now open to question. This inward turn is continued in the works of Conrad.[84]

In 'Geography and Some Explorers', Conrad inserts himself into European traditions of exploration just as Brooke did in his 'Prospectus'. He is, after all, trained and educated as an officer in the British Merchant Marine. However, he is also inescapably a Pole, identified with a nation which at that time had no legal existence, after its partition by the great powers. Perhaps equally important, whereas he entered the Congo as part of the European system of exploitation, his main professional involvement with the archipelago involved a different kind of complicity: when he sailed up the Berau river, he was an officer on board the *Vidar*, a steamship owned by Syed Mohsin Bin Salley Ali Jaffree, the original of the Arab trader to whom the fictional Willems betrays the fictional Lingard's secrets of navigation.[85] In other words, he 'follows in the footsteps' of the treacherous Willems rather than those of the romantic adventurer, Lingard, who is the central figure in the early Malay novels. Conrad's relation to the discursive formation 'Writing Malaysia' is thus doubly problematic: his identity as a British naval officer is always destabilised by his identity as a Pole, and his main experience of the archipelago is mediated through Arab rather than European trading networks.

The account of Conrad's fiction begins, in Chapter 4, with an exploration of mobility and cultural diversity in his first two novels, *Almayer's Folly* and *An Outcast of the Islands*. It examines hybridisation, the fetishising of originary identity, and the performance of identity in the context of shifting patterns of local politics and imperial rivalry. Chapter 5 explores the intertwining of issues of 'race' and gender – and the encounter with the sexual and/or racial Other – in the first phase of Conrad's Malay fiction. It begins with *Almayer's Folly* and *An Outcast of the Islands* and their representation of (Asian) women's power over both Asian and European men. In the second part of the chapter, 'Karain' and 'The Lagoon' are examined in relation to the male-bonding that was implicit in the two novels. Where the two novels tacitly assume a complicitous European male reader, 'Karain' self-consciously inscribes the male reader's scene of reading into the narrative pattern of written texts and spoken narratives; it writes the reader into the chain of narratives and narratees; and it implicates the reader in the various implications of the narrative.[86] 'Karain''s scrupulous attention to the differences between written and spoken story-telling leads into the consideration of writing and speaking in the archipelago in *Lord Jim* and *Victory* in Chapters 6 and 7. Where 'Karain' implicitly contrasts European print culture with Malay oral culture, *Lord Jim* is situated by Marlow within a European community that constitutes itself through the circulation of gossip. *Victory*, too, is situated by its narrator within the same European oral community. Like *Lord Jim*, it explores the encounter between different European cultures in the archipelago, while also attending to voices marginalised or silenced by European dominance. Chapter 8 explores the encounter of East and West through attention to dialogue, the staging of encounters involving switching between languages, and cultural cross-dressing. The chapter examines, through Travers and Lingard, how the class conflicts and sexual politics of metropolitan society are played out on the stage provided by the colonial setting; and, through Mrs Travers, how the coloniser's mimicry of the colonised acts as an appropriation of the costume of Otherness. *The Rescue* thus engages with the aestheticisation of the Other and, in doing so, problematises its own attempt to represent Otherness.

In this way Conrad's 'writing Malaysia' continues that 'turning inward' referred to by White. To begin with, in his first two novels,

Conrad attempts to represent a Malay world and to give voice to his Malay participants. With 'Karain', he comes up against the irreducible Otherness of the Malay reality. Subsequently, he explores European attempts to represent that Otherness – through his self-conscious engagement with the conventions of adventure romance in *Lord Jim*; by constructing his narrative through the discourses circulating among the expatriate European communities in *Lord Jim* and *Victory*; and, finally, by exploring the aestheticising of Otherness in *The Rescue*. From the outset, he asserts the heterogeneity of the culture of the archipelago: he does not produce Otherness as 'a thing', but rather as a strategy or a process.[87] As he proceeds through these fictions, European culture comes more and more to be explored through the complex cross-cultural encounters of the archipelago, and class and gender become at least as important as 'race'.

1
Problems of Historiography

It is tempting to begin with a chronological mapping of the region. A general survey might register the Indian influence beginning around the fifth century; subsequent Chinese influence; the impact of Islam from the ninth century; and contact with Europe from around 1500 marked by successive attempts by various European countries to dominate the spice trade.[1] A more detailed map would then mark a Portuguese period beginning, perhaps, with d'Albuquerque's visit to Sumatra in 1510 and his capture of Malacca in 1511.[2] It would register the early rivalry between the Portuguese and the Spanish: Magellan's 1519 expedition established a Spanish-controlled trade-route to Malacca from the east to avoid the Portuguese gunships in the Indian Ocean that protected the Portuguese sea-route from the west.[3] Although this eastward route was too dangerous and too expensive to be practical, it did have political consequences: by the treaty of Saragossa, in an analogue of the Tordesillas Line that divided South America, the region was shared between Spain and Portugal, with the Moluccas, the source of nutmeg and clove, located within the Spanish sphere.[4] By the end of the sixteenth century the Spanish had developed an entrepôt at Manila. The Portuguese, meanwhile, had established a commercial empire, based on Homuz, Goa and Malacca: they were encouraging the cultivation of pepper in Sumatra and the Malay peninsula, and were attempting to assert a spice monopoly.

This more detailed chronology would then note the subsequent struggle between Portugal and Holland for commercial dominance. The first Amsterdam company for trade in the Indies sent out a fleet of ships in 1595 and established contact with Bantam in Java. Several new Dutch companies were established in 1598, and the Dutch United Company (Vereenigde Oost-Indische Compagnie) was formed through the merging of these separate companies in 1602. The strategically-positioned new city of Batavia was set up from 1610; and Hendrick Brouwers opened up the Sunda Strait route in 1611. The Dutch attempted to monopolise the spice trade of the region after the 1641 capture of Malacca from the Portuguese.[5] But the Dutch position gradually weakened with the decreasing importance of the spice trade in the eighteenth century and the increasing importance of Bengal textiles and China tea.[6]

This more detailed chronology might then note the founding of the English East India Company in 1599; the first voyage to the archipelago in 1601, which set up a factory at Bantam, and brought back so much pepper from Achin as to cause a glut on the London market; and the relative failure of the East India Company in the archipelago during the first half of the seventeenth century as a result of Dutch opposition. The period of prosperity for the East India Company began with the Restoration, although it was not until the eighteenth century that the East India Company began to show interest in the Malay states.[7] From 1675 to 1772, the English connection with Malaysia was maintained by 'country traders', English merchants resident in Asia, who, by the 1740s, were making in-roads into Dutch preserves.[8]

Between 1760 and the start of the twentieth century, Southeast Asia as a whole was divided among different European empires. English dominance of Malaya was established in the second half of the eighteenth century, based on conquests in India and command of the European trade with China.[9] These interests in India and China determined British policy in the peninsula and archipelago: 'to defend an empire on the one hand, and to protect a trade route on the other'.[10] Britain's Asian policy was thus 'always affected by European considerations' – in particular, fears of 'French dominance of the continent'.[11] Relations with the Dutch and the Spanish were shaped by the need to protect both empire and trade in the region from the French.[12] Finally, the area underwent a radical change in the late-nineteenth-century with the displacement of the Spanish by the Americans in the Philippines, and the beginning of American imperialism in Southeast Asia.[13]

There are, however, a number of problems with this simple map. First, it confidently glosses over and conceals various indeterminacies. The archeological and epigraphic evidence for the early period in particular is very scanty. Wheatley estimates that 99% of the region's history was unrecorded.[14] Wheatley, however, is starting from the evidence of human presence in the area 250 000 years ago, with the first epigraphic evidence dating from the fifth century CE and no indigenous literary sources before the sixteenth-century. There are early foreign records – in Arab, Chinese and Indian sources – but these involve both translation and transliteration. Thus, while the Indian influence on the culture of the region is unmistakable, how that came about is the subject of dispute. Whether it was the result of conquest, colonisation, immigration, trade, active borrowing – or some combination of all these – is not clear.[15] Bellwood, however, convincingly argues that, since Malay borrowed words from Sanskrit and not from Prakrit, that Brahmins rather than traders were the crucial cultural influence. The model he produces begins with Indian trading to Southeast Asia (and complementary Southeast Asian trade to India) in the first few centuries CE, which stimulated the growth of trading 'states'. However, the major influence of Indian culture on religion and politics took place at court level – perhaps through the invitation of local rulers. Sanskrit inscriptions found in eastern Borneo and western Java, dating from the fifth century CE, suggest that local rulers were modelling themselves on the Pallava kings of Tamil Nadu.

In the later periods, where there is written evidence, local chronicles 'are shaped to make a point or to omit a discreditable episode', while European accounts are influenced by the role the writers wish to play in the history they write (BBB, 4).[16] However, there are also serious problems of a more theoretical kind to this simple mapping. First, like all periodisations, it presents a notion of homogenous temporality rather than the possibility of multiple temporalities.[17] Secondly, this mapping of the region is consistently from the perspective of successive external impositions on the archipelago. This is partly a problem of sources: written evidence – particularly written evidence available to non-Malay speakers – is predominantly that of visitors to the region. As van Leur put it, in his influential work on Southeast Asian history:

> With the arrival of ships from western Europe, the point of view is turned a hundred and eighty degrees and from then on the Indies are observed from the deck of the ship, the ramparts of the fortress, the high gallery of the trading house.[18]

As a result, the area is transformed into and reduced to a field of European activity.

Accordingly, a fuller map of the region would perhaps want to begin with the successive migrations into the region in prehistoric times: the

Melanesioid peoples, including the Alfurs of the Moluccas; the Nesiot peoples, including the Dayaks/Kayan of Borneo and the *orang laut*; the Pareoans, including the Bugis, Achinese and Balinese.[19] However, this mapping too is contested. After expressing impatience with the unexamined reproduction of the model of successive waves of immigration, Bellwood asserts that 'a Mongoloid phenotype predominates in the west and north, and gradually fades southwards and eastwards' (80). From this he deduces that a model 'of Mongoloid expansion into an Australoid sphere, allowing for considerable variation within each group, should suffice to explain the picture' (80).

This fuller map would record (with more certainty) the outward expansion to trade contacts with India, the Middle East, Europe; the seventh-century Srivijaya empire (centred near present-day Palembang), that, at its peak in the twelfth century, controlled Sumatra, the Malay peninsula, and the greater part of Java, and hence both the Sunda Strait and the Straits of Malacca; the Majapahit empire in the fourteenth century, that, from Java, extended supremacy over Bali, Sumatra, Borneo to Pahang in Malaya and Tumasik (present-day Singapore); the rise of the new state of Malacca in the fifteenth century to become perhaps the greatest of Malay commercial empires; the rise of the Mataram empire in Java in the late sixteenth century; the spread of the Bantam Sultanate and its rivalry with Achin and Johore; the development by the Bugis in the eighteenth century of a network of trading posts linking the Straits with Borneo and beyond in a loosely-articulated empire; the emergence of the Sulu Sultanate in the period after 1768; and so on.

It would certainly note how the area, from earliest times, has been made up of a range of different ethno-linguistic communities, and its history marked by complex cross-cultural relations. Thus Malacca was an important trading port long before the Portuguese arrived. In 1403, for example, the Emperor Yung-Lo ordered Yin Chi'ing to visit Malacca as part of a new positive policy towards nations of the 'Western Ocean'.[20] The following year, Admiral Cheng Ho arrived in Malacca, and Yung-Lo received a mission from Malacca. Subsequently, this 'special relation' between Malacca and the Emperor was formalised, when the Sultan of Malacca married one of the emperor's daughters. She settled in Bukit Cina (China Hill), which remains a Chinese area to this day. On another level, the level of material culture, 'Martaban' jars, large stoneware jars of Chinese origin, were imported into Malaysia through Martaban in Burma from the eleventh to the seventeenth century. These played an important part in daily domestic life as containers of rice, but they also acquired a rôle in spiritual customs and beliefs. Imported objects were thus fully integrated into local culture and even became part of customs and beliefs relating to the spirit world.[21]

This fuller map might also record the role of religion in the region – including the religious dimension of trade rivalries. For example, Tarling notes how the Hindu Raja of Pajajaran provided facilities to the Portuguese at Sunda Kelapa and, by doing so, indirectly prompted the founding of the Islamic state of Bantam in opposition.[22] It would record more generally the role of Islam as a basis for opposition to European colonisation. Achin, for example, was, from the sixteenth century, an important link to Muslim India and the Middle East. It became a centre of resistance to the Portuguese. Indeed, the Portuguese attempts to introduce Christianity actually served to spread Islam, and, through Islam, to produce greater cultural unity in the region.[23]

This fuller map should also, of course, include Malay accounts of the region. As Milner observes:

> In Malaysia and numerous other regions of Southeast Asia, indigenous writings (in the form of inscriptions and chronicles) survive from pre-colonial times and the existence of such documents permits us to attempt to construct indigenous perspectives from which to interpret the significance of the encounter with colonialism. (IPCM, 4)

The chronicles of the courts generally have, as their subject matter, 'the activity and proceedings of rulers and of those who carry out royal orders' (IPCM, 16). In these texts (which are known as *hikayat*, when written in prose), the raja is central: history is constructed around royal genealogy, and new lands and peoples are introduced by reference to royal agency. As Milner shows, from the *hikayat* can be deduced the concepts of *kerajaan* (the condition of having a raja), *nama* (reputation), and so on, through which the pre-colonial society was organised and understood (IPCM, 10–30). However, the existence of *hikayat* alongside European accounts often produces what Greenblatt has referred to, in the American context, as the 'radical incompatibility' of 'equally compelling stories' (NWE, ix). In his early paper 'On the Malayu Nation', Raffles included a Malay account of the arrival of the Portuguese at Malacca in 1511, based on the *Hikayat Hang Tuah*.[24] It records how, during the reign of Sultan Ahmed Shah 'at a time when that country possessed an extensive commerce, and every thing in abundance, when the affairs of government were well administered', ten Portuguese ships arrived from Manila for trade (17–18). After an extended stay and exchanges of presents, the Portuguese requested 'a small piece of ground' the size of an animal's skin.[25] They then cut an ox-hide into ribbons and measured out an extensive area of ground upon which they built 'a storehouse of very considerable dimensions, leaving large square apertures in the walls for guns' (18). The Portuguese brought in cannon by night and chests of small arms, 'saying their contents were clothes': at midnight, they opened fire on Malacca, destroying all the houses and putting the people to flight. The account emphasises the deceit and trickery of the Portuguese, while noting the suspicions of some of the Sultan's advisors, which the Sultan chose to ignore. In his *History of Sumatra*, Marsden gives a very different account, derived from European sources, which foregrounds the European captives held by the Shah from Diogo Lopez Sequiera's 1509 visit to Malacca. It emphasises how, out of concern to save the lives of these captives (who are not mentioned in the Malay account), d'Albuquerque 'negotiated with the King of Malacca before he proceeded to an attack on the place' (HS, 408).[26] The European and the Malay accounts are in conflict, and neither can be easily privileged over the other.[27] However, as Clifford notes in *Further India*, 'a great deal has been made of the treachery of the Sultan of Malacca' (FI, 50), but it is useful to remember that Diogo appeared in the guise of a trader, whereas his mission was to conquer Malacca.[28]

In his novel *Scorpion Orchid*, Lloyd Fernando makes fictional play with precisely this problem. Chapter 15 begins with the story of the *Eastern Queen* sent by the Royal Society on a voyage of exploration in the Pacific. The Captain's log records how, near Tumpat, he 'landed a boat with four people, Keppel, Mundy, Wallace and Brooke'.[29] This evocation of a European textual tradition is the first hint of the historical fabrication, the historical metafiction, that the chapter produces. As the chapter proceeds, Fernando presents competing narratives of the British takeover. According to the narrative provided by the British Protector, Thomas Lang, the white men asked for guides 'to help them gather specimens of flora and fauna'; the guides attacked the party of white men and, in response, the white men threatened the village with the ship's guns; during the night the Penghulu came on board to ask for their assistance against Hang Mahmud, who had deposed him; subsequently, after the death of Hang Mahmud and the surrender of the village, 'at the Penghulu's invitation', the captain 'agreed to remain as protector and adviser' (SO, 146). However, the *kampung* has a counter-narrative. According to this version, the white men were interested not in flora and fauna but in a mine and the villagers' silver; they captured the Penghulu and held him hostage; Hang Mahmud rescued the Penghulu, but the *Eastern Queen* then turned its guns on the village:

> After the fifth shot, some flimsy huts were ablaze, Hang Mahmud was among those fatally wounded, and the remainder surrendered. Captain Smith then annexed the territory to the British Crown ...' (SO, 146)

The events are differently infigurated in the different historical traditions. In *Scorpion Orchid*, the two narratives are set against each other, and then both are revealed to be 'bogus history ... a complete fabrication' (SO, 147) produced by a Malay student as part of an argument with an English academic over the British role in Malaya.

Bugis, Sulus and Piracy

There is, however, another kind of problem with this mapping – and that is the problem of terminology and concepts. Benedict Anderson notes that 'wherever in the islands the earliest clerics and conquistadores ventured they espied, on shore, *principales*, *hidalgos*, *pecheros* and *esclavos* (princes, noblemen, commoners and slaves) – quasi-estates adapted from the social classifications of late medieval Iberia'. In short, 'the "class-structure" of the pre-colonial period is a "census" imagining created from the poops of Spanish galleons'.[30] In the same way, the reference to 'empires' imposes a European conceptual framework onto what might have been very different political and social structures.[31] Geertz's *Negara*, for example, begins by drawing attention to the range of social structures in the region: the Malayo-Polynesian tribal systems of interior Borneo and Celebes; the traditional peasant villages of Bali, West Java, and parts of Sumatra; the fishing and smuggling villages of the Borneo and Celebes coasts; the half-modernised metropolises of Jakarta, Medan, Sourabaya, and Macassar.[32] His subsequent detailed account of Balinese political organisation presents a rhizomatic structure of dispersed power:

> an extended field of highly dissimilar political ties, thickening into nodes of varying size and strength at strategic points on the

landscape and then thinning out again to connect, in a marvellously convolute way, virtually everything with everything else. (*Negara*, 24)

As he had already noted in *Kinship in Bali*, the 'complex indigenous political system' that the Dutch encountered in Bali in the nineteenth century was 'basically not territorial' in nature.[33] It was made up of 'multiple interconnected networks of personal ... ties' forming 'highly unstable pyramids of authority' (*Kinship*, 24):

> no lord held as subjects the entire population of any one village. ... In any single village, the various members would typically owe fealty to a number of different lords. (*Kinship*, 25)

Indeed, any individual member of the village might owe fealty to one lord, pay tax to another, and work for a third, since military duties, taxpaying duties, and sharecropping duties belonged to separate, superimposed systems. Under Dutch rule in the nineteenth century, this non-territorialised subjecthood was replaced by 'rationalised' territorial government.

More recently, Anthony Milner has taken off from Geertz's idea of 'meaningful structures' to present a cultural analysis of Malay political activity 'in Malay terms'.[34] Through an analysis of the neglected *hikayat*, he has uncovered an understanding of political experience 'radically different' to that of European colonisers. The Dutch-British evidence acknowledges the central ceremonial role of the ruler but without understanding the implications:

> Political life could be subsumed under one term: men considered themselves to be living not in states or under governments, but in a *Kerajaan*, in the 'condition of having a raja'. (*Kerajaan*, 114)

Milner's analysis of the ceremonial polity of pre-colonial Malaya challenges the European emphasis on 'theatricality' or the reading of Malay politics in terms of a 'theatre state'.[35] In *Kerajaan* polity, royal subjects 'understand what we might call their identity and purpose' in terms of rajaship: the subjects' 'being' was defined in terms of official titles and status, and official titles had significance not only for this world but also for the after-life (IPCM24). Milner hints that this concept of *Kerajaan*, with its emphasis on the ceremonial and spiritual role of the raja (rather than on wealth and power for their own sake), might have been influenced by Buddhist or Hindu concepts (the relationship between the *Bhakti* teacher and his disciples has certain analogies). Whatever its derivation, it was eroded by Islamic and western challenges. Thus Milner particularly notes the impatience of Munshi Abdulla, a disciple of Raffles, with the conventionalised Malay world. Munshi Abdulla 'viewed the world not in terms of the Raja but from the perspective of the individual' (K115), and was 'one of the earliest indigenous authors to draw from western-derived concepts to undermine the *Kerajaan*' (IPCM11).[36] Milner concludes: 'the Raja's predominantly ceremonial "work" could not continue to play a critical role in a community of private men' (K115).

At the same time, it should be noted that Dutch domination of the archipelago, from the sixteenth to the nineteenth century, was itself not a matter of territorial occupation but rather of legal contracts and enforced monopolies, of spheres of influence, with the small Dutch naval presence carrying out a policing role.[37] Were the Dutch, perhaps, in part responding to cultural patterns already present in the archipelago? When Raffles made the treaty with Temenggong Abdul Rahman and Sultan Hussain that allowed the East India Company to establish a settlement at Singapore, their interpretation of the treaty, like the first Governor's, was 'that the dispersal of the land was vested in the native chiefs, that the government of the country was native and the port a native port'.[38] As Trocki observes, to the Malays Singapore was 'simply one more variation on a very old theme'.[39] Indeed, consciously, unconsciously, or merely ironically, Raffles had patterned his new settlement 'on the classic model of the Malay maritime empire' (Trocki, 52).

Certainly, within the archipelago, the Bugis, as Tarling notes, 'built a wide-spreading politico-commercial imperium without formalizing it'.[40] The Bugis – particularly the Wajo – reacted to the establishment of Dutch power in Celebes in the seventeenth century 'by making themselves the great traders between the distant eastern parts of the Archipelago and the parts to the West on the important China routes'.[41] During the eighteenth century the Bugis had made themselves 'the major traders between the eastern and western parts of the Archipelago, establishing a political influence and commercial control over many of the intervening petty states where Dutch influence was weak'.[42] It was in an attempt to enlist East India Company support against the Bugis of Selangor that the Sultan of Keddah negotiated the cession of Penang; while, as D. K. Bassett notes, in the 1780s, a number of English 'country traders' sufficiently valued the independence of

Riau from the Dutch to run guns to the Bugis who were in control there.[43] The Bugis did not develop a formal empire, and this loosely-articulated commercial and political network was flexible enough to be responsive to the shifting economics and politics of the region. Thus, although the foundation of Singapore in 1819 weakened the position of the Bugis establishment at Pontianak in west Borneo, instead of pro-ducing political disintegration or extensive piracy (which seems to have been the response of the 'sea people' of the Riau archipelago), this led to Bugis settlements such as that at Kutai in east Borneo developing trade with Singapore.[44]

The Bugis indeed were so successful that the power of their 'empire' was felt as a restraint by European traders. In *Piracy and Politics*, Tarling draws attention to the journalism of John Dalton in the *Singapore Chronicle* in the late 1820s. Dalton's target was the Bugis-dominated states of east Borneo. He attacks the Bugis for piracy, and he reports the Bugis as having taken a number of Europeans captive – including a European female (PP, 113).[45] He also presents himself, as Brooke was to do later, as the potential liberator of the Dayak/Kayan peoples of the interior of Borneo. He noted that 'all they desire is the opportunity of exchanging; this at present cannot be done, as they are compelled to sell their produce to some neighbouring raja or rich Bugis' (PP, 114). As Tarling suggests, Dalton's journalism and reports were designed 'to break down the Bugis influence ... as a means of expanding the Singapore entrepôt's traffic with the people of the interior' (PP, 114). It is also interesting to note how Dalton makes strategic (and very loose) use of the label 'piracy' to describe the commercial monopoly of the Bugis: 'They are all pirates who paralyze the exertions of thousands of individuals who would be otherwise active'.[46] Dalton thus interpellates the Bugis' commercial activities within a powerful and influential imperialist discourse. Raffles, by comparison, for his own political reasons, in his *History of Java*, presents a very different picture of the Bugis as traders:

> The enterprize of the Arabs, Chinese, and Bugis is very conspicuous. They are in general fair traders; and Europeans acquainted with their several characters can rely on their engagements, and command their confidence. Many of them, particularly the Bugis, are possessed of very large capital. (HJ, I, 203).

Raffles, nevertheless, laid great stress on the suppression of 'piracy' in his plans for an English empire in the archipelago.

As Tarling (1957) points out, the term 'piracy' was used fairly freely to cover a range of activities: trade disputes involving Malay 'states'; quarrels between or within Malay 'states'; even 'empires' established by Malays (such as Achin and Brunei). Where Malay states 'gained authority over lesser states, forced their trade to pay taxes, or to come to a central port' (14), such attempts at revenue collection were often labelled piracy. The Sulu attacks on the Philippines – which were part of a continuing struggle between Sulus and Spain since the sixteenth century and took place in the context of Spanish claims on the Sultan of Sulu's territories – were labelled piracy, while Spanish attacks on the Sulus were not.[47] In general, what was being demonised by the label of 'piracy' was indigenous agency which posed competition or resistance – or even just independent activity.[48] It was obviously in the interests of the mercantile community of the Straits Settlements, for example, to make allegations of piracy: 'For the merchants were anxious to ensure the breakdown of larger and more exacting forms of native government' (1957, 15). By this means they also gained naval backing for their own trading transactions.[49]

A further objection to all these mappings, however, might be that they maintain a 'trade and empire' approach that doesn't escape from van Leur's criticism. They present narratives of conquest and domination, which ignore the internal dynamics of the region and underplay the interactive aspects of the colonial encounter. James Francis Warren's study of 'the Sulu zone' attempts what he calls 'an ethnohistorical research strategy' (xii) in order to offer a reading of the Sulu zone as a single 'cultural ecosystem' (xxi) from a Sulu perspective.[50] The first point that needs to be made is again one of terminology: the term 'Sulu' has been used so far as if it represented a people, but the zone which includes the Sulu Sultanate is an ethnically and culturally diverse region. The dominant ethnic group is the Taosug, who are quite distinct from the indigenous Samal communities.[51] As Warren notes, the zone, which includes the Sulu archipelago, the north-east coast of Borneo, southern Mindanao, and western Celebes, brings together island and coastal peoples, nomadic fishermen and slash-and-burn agriculturalists in a loosely-integrated political system made up of a shifting network of interpersonal relations focused on the Sulu Sultanate. Sulu's ascendancy at the end of the eighteenth century derived from the expanding trade between India and China.[52] At the same time, from 1785 to 1845, Manila-Sulu trade was a vital link in Spanish-Philippine trade with China. In the first half of the ninetenth-century, however, the Taosug tried to diversify Sulu's commercial relations with the West. Their skill as diplomats and traders ended in a Pyrrhic victory. Treaties negotiated with the United States (1842), France (1845), and Britain (1849) alarmed Manila: the Spanish government then mounted a series of expeditions against the Sulu archipelago, and all trade between Manila and Sulu ceased. Later, in the 1870s, the Spanish set out to destroy systematically all Taosug shipping (119), and, in 1875, attacked and destroyed various Taosug towns and settlements, occupying Jolo until 1899. As Warren notes, 'the Spaniards could not come to terms with the Sultan' because the Taosugs 'insisted on their freedom of trade with foreign nations' (122).

Heavy ordinance and gunpowder were key articles of exchange in the early traffic between the East India Company and the Sulu Sultanate: the Bengal saltpetre used in English gunpowder was superior to local saltpetre. As a result, in the early nineteenth century, gunpowder and muskets were the main items desired by the Taosug in their dealings with European country traders.[53] The other important participants in Taosug commerce were the Bugis. The Bugis traded slaves, spices, cotton and coffee for iron, saltpetre, muskets, and gunpowder. This trade declined between 1846 and 1870 partly with the opening of the port of Macassar to free trade in 1846, partly as a result of Spanish naval patrols, partly through the competition of merchant venturers such as William Lingard.[54]

If the rise and fall of the Sulu Sultanate depended on its relations with the European presence in the region, and to that extent on European politics, its development was also shaped (as Warren shows) by shifts in the regional balance of power. External trade was the source of both the wealth and the political influence of the Taosugs. The external trading networks provided the goods for the Taosugs' dominance of intersocietal exchange networks within the Sulu archipelago and strengthened their hegemony over 'the Mingdanao and Iranun, the riverine agriculturalists of northeast Borneo, and the Bugis of Samarinda, Kylie and Berau' (66). Warren describes the Sulu Sultanate as 'a centralized political system whose territorial sovereignty was recognized most strongly at the centre' (xxii) but shades away at the peripheries.[55] Borneo is a case in point. In the late eighteenth century, any effort by Sulu to assert its hegemony was resisted by the neighbouring sultanates of Brunei and Cotabato. From 1770 to 1820, the Sultanate of Sulu was in conflict with the Brunei Sultanate. In succession, the Sultan of Brunei sought the assistance of the English and the Spanish against the Sulu Sultanate. There was also conflict with the

Bugis in the Tirun district, 'the southern extremity of the Sulu zone' (80), which is the setting for Conrad's first novels. The district marked an overlap of Buginese and Taosug spheres of influence, and trade centres such as Gunung Tabor, Sambaliung and Bulungan switched between Buginese and Taosug dependency. Thus, the Taosug exacted tribute and trade from Gunung Tabor for over half a century (88), even though Berau remained a predominantly Bugis trading base. It is in Berau that Conrad places the action of his first two novels.

2
The Advancement of Learning: Marsden, Raffles, Brooke

While Marco Polo seems to have been the first European to visit and write of the archipelago, the historiography of the area in English begins with William Marsden's *The History of Sumatra* (1783).[1] As Bastin notes, this was not the first work about the region to be published in English, but it was 'the first detailed account of Sumatra' to appear in any European language (HS, viii). More important, Bastin claims, it was the first to provide 'truly scientific categories of analysis' (HS, ix). As a result it laid the basis for the development of Southeast Asian studies.[2] The antecedents for its 'scientific categories of analysis' are the subject of this chapter; together with the textual tradition that developed from it. This chapter will suggest how a semiotic component derived from the practices of merchants combined with a material component derived from the practices of the landed gentry. This discursive formation will, in turn, be mapped onto the transition from the monarchical rule of the sixteenth century through the changes of seventeenth-century commonwealth and Restoration to the eighteenth-century development of the administrative machinery of government. To put it in other words, the chapter traces the writing of Malaysia as part of the Enlightenment project.

Marsden, Banks and enlightenment science

In the conclusion to the first edition, Marsden recorded how the writing of the *History* was 'encouraged by persons of the first consideration in the world of science' (HS, I,373). In fact, Marsden was encouraged to undertake the work by his association with Joseph Banks and other members of the Royal Society, whom he first met early in 1780.[3] Marsden (1754–1836) went to Bencoolen in West Sumatra as a Writer in the service of the East India Company in 1770 at the age of sixteen. He spent from May 1770 to July 1779 in West Sumatra before return-ing to London in 1780.[4] From 1780 onwards he was part of Banks's London circle.

Joseph Banks (1743–1820) was the eldest son of a wealthy, landed family. Like many of his fellow gentry, as a young man he displayed the tastes of a virtuoso. He started his collection of flora in 1763, and he had his cabinet of insects, butterflies and beetles. He combined these tastes with a sense of public service as the responsibility of a member of a privileged class. In his case, this took the form of 'the Scientific Service of the Public'. In *Joseph Banks and the English Enlightenment*, John Gascoigne traces Banks's passage from the unsys-tematic intellectual interests of the gentlemanly virtuoso and collector to the scientific specialist.[5] Banks had an interest in botany from his teens. At Oxford, he arranged to be taught botany at his own expense. But it was the work of Linnaeus which helped effect the transition from virtuoso to botanist.[6] As Gascoigne observes:

> At last there was a commonly agreed means of filing the products of the natural world into an orderly and rational system and thus of investing the interests of the naturalist and virtuoso with the dignity of a true science. (JBEE, 66)

Banks, however, was more than just a gentleman collector whose interest in botany became scientific. As Gascoigne has shown, Banks was 'a scientific statesman of enormous significance' (JBEE, 2). In the first place, the landed gentry's interest in the improvement of the estate, in Banks's hands, took on a global and imperial dimension. As Gascoigne puts it, Banks attempted 'to apply science' to the cause of increasing both the yield of the earth and 'the diversity of the products that could be derived from it' not just within Britain but in its Empire (JBEE, 4). One example of this is Banks's involvement in 'global transplantations'. Secondly, through Banks's extraordinary range of activities, the gentleman's culture of the eighteenth century, with its clubs and societies, became the basis of the material and institutional practices of nineteenth-century science. Thirdly, through Banks's wide range of public roles, the advancement of science was imbricated in the machinery of state that gradually developed in the course of the eighteenth century. Banks's access to the networks of political power enabled the development of scientific projects. Banks's involvement in bureaucratic power resulted in the assertion of power-knowledge on a global scale.

Banks became a public figure in 1771. In 1773, he took over informal direction of the Royal Botanic Gardens in Kew, which brought him into close association with George III.[7] His real power base, however, was the Royal Society.[8] He was elected to membership of the Royal Society in 1766; he became a member of the Society's Council in 1774; and he became President of the Royal Society in 1778, a position he held until his death in 1820. As President of the Royal Society, he was *ex officio* an overseer of the Board of Longitude and of the Royal Greenwich Observatory.[9] In addition, he was also (among many other things) a member of the Board of Agriculture, a trustee of the British Museum, and a founder member of the African Association, which sponsored a series of expeditions (including that of Mungo Park). From his position as President of the Royal Society, he became more and more involved in the workings of government, advising on a wide range of issues relating to science and empire, and becoming, in effect, almost a government department. By 1797, Banks was a Privy Councillor (as a member of the Privy Council Committee for Trade and Plantations). As a public figure, Banks's social connections meant that he was intimately involved in the networks of administrative power for half a century at the time when those networks of power were themselves evolving into the administrative machinery of the British imperial state.[10]

At the same time, from 1776 his home in Soho Square became 'a virtual scientific research institute' (JBEE, 26); and Banks positioned himself at the centre of a complex interchange between international scientific academies, networks of local societies, and a range of individuals at provincial, national and international levels. Thus Kew Gardens became the model for a series of colonial replicas (including, for example, Calcutta Botanic Gardens), between which Banks set up a practice of exchanges in a system of 'global transplantation'. On another level, Banks maintained an extensive national and international correspondence, which constituted a network for exchange of information and material. To take one example, Banks's correspondence with Johann Blumenbach: Banks supplied Blumenbach with skulls from voyages of exploration; Banks arranged for Blumenbach to have access to the mummies in the British Museum, when Blumenbach visited London; Blumenbach, in turn, supplied recruits for African Association expeditions and linguistic material from Africa, which Banks then passed on to Marsden for his later research into the relations between languages.[11]

Banks's experience of maritime exploration would no doubt have re-inforced his encouragement of Marsden's writing of *The History of*

Sumatra. In 1766 he had taken part in the *Niger* expedition to Newfoundland. More important, in 1768 he had sailed with James Cook in the *Endeavour* on a three-year circumnavigation of the globe, via Tahiti, New Zealand and Australia, which had passed through the archipelago.[12] In 1772, after withdrawing from Cook's second voyage, the *Resolution* expedition, he made a voyage instead to Iceland.[13] Again, what at the outset seems a variant of one of the practices of his class (in this case, the Grand Tour) became a scientific practice. Banks's presence on board the *Endeavour* as a scientific observer seems to have established the practice of combining scientific inquiry with naval exploration.[14]

Gascoigne suggests that the virtuoso's interest in collecting and in antiquities became the basis for scientific collecting and anthropology, respectively.[15] The study of natural and historical worlds were regarded as 'complementary parts of the map of knowledge of gentlemanly society' (JBEE60). These spheres of interest subsequently became specialised into the emergent disciplines of biology and anthropology. Thus, during the voyage of the *Endeavour*, in addition to assembling a natural history collection, Banks kept a journal, and Banks's journal does not confine itself to natural history.[16] Beaglehole observes that, from the arrival in Tahiti, the 'natural historian becomes the natural historian of man', and suggests that Banks's notes on material culture and customs make him effectively the 'founder of Pacific ethnology' (EJ, I, 40). At Raiatea in the South Seas, for example, he made notes on dress (EJ, I, 325); games (EJ, I, 325); dancing (EJ, I, 324, 328); canoe-building (EJ, I, 319); and religion (EJ, I, 318, 324). Similarly, on leaving Tahiti, he offers an extended account of the culture he has encountered in terms of hairstyles, tattoos, dress, houses, food, eating taboos, music, dance, making cloth, fishing, tools, boat-building, cosmogony, language, illness and medicine, ceremonies for the dead, creation myth, marriage, the social system (EJ, I, 334–86). In what might be seen as an anticipation of participant-observation as an anthropological method, he also takes part in a mourning ritual, which involves being stripped, blackened with charcoal, and running naked among the mourners (EJ, I, 288–9).

As an observer of natural history, Banks follows Linnaeus: he selects, names, lists, and classifies a range of creatures. When he extends natural history to include the human culture he encounters, he continues to name and list objects and practices. In doing so, he constructs (to use Foucault's terms) a corpus of knowledge which presupposes a particular way of looking at things, and he constitutes himself, the

speaking and seeing subject, as the locus of the registering and interpretation of information.[17] The source for both Banks's categories and
his constitution of the observer is to be found in the work of Francis
Bacon.

Francis Bacon, the Royal Society, and 'The New Atlantis'

The Royal Society was incorporated in 1662 and received its Royal
Charter in the same year. Although the founding of the Royal Society
coincided with the Restoration, its roots go back much further. The
founding of the Royal Society can be seen as 'both Bacon's deification
as a philosopher and the final victory of the Baconian project of collab-
oration, utility, and progress in natural enquiries'.[18] Thomas Sprat's
History of the Royal Society (1667) both records and is part of this
process. Sprat self-deprecatingly suggests the redundancy of his own
writing: 'there should have been no other Preface to the History of the
Royal Society' than some of Bacon's work.[19] The frontispiece to the
volume makes the same point: it shows a study, at the centre of which
is a bust of Charles II, flanked by two figures, Lord Brounker (the first
President of the Royal Society) and Francis Bacon (identified as 'Artium
Instaurator').[20] The three figures celebrate the patron and president of
the Society – and present Bacon as the official precursor.[21] The objects
in the study (navigation instruments, books, the gun) can be read as a
reference to Bacon's celebration of the navigational compass, printing
and gunpowder as the three great inventions that changed the course
of history by changing space, communications, and politics (CCB,
37).[22] They also obviously figure maritime exploration, the dissemination of information, and conquest.

Bacon's plan for a systematic methodology for the reform of knowledge had two principal strands: the use of inductive as against syllogis-
tic logic; and the compilation of a 'natural history', a vast collection of
material about natural phenomena, to serve as the 'primary material of
philosophy' (SSRE, 13). It is fair to say, however, that, although
members of the Royal Society 'claimed kinship' with Bacon, they in
fact 'ignored Baconian induction as a scientific method'.[23] As regards
the Baconian emphasis on 'careful observation and experiment', Bacon
'only gave a systematic statement of an approach that already existed'
(SSRE, 15). Nevertheless, Hunter concludes that 'Bacon's philosophy
provided a general programme' (SSRE, 17), while his idea of 'natural
history' had an impact on the contemporary image of science. *New
Atlantis*, in particular, was deeply influential (SSRE, 13).

Antonio Pérez-Ramos argues that Sprat's *History of the Royal Society* produced a 'canonical version of Baconianism' (CCB, 99), which ignored the inductive method but foregrounded natural history and theory-free experimenting. Bacon was thus re-invented by the Royal Society as a restoration virtuoso. In this re-invention, Bacon and the Royal Society were represented as sharing a common mission: the empirical observation of flora, fauna, and the inhabitants of the 'natural world'.[24] The Royal Society, however, also responded to those aspects of Bacon's work which dealt with the organisation of science (CCB, 314). Bacon's 'device', performed at Gray's Inn in 1594, showed him already thinking in terms of institutions for the advancement of learning: the library; botanical and zoological gardens; the museum; the laboratory.[25] As Banks's career demonstrates, these institutions would put in place the institutional components of a discursive practice. *New Atlantis* gave that project form and provided a semiotic model.

Rawley's address to the reader at the start of the first English edition of *New Atlantis* (1627) foregrounds Bacon's political agenda: to present 'a model or description of a College, instituted for the interpreting of Nature, and the producing of great and marvellous works for the benefit of men'.[26] Salomon's House is 'dedicated to the study of the works and creatures of God' (AL, 276). This formulation (like the College's alternative title, the College of the Six Days' Works) very carefully brackets out the religious and the metaphysical from its area of concern. Within these limits, the College aims at 'the knowledge of causes, and secret motions of things; and the enlarging of the bounds of human empire' (AL, 288). Bacon's narrative gives the College's mission statement and objectives a very precise embodiment. It emphasises the scientific method of observation and experiment.[27] It describes the use of botanical gardens and zoos for observation and experimentation with flora and fauna. It indicates experiments relating to heat, optics, sound, smell, taste, and motion. It suggests possible benefits in the form of such inventions as 'new artificial minerals' (AL, 288), telephones, flying machines, submarines, and 'instruments of war' (AL, 295). The account of the different categories of Fellows reaffirms the importance of the devising of experiments and the development of practical applications, but, alongside the research and development aspect of the College, great emphasis is put on the gathering of information. Indeed, the College actively sends out Fellows to gain knowledge of 'the sciences, arts, manufactures, and inventions of all the world; and withal to bring unto us books, instruments, and patterns in every kind' (AL, 277).[28]

New Atlantis is written in the form of the narrative of a voyage. One of Bacon's major sources was the English version of Joseph Acosta's *The Naturall and Morall Historie of the East and West Indies*.[29] Acosta, in his 'Advertisement to the Reader', describes the book that follows as 'partly historical and partly philosophical', meaning that it has a dual focus: 'the deedes and custome' of the people and 'the works of nature'. Book I includes an account of the ocean west of Peru and suggests the existence of a large land mass there. This verbal mapping of the western ocean includes references to 'the Ilands, which they call Salomon' (I, 20), to '*Moloco* ... which they called the Golden Chersonese', and to 'that great and famous Iland of Sumatra ... well-knowne by the ancient name of Taprobana' (I,37). Acosta, however, is keen to emphasise the priority of 'observation' over scriptural and classical authorities (I,20). Accordingly, he devotes most of the rest of the book to the 'West Indies' and gives details of metals; plants; animals; lakes and rivers; weather; as well as religion and customs, policy and government. The narrative of *New Atlantis* begins with the account of a voyage from Peru for China and Japan through the South Seas. After leaving Peru, the ship is carried up north into 'the greatest wilderness of waters in the world' (AL, 257), where it discovers New Atlantis. The account of New Atlantis that follows provides a model of scientific observation. After mapping the voyage, like Acosta's work, it offers a description of the land, of the inhabitants, of their dress, fruits, housing, customs, and institutions. It explores 'what laws and customs they had concerning marriage' (AL, 284), and it offers 'thick' description of a particular 'feast of the family' (AL, 279). In other words, Bacon's taxonomic skills provide a model for the scientific description of the encounter with other cultures. It is a model that Banks in his journals and Marsden in his *History* were to follow.[30]

At the same time, *New Atlantis* is marked by a scopic regime, a concern with the specular. While the Europeans subject Atlantis to their gaze, they are also conscious that they are potentially the objects of their hosts' gaze. They recognise, for example, that their attendants might also have the task of spying on them ('may withal have an eye upon us' [AL, 263]). The Governor's account of Atlantis emphasises this scopic regime. His account of traveller's from Atlantis, for example, stresses that 'we know well most part of the habitable world, and are ourselves unknown' (AL, 266). Peter Hulme and Ludmilla Jordanova have noted the importance of vision for the Enlightenment project: observation is 'at the heart of the acquisition of solid knowledge of the world'.[31] As Braidotti puts it, 'the scopic drive' becomes 'the paradigm of knowledge'.[32] But these unseen seers also emphasise asymmetries of knowledge and power. A speech by one of the Europeans raises exactly this point. He comments first on foreign travel:

> though the traveller into a foreign country doth commonly know more by the eye than he that stayeth at home can by relation of the traveller; yet both ways suffice to make a mutual knowledge, in some degree, on both parts. (AL, 270)

Then he compares this exchange of knowledge with the situation of travellers from Atlantis, which he likens to the 'condition and propriety of divine powers and beings, to be hidden and unseen to others, and yet to have others open, and as in a light to them' (AL, 270).[33] In fact, the extreme instance of the Atlantean travellers serves to expose the asymmetries of power and knowledge masked by the reference to 'mutual exchange, in some degree'. It epitomises the 'positional superiority', which Said describes as a founding strategy of Orientalism: Bacon's unseen seer, in other words, could be said to represent Said's 'sovereign Western consciousness'.[34]

Julie Solomon has argued that Baconian empiricist discourse derived from the material practices of renaissance merchants and traders. In opposition to the courtly mode of reading, which operated through activating the reader's identificatory desire, this discourse constructed a reader who did not invest himself in the text but distanced himself from it. Solomon argues that its 'objectivity' was derived from commercial class practices in encountering other cultures: she characterises these as the temporary suspension of aspects of the self – desires, values, habits, customs – in order to gain material benefit from alien circumstances. As Kenneth Andrews puts it:

> The approach of the Elizabethans and Jacobeans to non-Europeans was normally commercial and pragmatic. Business required a realistic, live-and-let-live relationship and merchants visiting or resident in parts of Africa and Asia had to conduct themselves in a manner acceptable to their hosts.[35]

Solomon takes this a step further. She suggests that 'in contemporary travel guides the specificity of the merchant traveller's self disappears from view to be replaced by nothing more than extensive lists of objects' (521). She then argues that Bacon draws on the experiences of 'trading merchants, commercial and other travellers' and codifies their way of knowing and reading the world.[36] Bacon lifts this structure of knowing the world out of its mercantile economic, political and cultural context to relocate it within courtly scientific discourse. He appropriates and de-contextualises a mercantile practice to present it as 'a cognitive stance that transcends all conditions of nature, nurture, class, nation, and history' (525). It becomes what Braidotti calls 'the fetishised false universal mode of Western humanism' (NS, 37). Clearly, however, the merchant traveller's self-distancing is not to be read as disinterest; 'commercial class discourse preserves a central place for self-interest ... but renders it powerfully invisible because radically contingent' (522). The self is withheld, but self-interest permeates the discourse. In the same way, the scientific knower 'disinterestedly perceiving and recording the world' (519) withdraws herself from the object of perception in order to gain mastery over it. Bacon both codified a discourse, as Solomon argues, and anticipated a discursive formation. But the Baconian project of knowledge is also a project of mastery.

Lisa Jardine notes that the renaissance merchant's transactions 'conform more to the pattern of intellectual service than to the simple model of manufacture':

> His profit derives from his knowledge and understanding of markets, his ability to anticipate rise and fall in demands, his judgement as to what goods are valued more highly in one location than another.[37]

To have an edge over his competitors, the merchant needed to be more quickly informed than anybody else, and 'the prime requirement' was to be included 'in as many as possible of the information networks'.[38] As Jardine observes, the figure of the merchant maps onto the international networker, onto the intellectual knowledge gatherer, and onto the political intelligencer. There are comparable slippages between knowledge transactions, commercial gain and political control in the writings of Marsden, Raffles, and Brooke.

Marsden and commerce

In the Preface to the third edition of *The History of Sumatra*, Marsden describes his aim as the provision of 'authenticated facts' for naturalists, not 'the marvellous' for entertainment. In the *History* itself, he champions scepticism against credulity, and he is even sceptical about scepticism.[39] Indeed, the scientific aspect of Marsden's work is manifested not so much in its organisation or its generation of categories, but in his concern with evidence. He notes the absence of comprehensive written sources for constructing a history (HS, v); he is scrupulous also about possibilities of bias in the information as a result of the European presence. Thus, he ends his account of Battu writing:

> as this was performed in the presence of Europeans, and upon our paper, they might have deviated from their ordinary practice ... the evidence therefore is not conclusive. (HS, 384)

He is sensitive also to cultural relativism. After offering the European view of Malay dancing, he instantly presents the Malay view of European dancing:

> Certain I am that our usual dances are, in their judgement, to the full as ridiculous. The minuets they compare to the fighting of two game-cocks, alternately approaching and receding. (HS, 267)

He is careful to specify at the outset the sources of his own information: his own immediate observation; 'matter of common notoriety'; and information received 'upon the concurring authority of gentlemen' of the East India Company. This not only indicates who is allowed to speak, but also points towards the institutional site of that speaking: the information-gathering of the servants of the East India Company.[40] His subsequent use of narratives of journeys written by various 'servants' of the Company in his *History* also evidences the extraordinary extent to which textual production was part of the Company's experience and practice.[41]

In the Preface to the third edition, Marsden describes his objectives and presents how he sees his task. He begins by noting that Sumatra has been 'unaccountably neglected by writers' (HS, iii), despite its familiarity to Europeans for centuries. He criticises the Portuguese: 'more eager to conquer nations than to explore their manners or antiquities' (HS, iii-iv). The Dutch and English have been similarly remiss: 'not one page of information respecting the inhabitants of Sumatra has been communicated to the public by any Englishman who has resided there' (HS, iv). His concern is with the natural history of Sumatra but also with 'the customs, opinions, arts, and industry of the original inhabitants' (HS, vi). He is not interested in 'the European powers who have established themselves on the island; the history of their settlements, and of the revolutions of their commerce' (HS, vi). He understands the problems a complete record of Sumatra faces, not only from the absence of comprehensive written sources, but also from the diversity of 'national distinctions' and 'independent governments':

> the local divisions are perplexed and uncertain; the extent of juris-diction of the various princes is inaccurately defined; settlers from different countries, and at different periods, have introduced an irregular, though powerful, influence, that supersedes in some places the authority of the established governments, and imposes a real dominion on the natives, where a nominal one is not assumed. (HS, v)

As with Raffles later, there is evident here a desire to recover the original indigenous culture. Said has suggested that this is a manoeuvre characteristic of the orientalist project: the target culture is first to be known and then to be re-created by European scholars, who disinter languages, cultures, to posit the true orient by which to judge and rule the modern orient. This knowledge is achieved by two standard proce-dures: essentialising the Other and asserting an originary identity. Marsden, however, is aware that 'complete originality' might be 'a visionary idea': he is prepared to content himself with 'antiquity at least' (HS, 54).[42]

The History of Sumatra begins with what are, in effect, a series of brief chapters on the geography, climate, geographical features, flora and fauna of Sumatra. The chapters offer comprehensive descriptive listings – of, for example, fruits and flowers, or animals and reptiles. Significantly, the striking exception to this pattern is the chapter on 'vegetable productions' (HS, 129). The account of pepper, nutmeg and cloves does not follow the pattern of preceding chapters of comprehen-sive description. All information is dominated by and subordinate to the importance of these 'vegetable productions' as commodities. Thus the chapter begins:

> Of those productions of Sumatra, which are regarded as articles of commerce, the most important and most abundant is pepper. This is the object of the East India Company's trade thither, and

this alone it keeps in its own hands; its servants, and merchants under its protection, being free to deal in every other commodity. (HS, 129)

The account of nutmeg and cloves focuses particularly on the triumph of transplanting nutmegs and cloves first to Sumatra and subsequently to Bengal after the British capture of Banda and Amboina in 1798. He quotes Robert Broff, then chief of the Residency at Fort Marlborough:

> The acquisition of the nutmeg and clove plants became an object of my solicitude the moment I received ... the news of the surrender of the islands where they are produced; being convinced, from the information that I had received, that the country in the neighbourhood of Bencoolen, situated as it is in the same latitude with the Moluccas, exposed to the same periodical winds, and possessing the same kind of soil, would prove congenial to their culture. (HS, 146)

Here, for the modern reader, cartography, climatology, and geology suddenly converge in a scheme of transplantation. Although this recalls the experimentation with 'variety of ground and soil, proper for divers trees and herbs' in *New Atlantis*, the interest of Broff and Marsden is, of course, not merely the scientific one of transplanting plants into congenial environments. Military action and scientific information-gathering are drawn together for commercial purposes. Marsden makes very clear the real reason for the tone of triumph. His account of nutmegs and cloves begins:

> It is well-known with what jealousy and rigour the Batavian government has guarded against the transplantation of the trees producing nutmegs and cloves from the islands of *Banda* and *Amboina* to other parts of India. (HS, 146)

The East India Company was concerned to keep the trade in pepper in its own hands, but it was equally keen to break the Dutch East India Company's monopoly of the trade in nutmegs and cloves.

If Marsden offers scrupulously detailed accounts of flora and fauna, his accounts of the human inhabitants of Sumatra, despite his best intentions, are more problematic. He presents certain tropes which will recur in subsequent English accounts of the people of the region. For example, in discussing the inhabitants of the eastern side of the island, he notes how 'they are settled at the entrance of almost all the navigable rivers, where they more conveniently indulge their habitual bent for trade and piracy' (HS, 421).[43] Elsewhere, he observes how, because of the favourable climate of Sumatra, 'the human machine is kept going with small effort' (HS, 54); as a result, 'the negative pleasure of inaction' is preferred to 'the enjoyment of any conveniences that are to be purchased with exertion and labour' (HS, 55).[44] This explains for Marsden the puzzling combination of 'high antiquity' with 'limited progress' in the arts and sciences of Asia. He follows a standard Enlightenment line in suggesting that climate had produced the different temporalities of Europe and Asia. This idea of Malay 'degeneration' led, in turn, to the trope of 'regeneration' which features later in the writings of Swettenham and Clifford.[45]

This construction of the inhabitants of Sumatra, with its assertion of European superiority, also underwrites Marsden's political agenda. Towards the end of his *History*, he praises the Company's Residents, noting that they are considered as 'the protector of the people from the injustice and oppression of the chiefs' (HS, 214), while also protecting the chiefs from each other: the districts over which the Company's power extends 'are preserved in uninterrupted peace'; if it weren't for this power 'every *dusun* [village] of every river would be at war with its neighbour' (HS, 214). Accordingly, he foresees 'the gradual and necessary increase of the Company's sway, which the peace and good of the country required' (HS, 215). He allows in a dissenting voice, but only to challenge and discredit it:

> Then let not short-sighted or designing persons, upon false principles of justice, or ill-digested notions of liberty, rashly endeavour to overturn a scheme of government, doubtless not perfect, but which seems best adapted to the circumstances it has respect to ... Let them not vainly exert themselves ... to infuse a spirit of freedom and independence, in a climate where nature possibly never intended they should flourish. (HS, 215)

The emphasis on structures of dependence and subordination in his account of civil society in Sumatra now comes into play. The people of Sumatra, he affirms, are 'free in the choice of whom they will serve' (HS, 216); the chiefs willingly accept Company domination; and any criticism of this arrangement fails to recognise the character of the people, the patriarchal and feudal nature of the society, the climate and, indeed, nature itself. Marsden's collection of information in his *History* thus in the end underwrites his political judgement: it gives him the authority to dismiss critics of the Company. More important, through its production of knowledges, the *History* creates 'a space for a "subject peoples"': its system of representation presents the population in terms of degenerate types 'in order to justify conquest and to establish systems of administration'.[46]

Raffles and political intelligence

Thomas Stamford Raffles (1781–1826), the son of a captain in the West Indies trade, became a clerk in East India House in 1795; in 1805 he was sent to the Penang establishment of the East India Company as assistant secretary. He took advantage of the sea-voyage to learn Malay, and, according to his widow, Lady Raffles, developed from the start the habit of 'associating with the natives, and admitting them to intimate and social intercourse' (*Memoir*, 8).[47] In 1806 he began his correspondence with William Marsden, and, by 1808, he was encouraged to collect information on 'the Eastern Isles' (*Memoir*, 14). The French annexation of Holland in 1809 produced a crisis for the English in Southeast Asia. To quote Lady Raffles again:

> France looked to Java as the point from whence her operations might be most successfully directed, not only against the political ascendancy of England in the East, but likewise against her commercial interests both abroad and at home. (*Memoir*, 22)

Lord Minto, Governor General of Bengal, was ordered to expel the Dutch from Java and destroy their fortifications. Instead, he established a provisional administration there under Raffles. Raffles's knowledge of the Malay language and his interest in Malay literature, customs and laws now proved its usefulness. It provided the means and the basis for forging political relations with Javanese chiefs and Bali rajas. Raffles had written to Minto (in a different context):

> The want of local information is, indeed, the rock on which the infant settlements of the English have at all times been wrecked.[48]

Raffles supplied just such 'local information': his precise and detailed knowledge of individuals, peoples, cultures, places was put to strategic use in the English takeover of Java.[49]

In August 1811 the English fleet reached Java; by September Java had capitulated, and Raffles was installed as Lieutenant-Governor. Significantly, while Minto was staying in Malacca, en route to Java, Raffles had organised a meeting of the Malacca Asiatic Society, and one of Raffles's early actions once he became Lieutenant-Governor of Java was to revive the Batavian Society of Arts and Sciences.[50] Lady Raffles notes that he availed himself 'of every opportunity of gaining local knowledge'; to this end, local chiefs were 'constant guests at his table' (*Memoir*, 123). To this end also the Batavian Society of Arts and Sciences was encouraged to undertake the learning of Javanese and the collection of Javanese manuscripts.[51] Raffles's own agenda can perhaps be glimpsed in his 1813 'Discourse' to the Society, where he drew particular attention to 'the great Island of Borneo, hitherto a blank on the chart of the world' (*Memoir*, 142). While re-organising the economy and administration of Java, replacing the Dutch enforcement system by a 'land-rent' system and a 'village-system' derived from India, Raffles was also busy making drawings of ancient monuments, collecting materials for a Javanese vocabulary, collecting specimens and information. As he wrote to Marsden (12 January 1813):

> No exertions are wanting in collecting the most useful and extensive information; and we are already far advanced in a statistical account of each district. (*Memoir*, 206)

Through this network of Societies, scholarly expertise was encouraged, organised, and put to colonial use: scholarly knowledge was institutionalised to make Malaysia accessible to European scrutiny.

Raffles left Java in March 1816 and returned to London, where he wrote *The History of Java*.[52] Raffles was very familiar with Marsden's *The History of Sumatra*, and clearly took it as a model for his own work.[53] In Chapter I, he offers a mapping of Java and an account of its seasons, fruits, trees, animals, and 'useful productions', generally (HJ, 42). Chapter II discusses the population; Chapter III agriculture; Chapter IV manufactures and handicrafts – and so on. Chapter VI deals with the 'intellectual and moral character' (HJ, 244) of the people of Java, their institutions and government; Chapter VII discusses 'usages and customs'.

According to the *Memoir*, Raffles believed in 'fixed and immutable principles of the human character' (*Memoir*, 212) – i.e. a homogeneous human nature despite superficial cultural differences. What those 'immutable principles' might be is suggested by the terms of his support, in the Introduction to his *History*, of Hogendorp's proposals for reforming the Dutch administration of Java:

> a system founded on the principles of property in the soil, freedom of cultivation and trade, and the impartial administration of justice according to equal rights. (HJ, xliii)[54]

This suggestion is supported by his explicit criticism of the Dutch administration in Chapter III:

> The Dutch Company, activated solely by the spirit of gain, and viewing their Javan subjects with less regard or consideration than a West-India planter formerly viewed the gang upon his estate, ... employed all the pre-existing machinery of despotism, to squeeze from the people their utmost mite of contribution, the last drop of their labour, and thus aggravated the evils of a capricious and semi-barbarous government. (HJ, 151)

In place of this, Raffles created a new system during 1814–15, which involved 'the entire abolition of forced deliveries at inadequate rates, and of all feudal services, with the establishment of a perfect freedom in cultivation and trade' (HJ, 155). As this implies, the replacement of the feudal system by a land rental system was designed to encourage enterprise:

> By ... continuing to the peasant the protection of laws made for his benefit, by allowing full scope to his industry, and encouraging his natural propensity to accumulate, agriculture on Java would soon acquire a different character: it would soon become active and enterprising ... capital would be fixed and augmented in the hands of the skilful and the industrious among the cultivators ... and an improved race would shew themselves, in some measure, worthy of the most fertile region of the globe. (HJ, 161)

In short, Raffles advocates the once-more familiar principles of free trade and enterprise in opposition to Javanese feudal controls and Dutch monopoly.[55]

These principles influence Raffles's reading of the character of the people of the archipelago. From early on, he takes a positive attitude towards the Bugis and the Malays:

> Both the Malayan and *Bugis* nations are maritime and com-
> mercial, devoted to speculations of gain, animated by a spirit of
> adventure, and accustomed to distant and hazardous enterprizes ...
> (HJ, I, 43)

He explains the alleged 'indolence of the Javans' by reference to the
Dutch system:

> Much has been said of the indolence of the Javans, by those who
> deprived them of all motives for industry. ... They are as industrious
> and laborious as any people could be expected to be, in their
> circumstances of insecurity and oppression. (HJ, I, 251)

Anthony Forge offers a useful summary of Raffles's position:

> Raffles presents his own attitudes as essentially opposed to those of
> the Dutch and their system in virtually all respects. This is perhaps
> most clear in his views on the economic nature of the Javanese. To
> Raffles the Dutch justified slavery and the forced delivery of prod-
> ucts on the grounds that the Javanese would only work if they were
> forced to. ... For Raffles the Javanese were civilised and like all
> civilised men, an example of 'economic man'.[56]

Raffles submerges difference through the imposition of 'economic
man' as his model for civilised humanity. As part of this process, he
emphasises the civilised nature of the Javanese: as Forge notes, he
'constantly compares the customs and laws of the Javanese to those of
ancient Greece and Rome'. The illustrations were an integral part
of this strategy. Forge states that there were 'no reliable published
images of the inhabitants of the East Indies before the nineteenth
century' (RO, 110).[57] He argues that this is partly the result of
eighteenth-century traditions of representation: the two models for
non-Europeans were either the Europeanised image of the Noble
Savage or the non-European image of the 'depraved, fierce, subhuman'.[58] It is significant that Marsden's *History of Sumatra* had no
illustrations before the 1811 edition, and, even then, most of the
illustrations were natural history subjects.[59] In this context, Raffles's
illustrations can be seen as an important innovation. Raffles's *History
of Java* had ten colour plates, 'all dominated by humans of various

ranks'; no natural history or landscape images; and more than fifty monochrome full-page plates of man-made objects. Most significant, where Marsden's frontispiece was an anonymous 'Sumatran', Raffles's frontispiece is a portrait of a named Javanese prince. As Forge observes, 'every plate in Raffles is directed to showing the Javanese and the products of Javanese culture' (RO, 114). In other words, while clearly taking Marsden's *History* as his model, Raffles nevertheless shifts the genre from 'natural history' towards what was to become 'cultural anthropology'.

In his more detailed analysis of the genesis of the colour plates, Forge shows how Raffles intervened, at successive stages, to produce images which asserted the human form and Javanese civilisation. Daniells, whose technical skills were developed in relation to a market for 'romantic picturesqueness' (RO, 120), and who was to go on, later in life, to produce 'Orientalist' drawings, had already developed a repertoire of visual clichés to signify the 'Orient': 'exotic plants, native huts, distant boats, palms' (RO, 121). Raffles seems to have persuaded Daniells to reduce these clichés in the final plates in order to emphasise, instead, the human figure and Javanese civilisation. Accordingly, Daniells's trees and vegetation are cut back, and houses and other signs of cultural activity are foregrounded (RO, 122). In 'A Javan Woman of the Lower Class' (HJ, I, 86), for example, the foreground is occupied by a rice-threshing trough; an ox-cart with oxen is in the middle-ground; a house with human figures in the background. The dominant human figure is thus carefully placed among signs of labour and evidence of cultivation. 'A Madurese of the Rank of Mantri' (HJ, I, 94) similarly presents an image of peaceful, ordered community. The title emphasises an ordered, hierarchical society, and the fence (which Raffles had added in the middleground) intimates both cultivation and a proper sense of property and boundaries. As Forge notes, Raffles's changes produce the impression 'of a well-tended land with a numerous, prosperous and peaceful population' (RO, 146). In contrast to Marsden's verbal picture of indolence and degeneracy in Sumatra, the illustrations to *The History of Java* convey the message of a hard-working and civilised people.

Forge also draws attention to a curious anomaly. While the frontispiece presents the portrait of 'a calm and civilised aristocrat', the final plate in volume II is a 'nearly naked savage' (RO, 150). All the other plates in the two volumes are of Javanese subjects; for the final plate Raffles chooses 'A Papuan or Native of New Guinea'. Forge suggests that Raffles was thus emphasising the contrast between the civilised Javanese and 'the undifferentiated savages with which the popular imagination peopled the whole archipelago' (RO, 150). It is possible that, given Cook's fate, Raffles was consciously setting the boundary between Cook's Pacific and his own East Indies. The final plate in the book clearly asserts a difference between Java and New Guinea which is more than just geographical: it presents an image of the Other – which is an Other to both English and Javanese – as the basis of a bond between English and Javanese.

During his time as Lieutenant-Governor of Java, Raffles had sought to negotiate a series of treaties with the Malay states so that, even if Java were returned to the Dutch, the British would have an empire in the archipelago based on posts in Bangka, Bali, Celebes and Gilolo and the settlement in northern Borneo, deriving from these treaties 'a general right of superintendence over and interference with' all the Malay states (*Memoir*, 69–71). The Anglo-Dutch Treaty of London of 1814 restored the Dutch possessions taken during the Napoleonic War: Raffles was relieved of his post and returned to London. Between October 1816 and May 1817, he wrote *The History of Java* in part as propaganda for his scheme. Even his Introduction to Leyden's translation, *Malay Annals*, carries on this battle.[60] He criticises the 'greedy policy' of the Dutch, which 'swallowed up the resources of this extensive Archipelago in a narrow and rigid monopoly' (MA, viii). He makes clear what those resources are: 'the cultivation of the soil, the treasures of the mines ... the raw produce of its forests' (MA, xii). The region also constitutes a potentially important market, since the 'whole of this population' has acquired 'a taste for Indian and European manufactures' (MA, xii). Besides these commercial possibilities in terms of produce and as a market, there is also another pay-off:

> In proportion as their intercourse with Europeans increases, and a free commerce adds to their resources, along with the wants which will be created, and the luxuries supplied, the humanizing arts of life will also find their way ... (MA, xiii)

By the time this was published, Raffles's scheme was already beginning to bear fruit. Raffles had returned to the archipelago as Lieutenant-Governor of Bencoolen in 1818. In 1819, after a treaty agreement with Temenggong Abdul Rahman, Raffles had founded a settlement at Singapore. He had written to Colonel Addenbrooke

(June 1818): 'Our object is not territory, but trade; a great commercial emporium, and a *fulcrum*, whence we may extend our influence politically'.

Brooke and one-man imperialism

Raffles's founding of the settlement at Singapore stirred up diplomatic activity between England and Holland. Relations between the Dutch and the English in the region were subsequently regularised by the Treaty of 17 March 1824, which divided it up between them, effectively granting England an interest in peninsular Malaya, while affirming Dutch dominion in the archipelago.[61] In this treaty, the English withdrew from Sumatra and agreed to make no settlements or political connexions there or in the islands south of Singapore, while the Dutch made the same undertaking in regard to the peninsula, withdrawing their suzerainty over states like Perak and Selangor. The spirit of the treaty was 'to confirm a territorial dominion to the Dutch, while providing opportunities for British commerce'.[62] Accordingly, England retained Singapore and acquired Malacca and its dependencies, while the Dutch Moluccan monopoly was recognised and Dutch authority over native states was extended. Interestingly, nothing was said about Borneo. Between 1824 and the second treaty with the Netherlands in 1871, Borneo became a focus of British activity, and Foreign Office policy was intertwined with 'the varying fortunes of Sir James Brooke of Sarawak'.[63]

James Brooke (1803–1868) was the son of an East India Company official. In 1819 he became a cavalry officer in the Indian Army. He was wounded in 1825 in the Anglo-Burmese War, and, after a lengthy, unsuccessful convalescence, was forced to resign his commission in 1830. He spent 1830–1 visiting the Straits Settlements and China, and, in 1834, he made an unsuccessful trading trip to China. Brooke's father died in 1835, leaving him £30 000. Brooke bought a yacht, the *Royalist*, and, in 1838, he published his 'Prospectus' for a voyage of exploration in the archipelago. In 1839, he made his first visit to Kuching and found the country up in arms. Kuching had been founded in the 1830s by the Brunei ruler to exploit the wealth of Sarawak, but the Governor, Pangeran Makota, had driven the local Malays to opposition through his extortions. The Sultan, Omar Ali Saiffudin, had sent his uncle, Raja Muda Hassim, to quell the trouble. In 1840, on Brooke's return visit to Sarawak, the country was still in disorder. He agreed to assist Raja

Muda Hassim to put down the revolt. In exchange, in 1841, Brooke was declared Raja and Governor of Sarawak.

Between 1843 and 1850, Brooke was busy crushing his Iban and Malay adversaries in Sarawak in order to safeguard his own position there. This was Brooke's 'war against the pirates'. In 1843 and 1844, Brooke, assisted by his friend Henry Keppel, the Captain of the *Dido*, led a series of punitive raids against the Iban. The Iban had moved into Seribas, Batang Lupar, and the Sekrang River in the late eighteenth century. In 1844 Brooke attacked and destroyed the village of Patusan, the base of Sherif Sahab. These raids severely damaged the Iban through the great loss of life, the capture of guns and gunpowder, and the loss of over 200 warboats. The following year, 1845, Sir Thomas Cochrane led an expedition against Sherif Osman and his Ilanun followers in Maruda Bay. This resulted in the death of Osman, the complete destruction of the Ilanun base, and the eclipse of Ilanun power. As Tate notes, Brooke's role in Sarawak had offended the Governor of Sarawak, Pangeran Makota, who backed the Sherifs of Seribas and Sekrang against Brooke.[64] In other words, their opposition to Brooke was an extension of Brunei court politics.[65] Similarly, Sherif Osman, the Ilanun chief at Maruda Bay, was an ally of Pangeran Usop, who was Hassim's main rival at the Brunei court. Cochrane's Maruda Bay expedition thus removed an opponent of Raja Muda Hassim – and an opponent of Brooke's presence in Borneo. When Cochrane subsequently turned the guns on Pangeran Usop, Raja Muda Hassim was (temporarily) left supreme in Brunei and Brooke secure in Sarawak.[66]

For Brooke, as for Raffles, commerce was an instrument of 'progress'. Like Raffles, he saw commerce as the key to relieving interior peoples from oppression, but he also saw it as a way of reforming Malay states under British guidance.[67] As Tarling puts it:

> Intervention in the eighteenth century was a commercial technique; with Raffles it was part of a grandiose imperial scheme; with Brooke it gained special character of its own, intimately connected with his own individuality. (BBB, 38)

In 1838, Brooke prepared the prospectus for his voyage for the Royal Geographical Society.[68] The prospectus begins by describing how his voyage to China had 'opened an entirely new scene' to him, showing him for the first time 'savage life and savage nature' (EB, II, i). He invokes the map of the archipelago 'with its thousand unknown islands and tribes' (EB, II, i), which becomes the sign of both 'a large field of discovery and adventure open to any man daring enough to enter upon it' (EB, II, i) and, more prosaically, 'an extended field for Christianity and commerce, which none surpass in fertility, rich beyond the Americas in mineral production' (EB, II, ii). After a roll-call of heroic predecessors (Drake, Dampier, Cook), he presents a picture of the archipelago and its peoples which is clearly derived from his reading of Marsden, Raffles and others.[69] He presents them as lands 'degraded and brutalised by a continued course of oppression and misrule' (EB, II, v). Contemplation of the map leads to the thought that 'there are yet lands unknown which might be dis-covered' (EB, II, ii). This image of the archipelago constructed from his reading of the literature prompts 'imagination' to fantasies of rescue and regeneration. He glances at the possibility 'to relieve the darkness of Paganism, and the horrors of the eastern slave-trade' – described with some exaggeration as 'slavery in its worst and most aggravated form' (EB, II, v).[70] Then he describes more practical objectives: a stay at Singapore, 'gaining a general acquaintance with the natural history and trade of the settlement, and some knowledge of the Malay language' (EB, II, vi), followed by an expedition to Malludu Bay, where 'something may be added to our geographical knowledge of the sea-coast of this bay, its leading features, productions, rivers, anchor-ages, and inhabitants, the prospect of trade and the means of navigation' (EB, II, ix). The prospectus invokes science, commerce and Christianity: the romantic and heroic quest for knowledge combines careful, scientific preparation with both an orientation towards commercial possibilities and an idealistic rhetoric of rescue and regeneration.

Keppel records how Brooke, on leaving Calcutta for China in 1830, saw the islands of the archipelago for the first time – 'islands of vast importance and unparalleled beauty – lying neglected and unknown' (EB, I, 3). Brooke's first sight of the islands, in other words, in a classic imperialist procedure, denudes the islands of their humanity and deprives them of their history. This procedure is repeated even as he comes to know Borneo and its inhabitants. Thus, in August 1839, when he first arrives in Borneo, he produces his encounter with primary jungle as a primal scene:

> The foot of European, I said, has never touched where my foot now presses – seldom the native wanders here. Here I indeed behold nature fresh from the bosom of creation, unchanged by man, and stamped with the same impress she originally bore! (EB, I, 19)

The elision of the 'native' presence in this passage is repeated elsewhere, as when Brooke is rowed up the Samarahan river by his crew of Malay boatmen: 'we were proceeding up a Borneon [sic] river hitherto unknown, sailing where no European ever sailed before' (EB, I, 37). The 'unknown' islands and rivers are now made known to Europeans; the 'neglected' land calls for European intervention.

Brooke's response to his first sight of the 'unknown and neglected' islands is also characteristic: 'he inquired and read' (EB, I, 3). As his journal and the prospectus make clear, Brooke read widely in the available literature.[71] This textual attitude, in turn, produces the recurrent phenomenon of western writing and oriental silence. The textual tradition creates knowledge, but it also creates the reality it purports to describe (as Brooke's prospectus exemplifies). Having read Marsden's account of the Malays of Sumatra, Brooke arrives in Borneo with definite expectations about Malays. However, after his reception by Raja Muda Hassim, he notes how his expectations have not been fulfilled:

> I expected to find an indolent and somewhat insolent people, devoted to sensual enjoyments, addicted to smoking opium, and eternally cock-fighting or gambling. (EB, I, 78)

Marsden's account of Malays in Sumatra, in other words, is read as describing 'the essential Malay', whom Brooke then expects to find in other Malay communities. Nevertheless, the textual attitude maintains its grip on him. Not only does the essentialising habit remain ('there is a straightforwardness about the Dyak character' [EB, I, 149]), but the trope of the lazy native still governs Brooke's thinking. Thus, after meeting the Bugis in Celebes, he comments 'the Bugis are not an indolent race' (EB, I, 127); conversely, by the time of his second visit to Sarawak in August 1840, he has come back to thinking of the Borneans that 'indolence is the root of their evils'.

Brooke's account of Borneo and Celebes comes not in the form of a 'history' but as first-person narrative. Curiously, this narrative is not presented directly by Brooke: Brooke's journal is mediated through two sea-captains, Keppel and Mundy. Henry Keppel's *The Expedition to Borneo of H.M.S Dido for the Suppression of Piracy* uses Keppel's presence in the archipelago as captain of the *Dido* as the thinly-realised narrative frame for the inserted narrative of Brooke's journal. Rodney Mundy's *Narrative of Events in Borneo and Celebes* begins with a brief introduction in which Mundy sketches his association with Brooke; it then presents

Brooke's journals for 1838–1846, before turning, in Volume II, to Mundy's own journal. In each of these volumes, Brooke's narrative, like Lord Jim's, is mediated through another's narration. Keppel, in a dedicatory letter to his father, refers to his 'good fortune' in being entrusted by Brooke 'with a narrative of his extraordinary career'. Mundy expresses his gratitude that Brooke's journals were 'made available' to him. The effect is that of the 'messianic strategy' Pratt ascribes to Linnaeus, with his 'disciples' fanning out across the globe.[72] Keppel and Mundy offer Brooke's narrative and establish an interpretative tradition. In his Introduction, for example, Mundy refers not just to 'the enlightened policy and progressive measures of Mr Brooke' (NEBC, 1), but to 'the sacredness of the enterprise he was engaged in' – namely, 'the desire to relieve and disenchain millions of our oppressed and enslaved fellow-beings' (NEBC, 2). Keppel rounds off Brooke's account of his role in putting down the revolt against Raja Muda Hassim and of his becoming Raja of Sarawak with the editorial comment:

> By accident – or, more properly, by Providence – he appears to have been sent to put a stop to an unnatural war, and to save the lives of the unfortunate rebels; and the benefit he had conferred on so many of his fellow-creatures, the good he had already done, and the infinity of good which he saw he still might do, made him anxious to return. (EB, I, 200)

Clearly, through their staging of Brooke's journal and their commentary on it, they can present Brooke in ways in which he could not present himself through first-person narrative. They raise the figure of Brooke to a mythic level through these messianic undertones; they present his activities through a consistently idealising rhetoric; they present Brooke himself as, if not a messiah, at least an exemplary romantic hero. Thus Keppel describes Brooke as 'truthful and generous; quick to acquire and appreciate; excelling in every manly sport and exercise' (EB, I, 4); and Brooke's farewell speech on his departure from England for the East Indies is given in a style that comically merges the rhetoric of a juvenile lead's curtain speech with that of a Civil Service memo: 'I go ... to awake the spirit of slumbering philanthropy with regard to these islands; to carry Sir Stamford Raffles' views in Java over the whole Archipelago' (EB, I, 4).[73]

The internal dialogism of this farewell speech anticipates the conflict in Keppel's narrative between philanthrophic language and imperialist ideology, between idealising commentary and the evidence of Brooke's own journal. The genre to which the journal belongs is obviously not that of the Baconian 'natural history': it is rather that to which Conrad's 'Congo Diary' and 'Upriver Book' also belong. It is clearly the product of the same professional training in observation, the same protocol of description:

> Squally bad night. This morning, the clouds clearing away, was delightful, and offered for our view the majestic scenery of Borneo. At nine got under way, and ran in on an east-by-south course 4 or 5 miles towards Tanjong Api ... (EB, I, 6)[74]

In entries like this, Brooke displays the sea-captain's attention to weather conditions and the sea-captain's duty to record the ship's progress. However, Brooke's journal goes beyond the ordinary requirements of a sea-captain to an orgy of measuring and surveying. At times, as in Conrad's 'Upriver Book', he is concerned to record landmarks and sand-banks in order to enable a safe repetition of the voyage:

> The leading mark to clear this sand is to bring the hollow formed between the round hill at the right entrance of the Sarawak river and the next hill a-head, and as you approach the river's mouth, steer for a small island close to the shore, called Pulo Karra, or Monkey Island. (EB, I, 25)

Captain Whalley, with the same professional training, is similarly attentive to precise navigational signs:

> From Low Cape to Malantan the distance was fifty miles, six hours' steaming for the old ship with the tide, or seven against. Then you steered straight for the land, and by-and-by three palms would appear on the sky ... The *Sofala* would be headed towards the sombre strip of the coast, which at a given moment, as the ship closed with it obliquely, would show several clean shining fractures – the brimful estuary of a river. (Y, 165–6)

At other times, as Brooke measures barometric pressures, sounds depths of bays and channels, journeys up rivers, takes latitude and longitude, and checks the earlier charts of Horsburgh and Dalrymple, it is evident that a more extensive survey of the area is taking place. His résumé of his activities on October 5 makes this clear:

> Beginning from Tanjong Api, we have delineated the coast as far as Tanjong Balaban; fixing the principal points by chronometer and observation, and filling in the details by personal inspection. ... plans of all these rivers have been taken as accurately as circumstances would permit, by observations of the latitude and longitude, and various points, and an eye-sketch of the distance of each reach, and the compass-bearing. (EB, I, 94–5)

The reason for this precise mapping of the area is also clear from other information Brooke records: 'Tin, the natives confidently assert, can be procured' (EB, I, 42); 'The principal production at present is rice' (EB, I, 42). Brooke's excitement at the discovery of 'wild cloves growing' is particularly revealing. Again, this is not just a 'cartographic eye', but an eye to commercial – and even political – intelligence. Thus, when he sails to Celebes, which the Dutch had closed to trade, he makes the following record of Bonthian Bay:

> The small Dutch fort or entrenchment stands rather on the eastern bight of the bay, and is composed of a few huts, surrounded by a ditch and green bank. Two guns at each corner compose its strength, and the garrison consists of about thirty Dutchmen and a few Javanese. (EB, I, 110)

Brooke's status, however, was a recurrent puzzle to the local rulers that he encountered. Spenser St John reports that, during Brooke's first visit to Kuching, the Pangeran Makota regularly visited the *Royalist* to try and discover the 'real object' of Brooke's visit to Borneo:

> It was natural for the Malay chiefs to doubt whether any man would give himself the trouble to make so long a voyage, at so great an expense, merely to explore a country, survey its coasts, and collect specimens of natural history. They expected every moment to hear that Mr Brooke was the agent of the British Government, or at least the chosen envoy of the Governor of Singapore. (LSJB, 20)

Keppel, too, records how in discussions with the Raja, Brooke 'began by saying' that, 'as a private gentleman, unconnected with commerce' he 'could have no personal interest' in what he was about to say

(EB, I, 73). When he visited Celebes, Brooke found that 'the rajahs of Wajo look to me for assistance, and think me able to perform far more than is in my power' (NEBC, I, 54). On 27 March 1840, Brooke met the patamankowe, the Wajo chief at Boni, and the dialogue that he records taking place between them points up the ambiguities following from his asserted status:

> I expressed myself gratified at his receiving me, as he was aware that I was only a private English gentleman, travelling for my own pleasure, unconnected with any government. He replied he was fully aware of it, and he likewise was a private gentleman on this occasion. (NEBC, I, 132)

St John records that, when Makota could not discover the 'real object' of Brooke's visit, 'instead of believing Mr Brooke's assurances that his was a private voyage', he only acknowledged 'that he had discovered a cleverer diplomatist than himself' (LSJB, 20). The Wajo chief at Boni seems to have similar doubts about Brooke's statement, but, as a clever diplomat, answers him with the same card.[75]

Useful science

Pratt has noted a number of intersecting processes in the second half of the eighteenth century: the emergence of natural history as a structure of knowledge; the shift from maritime exploration to the exploration of interiors; the consolidation in Europe of bourgeois forms of subjectivity and power. As she observes, natural history articulates Europe's contacts with the imperial frontier and is itself articulated by them. In particular, the natural history project naturalises the European's own global presence and authority. As Pratt also points out, the international scientific expeditions of the second half of the eighteenth century marked an alliance of intellectual and commercial élites. These produced the ideational and ideological apparatus that mediated relations to other parts of the world. This chapter has traced the evolving discourse produced by these intellectual and commercial élites in relation to Malaysia.

The disinterested pursuit of knowledge for Bacon was already permeated with interest; by the time we reach Marsden, not to speak of such servants of empire as Raffles and Brooke, the pursuit of knowledge is quite openly tied to commercial and political interests. Bacon had appropriated the discourse of merchants and attempted to bring it to court. It was, however, only with the Restoration that the Baconian project was taken up. Gascoigne suggests that 'enlightened values became part of the ideological armoury of the apologists for the Hanoverian constitution who looked back on the Revolution of 1688 as the victory of rational government over the forces of mysticism and reaction' (JBEE, 29). With the shift of government from the whim of the monarch, the oligarchical rule of the eighteenth century and the gradual development of state administrative machinery, Bacon's project was moved closer to the heart of Government. Banks was Bacon's inheritor and successor. Banks shared Bacon's valorisation of 'useful science'. He was instrumental in the creation of institutional support for 'useful science' and in bringing scientific concerns into government. The class practices and values of the landed gentry became the Trojan Horse for an intertwining of science, commerce and exploration that ultimately challenged those class practices and values. This challenge is embodied in Raffles and his model of the private man, economic man. The next chapter considers the breakdown of the authority of both scientific and administrative discourses.

3
The Inward Turn: Wallace and Clifford

Hugh Clifford arrived in Malaya in 1883 as a junior cadet in the Perak Civil Service, and served as private secretary to Hugh Low, Resident in Perak.[1] In 1887, Clifford was appointed the first British Consular Agent in Pahang. In 1895, at the very early age of thirty, he was appointed Resident of Pahang, where he remained until 1902, when he returned to England on half-pay as a result of ill-health and turned to writing to make a living.[2] He had already been writing professionally since 1895, when Arnot Reid, the editor of the *Straits Times*, had invited him to contribute a series of sketches following the example of Frank Swettenham.[3] He had published his first novel, *Since the Beginning*, in 1898; a collection of his sketches, *In a Corner of Asia*, in 1899; and a second collection, *Bushwacking*, in 1901. He had also written numerous book reviews. From March 1898 to May 1899, he had written a regular review column for the *Singapore Free Press*.[4]

Clifford's best-known review, 'Mr Joseph Conrad at Home and Abroad' (*Singapore Free Press*, 1 September 1898), attacked *Almayer's Folly* for its 'complete ignorance of Malays and their habits and customs'. However, Conrad and Clifford had already made textual contact prior to this review. On 23 April 1898, Conrad's review of Clifford's *Studies in Brown Humanity* was published in the *Academy*.[5] Conrad's review praised the book for its 'truth' ('truth unadorned, simple and straightforward'). However, as the review makes clear, Clifford's attention to the 'truth' was both a strength and a limitation: while Clifford clearly writes out of a body of knowledge and experience of the peninsula and its people, 'art veils part of the truth of life to make the rest appear more splendid, inspiring, or sinister'.[6]

In a letter to William Blackwood, Conrad commented defensively on Clifford's article: 'I never did set up as an authority on Malaysia'.[7]

At the same time, he answered the accusation of ignorance by observing that 'all the details' picked out in the article were taken from 'undoubted sources – dull wise books'. One of those 'dull, wise books' was A. R. Wallace's *The Malay Archipelago*. Richard Curle recorded Conrad's love for 'old memoirs and travels' and expressed his belief that Wallace's *Malay Archipelago* was Conrad's 'favourite bedside book':

> There were certain books which Conrad read over and over again. Of all such books I fancy that Wallace's *Malay Archipelago* was his favourite bedside companion ... of Wallace, above all, he never ceased to speak in terms of enthusiasm.[8]

Florence Clemens was the first to show how Conrad made use of Wallace's work in his fiction.[9] She demonstrated how, in *Lord Jim*, Conrad used Wallace's account of his visit to the Rajah of Goa as the basis for his description of Doramin's household; how he used Wallace's account of his friend, Mr Mesman, in describing Stein; how he drew on Wallace's own experiences for his presentation of Stein's activities as a naturalist. She argued that Conrad used *The Malay Archipelago*, in particular, 'for backgrounds with which he was unfamiliar'. Conrad, for example, had never visited Bali or Timor: 'all the information which Dain Maroola of *Almayer's Folly* gave Nina Almayer about his country on Bali could have been gleaned' from Wallace; similarly, 'all that is told in *Victory* of the Timor scene and government' in the account of Morrison's experiences in Delli derives from Wallace also.[10]

The Malay Archipelago was acknowledged by Conrad as one of the sources for his Malay fiction, while Clifford and his work were known to Conrad throughout his writing career. This chapter is not concerned with locating sources for Conrad's fictions, but rather with analysing the discourses present in Wallace's work as a precursor text and in Clifford's work as texts with which Conrad's were, to some extent, in dialogue. In particular, the focus will be the problematising of the scientific project in Wallace and the problematising of the colonial project in Clifford.

Wallace: 'civilisation' and 'progress'

In 'Geography and Some Explorers', Conrad wrote of what he called 'scientific geography', where the 'only object was the search for truth', and the explorers 'devoted themselves to the discovery of facts in the configuration and features of the main continents' (LE 14). Where Clifford was a colonial administrator with literary pretensions, Alfred Russel Wallace was writing as a member of this group of 'travellers and men of science' (MA, I, 3). Wallace (1823–1913) left school at fourteen and came to London, where he read Tom Paine and became involved in Owenite socialism. From 1837 to 1841, he worked as a surveyor with his older brother. He also began the scientific collection of wild flowers and insects. In 1844 he met up with Henry Walter Bates, who introduced him to the study of beetles and butterflies, and, in 1848, the two of them took off for South America on an expedition that would last more than four years.[11] In 1854, Wallace left England for Singapore, and he spent the next eight years wandering through the Malay Archipelago, staying with Brooke in Sarawak, but otherwise relying on the hospitality and friendliness of the local people. In 1862 he returned home with his collection and his papers. *The Malay Archipelago* was published in 1869. Subsequently, Wallace involved himself again in socialism – and, in particular, in land nationalisation. He published a pamphlet, *Land Nationalisation: Its Necessity and Its Aims*, and was President of the 'Society for the Nationalisation of Land'. Wallace's advocacy of land nationalisation resulted from his early experiences while surveying – in particular, his awareness of the hardships of the rural population in the context of private ownership of land and the Enclosure Acts. More generally, he was critical of the unequal distribution of wealth, the situation of want in the midst of wealth, and the resulting deaths by starvation and preventable disease. In 1914, he published *Social Environment and Moral Progress*, in which he advocated a reorganisation of society on the rational basis of mutual help as opposed to the current system of 'mutual antagonism and degrading competition'.[12] As this chapter will show, his early socialism had also been reinforced by his observation of other lifeways – in South America and Malaysia.

Wallace's *Malay Archipelago* (which describes Wallace's journeys in the archipelago from 1854 to 1862) is dedicated to Charles Darwin, with whom Wallace was in correspondence during his travels. It adopts an evolutionary model in its account of organic life, and the same taxonomic impulse is directed to 'beetles and butterflies' (MA, I, vii), birds and humans. The main category he uses for humans is supplied by the concept of 'race', but what exactly the term means is somewhat unclear. After noting the way in which the physical geography of the area divides the archipelago into Indo-Malayan and Austro-Malayan masses, he observes how the physical division is repeated in the organic life of the areas – including the human. He notes there are 'two radically distinct races' (MA, I, 29), one Malayan, the other Papuan. However, subsequently, he refers not just to a Malayan 'race' but to Malayan 'races'. Although the concept 'race' carries with it the authority of the scientist and of scientific discourse, the unscientific nature of the category is suggested by the shifting and unstable use of the term. Are the Malays a 'race' (as in the first example) or are they a group composed of various races (as in the second)?[13]

Although the category is unstable, it nevertheless has very clear implications. In the first place, it is an hierarchical taxonomy; and, in the second, it is constructed on – and constructs – a savage/civilised axis. Wallace's account of the Portuguese in Malacca suggests one direction that this discourse can take. He notes that, among the various 'races' in Malacca are 'the descendants of the Portuguese – a mixed, degraded and degenerate race' (MA, I, 42) That word 'degenerate' is effectively illustrated by his account of the kind of Portuguese spoken in Malacca; the verbs 'have mostly lost their inflexions'; adjectives 'have been deprived of their feminine and plural terminations'; and there has been an 'admixture of a few Malay words'. The resulting language he describes as 'puzzling to one who has heard only the pure Lusitanian' (MA, I, 42). The word 'degenerate' prompts this vision of linguistic miscegenation, and hybridisation, set against the standard of 'the pure Lusitanian'. However, Wallace's attitude to 'civilisation' and to his own taxonomy is more reflective and less monolithic than this might suggest. For example, after offering, as an explanation of the low population growth of the Hill Dyaks, the hard labour of Dyak women at home and in the fields, he speculates on the impact of 'civilisation' on the Dyaks:

> The precept and example of higher races will make the Dyak ashamed of his comparatively idle life, while his weaker partner labours like a beast of burthen. As his wants become increased and his tastes refined, the women will have more household duties to attend to, and will then cease to labour in the field...
> (MA, I, 143–4)

Under the influence of 'civilisation' and the example of 'higher races', the Dyak woman will be domesticated and the Dyak man will adapt to the European model of division of labour, but Wallace also wonders 'with the sharper struggle for existence that will then occur, will the happiness of the people as a whole be increased or diminished?' (MA, I, 144).

The final chapter, 'The Races of Man in the Malay Archipelago', follows a similar trajectory. Wallace begins with a careful taxonomy of the peoples of the Malay Archipelago. He offers a familar, essentialising account of the 'character' of the Malay:

> In character the Malay is impassive. He exhibits a reserve, diffidence, and even bashfulness ... He is not demonstrative. His feelings of surprise, admiration, or fear are never openly manifested ... . He is slow and deliberate in speech, and circuitous in introducing the subject he has come expressly to discuss. (MA, II, 442)

The position of observer has been effaced: there is no suggestion, for example, that the 'character' of the Malay might have been influenced by the other party in this encounter. This erasing of the observer is most obvious in Wallace's account of Malay women, where the presence of the European is mentioned but the significance of that presence is ignored:

> Children and women are timid, and scream and run at the unexpected sight of a European. In the company of men, they are silent, and are generally quiet and obedient. (MA, II, 442)

In these two instances, Wallace signals both cross-cultural and cross-gendered encounters without considering fully the significance of the nature of the encounter. However, he is much more ready to question the ideas of 'progress' and 'civilisation':

> We most of us believe that we, the higher races, have progressed and are progressing. If so, there must be some state of perfection, some ultimate goal, which we may never reach but to which all true progress must bring us nearer. (MA, II, 459)

He sets against this comforting belief the observation that 'among people in a very low stage of civilisation, we find some approach to such a perfect social state' (MA, II, 459), whereas 'that severe competition and struggle for existence, or for wealth' (MA, II, 460), which constitutes European civilisation produces 'such an amount of poverty and crime, and ... the growth of so much sordid feeling and so many fierce passions' that 'the mass of our populations have not all advanced beyond the savage code of morals, and have in many cases sunk below it' (II, 461). This leads him to the challenging conclusion that 'our system of government, of administering justice, of national education, and our whole social and moral organization, remains in a state of barbarism' (MA, II, 461–2). His experiences in Malaysia, among what he has referred to as 'savages' and 'lower races', have produced this perception that European 'civilisation' is in fact 'a state of barbarism'. As Wallace puts it, the 'mass of human misery and crime' produced by 'our vast manufacturing system, our gigantic commerce, our crowded towns and cities' constitutes 'this failure of our civilisation' (MA, II, 462).

Wallace's *Malay Archipelago* thus evidences what Robert Young has described as the 'gap opening up between material civilisation and spiritual or moral values' (CD, 34). Young cites John Stuart Mill's 1836 essay on 'Civilisation':

> We are accustomed to call a country more civilised if we think it more improved; more eminent in the best characteristics of Man and Society; farther advanced in the road to perfection; happier, nobler, wiser. This is one sense of the word civilization. But in another sense it stands for that kind of improvement only which distinguishes a wealthy and powerful nation from savages and barbarians.[14]

Wallace's troubling perception is that, in the first sense, the archipelago is more civilised than England; while the second sense, which is merely a measure of power, means that the failed civilisation of Europe is nevertheless likely to overcome the happier 'social state' of the archipelago.

Wallace continued to draw on his experiences in the Archipelago in his criticism of capitalist society. D. A. Wilson, who visited him in 1912, noted his opposition to 'the selfish, wild-cat competition which made life harder and more horrible today for a well-doing poor man in England than among the Malays or Burmese before they had any modern inventions' (LR, 151). Wilson noted Wallace's continuing conviction that 'there were many individuals among us today who were in body, mind, and character below the level of our barbarian ancestors or contemporary "savages", to say nothing of civilised Burmese or Malays' (LR, 151). It was in this context that Wallace promoted nationalisation:

He defended the old Dutch Government monopolies of spices, and declared them better than today's free trade, when cultivation is exploited by men who always tended to be mere money-grabbers, selfish savages let loose ... (LR, 152)

Here Wallace stands in direct opposition to that 'free trade' tradition of Raffles. In another reversal of imperialist rhetoric, for him it is the 'free traders' who are the 'savages', just as for Conrad the 'true anarchist' was the millionaire.[15]

The invention of 'race'

Marsden's *History of Sumatra* used the idea of 'degeneracy' to distinguish two groups of inhabitants of Sumatra: those he terms Malay, and those he identifies as the indigenous people:

the Malay inhabitants have an appearance of degeneracy, and this renders their character totally different from that which we conceive of a savage .... They seem to be rather sinking into obscurity, though with opportunites of improvement, than emerging from thence to a state of civil or political importance. (HS, 207)

This distinction between degeneracy and savagery derives from Marsden's typology of the human race. He divides humanity into five groups. In the first group he puts ancient Greece; Romans of the Augustan period; 'France, England, and other refined nations of Europe'; 'and perhaps China' (HS, 204). In the second group, he places 'the great Asiatic empires at the period of their prosperity' (Persian, Mogul, Turkish) and some European countries. In the third group, he places Sumatra; a few other states of the eastern archipelago; the north coast of Africa; and 'the more polished Arabs' (HS, 204). In the fourth group come the 'less civilised' Sumatrans; newly discovered islands in the South Seas; perhaps the Mexican and Peruvian empires; the Tartar hordes; and others 'possessing personal property, and acknowledging some species of established subordination' (HS, 204). In the last group, he places what he calls Caribs, New Hollanders, Laplanders, and Hottentots – in short, those whom he considers to 'exhibit a picture of mankind in its rudest and most humiliating aspect' (HS, 204).

Although this typology is hierarchical, it is quite explicitly a cultural hierarchy (rather than a genetic one): there is no suggestion of fixed essences.[16] Degeneracy, accordingly, refers to a state of cultural decline.

Marsden's mapping of human development thus remains within an Enlightenment framework.[17] Young writes of the Enlightenment progressivist position:

> The account of the history of humanity did at least ... assume universal values and equal rights for all. Though unilinear and hierarchical, such a view generally considered any hierarchy as a temporary one, merely a difference of stage at the present which could be transformed through education, not a constitutive basis of difference. (CD, 32)

One particular version of this progressivist position typically consisted of an admittedly Eurocentric reading of history, which presented the progress of knowledge westwards through Greece and Rome, through the rise and fall of civilisations, arriving at the civilisation of present-day Western Europe.[18] In the same way, Marsden's view of the Sumatran Malays as 'degenerate' was an historical observation, based on the perceived rise and fall of civilisations: it did not carry the biological baggage that the term 'degenerate' had acquired by the 1890s.

In *Colonial Desire*, Robert Young situates the mid-Victorian development of ideas about race and culture in relation to two sets of antitheses. In the first place, the eighteenth-century opposition between the 'progressivist' Enlightenment view and the 'degenerationist' view, derived from the Bible, that humanity had in certain circumstances degenerated into savagery. The second antithesis Young sets up is the conflict between the 'monogenist' view (that all human beings were one species) and the 'polygenist' view ('that the diversity of human beings was such that it could only be accounted for by treating the different races of mankind as different species' [CD, 47]). These opposed views had obvious political implications: the racist polygenist view, for example, was particularly favoured by supporters of slavery in the United States. As Young notes, by the 1850s, it was harder to assert the Enlightenment ethos of the equality of humanity in the face of the obvious diversity of human societies. In this context, the only way to maintain the idea of the unity of humankind was to treat differences as different stages in the same overall evolutionary process (CD, 47).[19] This had the effect of conceptualising the cross-cultural encounter as 'a process of the deculturation of the less powerful society and its transformation towards the norms of the West' (CD, 4).

At the same time, Young draws attention to the dominance of racial theory by the mid-century: it worked as an ideology, permeating almost all areas of thinking and producing a 'racialisation of knowledge' (CD, 64). J. F. Blumenbach's classification of humankind, based on his work on human skulls, was influential in this development. Linnaeus had already extended his scheme to include humanity. In *De Generis Humani Varietate Nativa* (1775), Blumenbach had followed Linnaeus's division of humankind into four races: European, Asian, African, and American (which he labelled Caucasian, Mongolian, Ethiopian, and American). In the third edition (1795), he was obliged to add a fifth ('the Malay') to this list of principal races to take account of 'the new southern world', including 'the Sunda, the Molucca, and the Philippine Islands'.[20] However, this scheme begins to break down almost at once, because Blumenbach then immediately notes the complication of the Pacific archipelago with its two groups ('two tribes'): the Otaheitans and the 'New Zealanders', on the one hand, and the inhabitants of New Caledonia and New Hebrides on the other. Blumenbach had already indicated the question his work was designed to address: 'Are men, and have the men of all times and of every race been of one and the same, or clearly of more than one species?' (97–8). He had also already indicated his own answer. He asserts 'the unity of the human species' (98): 'one variety of mankind does so sensibly pass into the other, that you cannot mark out the limits between them' (99). Despite these clear affirmations, however, he also curiously privileges whiteness and the Caucasian: whiteness is 'the primitive colour of mankind' (269), from which the other varieties have degenerated; similarly, the 'Caucasian' is both the original type (*Varietas primigenia*) and has the most beautiful skull: 'from which, as from a mean and primeval type, the others diverge by most easy gradations on both sides to the two ultimate extremes' (269). As Braidotti observes, while Europe's true face is 'a concoction of diverse cultural, linguistic, and ethnic groups with a high level of conflicts', it managed to pass itself off as 'the norm, the desirable centre, confining all "others" to the position of the periphery' (NS, 10). Blumenbach's invention of 'the Caucasian' played an important part in this process.

The new scientific theory of race that developed in the mid-nineteenth century made physiological and anatomical dissimilarities the basis of essentialised racial differences. This theory was developed by such as Robert Knox, an Edinburgh anatomist, author of *The Races of Men* (1850).[21] It also led to the founding of the Anthropologial Society of London (in 1863) in opposition to the older Ethnological Society.[22] In 1865, the Anthropological Society published a translation of Blumenbach's work. The editor's preface gives Blumenbach's work a particular spin. It suggests, as one of the two 'advances' his work made, that 'he was the first who devoted himself to determine exactly, by the assistance of a great number of observations, the essential elements which distinguished the types of man'. The use of the word 'types' here is significant; this statement is then re-phrased as 'the first who made a very clear distinction of several races' (x).[23] Blumenbach's five principal varieties are now presented as five 'races'. This construction of five 'races' is then given a further spin in response to the question: 'is it proper to place them in the same rank, and allow them all the same zoological value?' (x). Here Blumenbach's reference to Caucasian skulls as 'the most beautiful' – and his presentation of the Caucasian as the original from which others have diverged – comes into play. The editor presents 'the Mongolian and the Ethiopian' as 'the extreme degenerations of the human species' (xi) with the Americans and Malays as 'transitional' races between the Caucasian and these extremes. 'Degeneration' here carries quite a different rhetorical force from its quasi-mathematical use in Blumenbach. Finally, the editor arrives at the re-iteration of certain 'truths' established by Blumenbach, including 'the plurality of races' (where Blumenbach insisted on the unity of *homo sapiens*) and 'the *necessity* of not placing in the same rank all the divisions of mankind' (xi). Through the editor's preface, Blumenbach's work is appropriated for a quite different agenda from his own.

One of the complications for nineteenth-century debates about 'race' was that the process of genetic inheritance was not yet known. Mendel's experiments with plant breeding, which led to his discovery of the mechanism of inheritance, took place between 1856 and 1863, but this discovery did not make any impact until around 1900. If Darwin's undermining of the fixity of species should have caused problems for theorists of race, then the Mendelian demonstration of the process of genetic inheritance should have ended racist fantasies about 'degeneration' and 'blood'.[24]

The construction of gender

In the Preface to *In Court and Kampong* (1897), Clifford refers to 'the many weary years' that he has spent 'in the wilder parts of the Malay

Peninsula'.[25] He notes (like Swettenham before him) that the 'conditions of life' which he is describing 'are rapidly passing away', describing this process as 'the natural' being 'replaced by the artificial' (ICK, viii). Clifford's ambivalent attitude towards this process becomes evident later, when he observes that 'the Malay in his natural unregenerate state is more attractive an individual than he is apt to become under the influence of European civilization', but then asserts his contradictory belief that 'the only salvation for the Malays lies in the increase of British influence in the Peninsula' (ICK, viii–ix). Although Clifford was a devout Catholic, Christianity is conspicuous by its absence from the stories that follow. Nevertheless, he at times uses a Christian discourse implicitly to legitimate his mission in Malaya, even as he justifies it explicitly in terms of 'the horrors of native rule, and the misery to which the people living under it are ofttimes reduced' (ICK, viii).

The first two chapters of *In Court and Kampong*, descriptive accounts of 'The East Coast' and 'The People of the East Coast', repeat this ambivalence. 'The East Coast' begins:

> In these days, the boot of the ubiquitous white man leaves its marks on all the fair places of the Earth, and scores thereon an even more gigantic track than that which affrighted Robinson Crusoe in his solitude. It crushes down the forests, beats out roads, strides across the rivers, kicks down native institutions, and generally tramples on the growths of nature, and the works of primitive man, reducing all things to that dead level of conventionality, which we call civilisation. Incidentally, it stamps out much of what is best in the customs and characteristics of the native races against which it brushes; and, though it relieves them of many things which hurt and oppressed them ere it came, it injures them morally almost as much as it benefits them materially. (ICK, 1–2)

Clifford invokes Defoe's paradigmatic imperialist adventure-romance, but he reverses *Robinson Crusoe*'s primal scene. Instead of the white man's first sight of the footprint of his future subject, this is a reading of the white man's traces, and Friday's naked foot is supplanted by the white man's boot. Clifford deploys the opposition of primitive/civilised, but, like Wallace, questions the value of 'civilisation': if colonialisation brings material benefits, it also brings moral damage. At the same time, the clothing metaphor, which is another trope of imperialist discourse, is also reversed or problematised. Clifford uses it again when he describes his mission as 'to clothe in the stiff garments of European conventionalities, the naked, brown, limbs of Orientalism' (ICK, 2), where the contrast between the 'naked, brown, limbs' and 'the stiff garments of European conventionalities' suggests another dimension to Clifford's ambivalence. Clifford's subsequent offer to uncloak 'the average Malay woman' (27) intriguingly intertwines knowledge, power, and desire.

Knowledge, power, and a particular construction of gender links Clifford with what seems to have been his model for *In Court and Kampong*: Kipling's short fiction – and, in particular, his Indian tales.[26] *In Court and Kampong* has the same format as *Plain Tales from the Hills* or *In Black and White*: it follows Kipling in his use of verse epigraphs for each story and in his use of a verse *envoi* for the volume as a whole. Clifford follows Kipling in other ways as well. For example, the first story, 'The Experience of Raja Haji Hamid', begins by noting that 'These things were told me by Raja Haji Hamid, as he and I lay smoking on our mats during the cool, still hours before dawn' (ICK, 30). This establishes the kind of intimacy which Kipling also frequently flaunts. It is foregrounded in Kipling's story 'Dray Wara Yow Dee' and provides the basis of the *Soldiers Three* stories. Clifford's story is also more deeply and subtly Kiplingesque. At one point, the narrator observes:

> He tossed about uneasily on his mat for some time, and I let him be, for the memory of the old, free days to a Malay *raja*, whose claws have been cut by the Europeans, is like new wine when it comes back suddenly upon him, and it is best, I think, to let a man fight out such troubles alone and in silence. (ICK, 30)

As often in Kipling's work, the narrator observes the individual and then claims to know the species. Like his naturalist precursors, he clearly uses his observer's distance and knowledge as a form of power. Secondly, the narrator's judgement is controlled by a particular construction of masculinity, of how 'men' deal with trouble, 'alone and in silence', which also dominates Kipling's work.[27] Clifford also follows Kipling in the way he uses the Oriental to attack European developments. Kipling's 'The Sending of Dana Da' takes off from events in Simla in the 1880s to launch an ironic attack upon Theosophy generally. In the same way, in 'The Battle of the Women', Clifford's account of a Malay incident is explicitly angled to attack the New Woman in Europe and America. This is implicit in the epigraph from Tennyson's 'Locksley Hall':

Woman is the lesser man, and all her passions, matched with mine,
Are as moonlight unto sunlight, and as water unto wine.

It is made explicit in the opening sentences: 'unlike most of the tales
which I have to tell concerning my Malay friends, [this] is garnished
with a moral; and one, moreover, which the Women's Rights
Committees would do well to note'. And it is stated explicity at the
close:

> One has heard of the Women's Rights Meeting in Boston, which
> was broken up by the untimely appearance of three little mice;
> and of that other meeting, in which the aid of the Chairwoman's
> husband and brothers had to be sought, in order to eject a solitary
> derisive man, who successfully defied the assembled emancipated
> females to move him from his position; but neither of these
> stories seems to me to illustrate the inherent feebleness of women,
> when unaided by the ruder sex, quite as forcibly as does the
> pleasant story of Tungku Aminah and her brother, Tungku Indut.
> (ICK, 44–5)

Tungka Aminah's army of 300 women are mocked for the culinary
weapons with which they have equipped themselves, for their 'shrill
feminine yelping' (ICK, 42), and for 'that queer, half-tripping, half-
running gait, which Malay women always affect when they go abroad
in a crowd at the heel of their Princess', a scene which is compared to
'young chickens trying to seek shelter under their mother's wing'
(ICK, 41). They are mocked when the entire 'army' panics and flees as
soon as Tungku Indut asks for his sword. But what is most striking is
the tone of amused detachment that pervades the story, the sense of
superiority that the narrator asserts over his subjects (both women and
Malays), and offers to share with the reader. Clifford here uses the
Malay world as an 'imaginary zone' onto which European concerns
can be projected, and through which European male superiority over
both European women and Malays can be affirmed.[28]

Negotiating boundaries

In his 'Preface' to *Studies in Brown Humanity* Clifford sets up the opposition which controls the tales he recounts: an opposition between 'the
Peninsula and its sepia-coloured peoples' and 'the men of the race
which has taken the destiny of the Malays of the Peninsula under its

special charge'.[29] The implicit context for this opposition was articulated in *In Court and Kampong*:

> What we are really attempting ... is nothing less than to crush into twenty years the revolutions in facts and in ideas which, even in energetic Europe, six long centuries have been needed to accomplish ... one cannot but sympathise with the Malays, who are suddenly and violently translated from the point to which they had attained in the natural development of their race, and are required to live up to the standards of a people who are six centuries in advance of them in national progress. (ICK, 3)

In *In Court and Kampong*, this familiar figuring of social arrangements in Malaya as comparable to the situation in medieval England becomes the basis for a kind of relativism, which is very far from ideas of equivalence or equality: 'We should be cautious how we apply our *fin de siècle* standards to a people whose ideas of the fitness of things are much the same as those which prevailed in Europe some six centuries agone' (ICK, 5). In *Studies in Brown Humanity*, this opposition is implicitly hierarchised through the expressed aim to make the '-sepia-coloured peoples' better known to the Europeans, and is repeated in some of the recurrent tropes. In the first tale, for example, 'In the Valley of the Telom', the Malay narrator is described as telling his tale 'brokenly as a child might do' (SBH, 8), while 'the semi-wild tribes' (SBH, 4), who feature in the tale, are figured in animal terms as behaving 'like any other forest creature' (SBH, 10). In the same way, in 'The People of the East Coast', Clifford asserts, as evidence of his liking for the Kelantan Malays, that he 'shot over one of them for four years', and, 'until he went blind, he was as a good a retriever as one would desire to possess (ICK, 28). Elsewhere, he slips into the essentialising of Orientalism and reproduces European stereotypes of Malay men and women. In the second story, 'The Fate of Leh the Strolling Player', for example, he refers both to 'the propensity, which the Malay can never resist, to scamp every bit of labour' (SBH, 27) and to 'the facile heart' of the average Malay woman (SBH, 31).[30] The penultimate story, 'From the Grip of the Law', begins with an elaborate essentialist comparison of 'the White Man' and 'the Brown Man': for example, 'the White Man seeks to build up What Ought To Be; the Brown Man longs to reconstruct What Has Been' (SBH, 225). This is presented as a truth about 'the nature' of each, as if it had no reference to the colonial situation.

Elsewhere, the desire to make 'better known' leads Clifford into an anthropological approach, which the book's title signals. The anthropological impulse is most clearly evident in the stories 'Umat' and 'The Spirit of the Tree'. In 'Umat', Clifford offers a detailed account of taboos among Kelantan Malays surrounding birth and the eclipse. He notes, for example, that Umat no longer shaves or cuts his hair during his wife's pregnancy (SBH, 48). Equally, Umat has to give up his favourite seat in the doorway of his house: 'Umat may not block the doorway, or dreadful consequences will ensue' (SBH, 49).[31] On the other hand, 'The Spirit of the Tree', which offers a description of a custom of tree-worship among the Chinese coolies, begins with a relativistic awareness of a Cornish tin-miner's 'extraordinary fund of Old-World superstitions, all of which he accepted as Gospel' (SBH, 108); and its narrative, which pits Trimlett's pleasure in destruction against superstitions surrounding a tree, ends with the supernatural confounding of Trimlett's pleasure. 'The Schooner With a Past' operates with a similar relativism. It begins by asserting that 'the eyes of the East and the eyes of the West are of different focus, the one seeing clearly where the other is almost blind': 'No given circumstances have precisely the same value when they are related by a Native or by a European, yet each may speak truly according to his vision' (SBH, 68). Interestingly, its narrative of a series of mysterious killings seems explicable only in the supernatural viewpoint of the Sulu crew. The 'White Man' who owns the schooner (who has no other designation in the story) is left in the discomfort of his different reality, watching 'the frightened faces of the Malays, gazing with protruding eyes at something that he could not see' (SBH, 80–81). As in 'The Spirit of the Tree', it is the Malay reality rather than the European which underwrites (and is underwritten by) the narrative.

A recurrent interest in the stories of *Studies in Brown Humanity* is sexual relations. 'The Fate of Leh the Strolling Player', for example, recounts the disruptive impact of the wandering players on the domestic life of the inhabitants of Pahang. When the travelling players arrive, the 'gates of Lust and Passion, the gates of Desire and Longing' (SBH, 26) are thrown open, and many 'lawful wives found themselves deserted by their men', while 'the husbands and fathers in the villages had to keep a sharp eye upon the doings of their wives and daughters' (SBH, 27). Similarly, 'TuKang Burok's Story' recounts TuKang Burok's revenge-killing of the man who put a spell on his fiancée so that she was filled with desire for him. The story involves the transgression of a moral and social code:

For, even among our own folk, no maiden willingly throws herself into the arms of her lover, though she love him dearly, for women are fashioned in such a wise that they feel shame like an overwhelming burden ... Allah, in his wisdom, has done well so to order, for otherwise, were there no shame among women, their passions being more fierce than those of man, great trouble would ensue ... (SBH, 147)

In addition, the woman has been compelled to chose as the object of her passion a man who is not only represented as physically repulsive ('of an evil odour, dirty, and covered with skin disease') but is also a member of a people looked down upon by the villagers as 'sorry animals' (SBH, 144). Accordingly, her desire for this 'wild man of the woods, an Infidel' (SBH, 147), is represented as degrading and, indeed, decivilising her, reducing her to an 'animal-like' state (SBH, 149).

'TuKang Burok's Story' has its counterpart in the final story of the volume, 'The Strange Elopement of Châling the Dyak'. This begins with an assertion of common humanity:

If you study the manners and customs of the various races of the Earth with a little care, you will find the ways of humanity strangely similar, though the men you watch be clad in loin-cloths or in dress-coats, though the scene be a French *salon* or a Malay hut. (SBH, 245)

This then becomes the context for an anthropological account of Dyak courtship customs:

the Dyak custom of allowing unmarried girls to receive their own guests, and to practically manage all the preliminaries to their own marriages with the youth of their choice, without reference to, or interference from, their elders, more nearly approximates to the American system, and would seem to show that even the emancipated girls of that energetic race have not got so very far ahead of primitive people and their beginnings ... (SBH, 245)

What might at first glance seem a relativising equation of Dyak and North American courtship customs is quite clearly no such thing: the comparison is aimed as a humorous deflation of American customs through its equation of 'advanced' and 'primitive' systems, and the final sentence unmistakably imposes an evolutionary grid over the picture. This evolutionary grid is visible at other times in the representation of the Dyaks:

> Châling stretched out a prehensile foot to grasp the knife, for, like most Dyaks, he would on occasion pick a sixpence off the ground with his toes ... (SBH, 252)

Later, after he has been hauled up into a tree by his captor,

> he balanced himself instinctively upon the limb of the tree, on which he was now seated, for the Dyaks had never quite deserted the arboreal habits of the human race, and they are still as much at home among the branches and tree-tops, as is possible for a people who have learned to build huts upon the ground. (SBH, 253)

Given his 'prehensile foot' and his 'arboreal habits', it is less surprising when the 'lady' who has seized Châling turns out to be an *orangutan*. She, for her part, is described as 'a creature so strangely, hideously human' (SBH, 256). Having begun with the assertion of a common humanity under the cultural differences of the human race, the story has set up an encounter between a human and an ape to problematise another boundary, and, arguably, in displaced form, to explore the question of miscegenation.[32] Donna Harraway has observed that 'western people produce stories about primates while simultaneously telling stories about the relations of nature and culture, animal and human, body and mind, origin and future'.[33] What is at issue is 'an Order, a taxonomic and therefore political order that works by the negotiation of boundaries achieved through ordering differences' (PV, 10), and the axes here are animal/human explored in relation to gender and 'race'.[34]

The earlier account of Châling's courtship of Minang had described the late phase of the relationship 'when she had begun to love him, and when there no longer remained any doubt in her mind as to Châling's passionate devotion to herself.' At this stage, 'she had invited him to stretch himself to rest upon the mat beside her, and Châling had lain there, listening to her even breathing, longing for the time when she would be his wife, but fearing to touch even the edge of her garment' (SBH, 246). His first night with the *orangutan*, which coincides with what should have been the celebration of his wedding to Minang, is a burlesque of Minang's conduct:

she threw herself down by his side, and pressed him fiercely against her great hairy body. Her limbs wound about him, crushing him with a strength of which their owner was quite unconscious .... The reek of the beast filled his nostrils with a horrible odour ... (SBH, 256)

Given this parallel, it is hard not to see this narrative as a displaced expression of male fears of female sexuality. 'TuKong Burok's Story' – in which the fiancée becomes enchanted with another man shortly before her wedding – had contained the observation that Malay women's passions are 'more fierce than those of men' (SBH, 147). That ferocity of passion was enacted by the enchanted Hôdoh and again here by the female *orangutan* who has seized Châling and taken him off to be her mate. If writing about Malay women allowed Clifford to describe passions and sexual feeling he couldn't include in portraits of European women, his depiction of the *orangutan*'s rape of Châling allows him to explore sexuality more explicitly than he could even in relation to Malay women.[35] Certainly, Châling's 'horrible slavery' (SBH, 257), the term used to describe his capture by the *orangutan*, is 'horrible' in part because it is sexual slavery. The *orangutan* is described in ways which gesture towards human sexual relations (she 'snuggled up against him, blowing hot, fetid breaths over his face, and licking his cheeks' [SBH, 257]). Or again, she 'lay upon her back, with arms and legs extended widely', while 'her hideous, leathery face looked strangely and most repulsively human' (SBH, 261). By this means, the 'unclean monster, at his side' (SBH, 261) serves to express anxiety about human sexuality as 'unclean' and monstrous.

When Châling at last returns to Minang, and sexuality is, at least, domesticated through their marriage, the equation of human and animal sexuality is maintained. When young women from the village try to persuade Minang not to marry Châling after his capture by the *orangutan*, Minang responds: 'What did it matter to her ... that Châling should have been forced to mate with a Mais, whom he assured her that he had never loved' (SBH, 263). In this joke that isn't a joke, extra-marital sexual relations are equated with cross-species sexual activities. And this first explicit acknowledgement of the sexual nature of Châling's encounter with the *orangutan* also pin-points the precise anxiety upon which the story turns. The word 'mate' signals the complex of feelings that surrounds sexuality in this story – which includes an anxiety about the stability of the human/animal opposition. The story began by asserting a 'common humanity' but almost immediately placed over that picture an evolutionary grid, in which 'dress-coats' and 'loin-cloths' are signs not just of cultural difference but of cultural hierarchies. In this scale, the 'prehensile' and 'arboreal' Dyak might be taken as marking a limit, and the Dyak's limit-position is marked, in turn, by the *orangutan*'s sexual interest in him. However, the *orangutan*'s sexual interest in Châling also destabilises the human/animal opposition, and the scale now runs not just from 'dress-coats' to 'loin-cloths' but down through the apes. And, as the story suggests, the erasure of the line between human and animal raises particular problems in relation to human sexuality.

The threat of seduction

Greenblatt has written about 'improvisation', the 'ability and willingness' to 'transform oneself ... into another', as part of the 'mobile personality of western society' which was instrumental in exploration and colonisation.[36] However, as he suggests in his account of Edmund Spenser, the other face of this 'mobile personality', for the colonial administrator in particular, was the 'threat of seduction', which was 'always present' (RSF, 187).[37] Clifford's first two novels, *Since the Beginning* (1898) and *A Free Lance of Today* (1903), show that Clifford was acutely conscious of this problem. Frank Austin, the hero of *Since the Beginning*, is warned by his older colleague, Gregson, that 'it takes a pretty strong man to study native life thoroughly ... without getting his own ethics and morality a trifle jumbled'.[38] These two novels explore the dangers of getting close to 'native life' under the aspects of sex and politics.

Since the Beginning starts with 'the soft, fragrant, enervating, voluptuous night of the Malay Peninsula' with the moonlight 'pouring down upon the squalid native town' (SB, 1). That opening sentence establishes the binary of fascination and repulsion which dominates the novel and characterises, in particular, its attitude towards Malay women. Frank Austin is introduced as 'one of those White Men' for whom 'things Oriental' possess 'an overpowering fascination' (SB, 22). Following his quest for 'a complete understanding of the secrets of an alien race' (SB, 23), he spends his leave in the remote country of Pelesu, where he becomes involved with Maimunah, a slave-girl at the court.[39]

Before Austin meets her, Maimunah's character is suggested through the control she exerts over her Malay lover, Pendekar Aris. The fascination she has for him and the desire he feels for her render him 'powerless' before her. Chapter V shows her using her erotic power over him to punish him. Through her taunting rejection of him, this 'strong man' becomes 'distracted by the fury of his desire, lost to all sense of self-respect, abject in his self-abasement' (SB, 83). Subsequently, when Austin sees her at the bathing place, having been told in advance of her love for him, his surrender is immediate: 'Almost before he realised what he was doing, he had made a quick answering sign' (SB, 91). Just as Jim tries to deny his responsiblity for his jump from the *Patna* ('I had jumped ... It seems' [LJ, 111]), Austin tries to deny responsibility for this 'answering sign'. However, if he leaves the scene 'disgusted with himself', that sense of disgust is immediately undermined by 'a feeling of joy and triumph .. a wild longing' (SB, 92).[40]

The narrative also attempts to make excuses for him. Thus, on the one hand, although Maimunah has Malay parents, in both face and figure she 'belonged to the pure Arab type', and 'her mind and charac-ter likewise were hierlooms from the race that invented algebra' (SB, 6–7).[41] For his part, Frank 'had been long removed from all intercourse with women of his own race' so that his 'standard of feminine beauty had, perhaps, become somewhat debased' (SB, 91). Clifford clearly finds it necessary to try to excuse Austin's attraction to Maimunah and eventual surrender to her. Indeed, part of the attempt to excuse Austin is precisely this emphasis on his surrender to her. Thus, when she swims out to his raft and settles herself on his bed, he forces himself to send her away. However, he is not able to resist her advances a second time, when she ambushes him during the horseplay to celebrate a wedding: 'the glowing eyes of Maimunah burned into his own, and her clinging arms drew him down, down, down, impotent and unresisting, into a measureless oblivion, which obliterated all the memories of a lifetime' (SB, 153). These various strategies clearly serve to minimise or deny his desire for her.

In the second half of the novel, seven or eight years have passed, and Austin is back in Malaya with his 'young wife', Cecily. It is revealed (to the reader but not to Cecily) that Austin lived for some years with Maimunah, but then sent her back to Pelesu, when he returned to England. He made financial arrangements for her, but has no sense of emotional attachment to her. Instead, he excuses himself by thinking that she belonged 'to a race of which the womenkind were accustomed to be put away without explanation or pretext when the fickle men-folk wearied of them' (SB, 178). Interestingly, the narrative does not allow Austin this excuse: it stresses instead that he has 'con-sistently underestimated the strength of the passion' that she feels for him (SB, 179). For him, she has become the 'savage, half-animal creature' to whom he was once 'the willing slave' (SB, 176), and the whole episode has become for him, in an obvious manoeuvre of denial of desire, his 'incomprehensible ill-doing' (SB, 180). The second half of the novel then sets up a contrast between his new wife, 'the saint he revered as intensely as he loved her' (SB, 216), and the 'human devil', Maimunah (SB, 225). The narrative, in the second half of the novel, thus supports Austin's view of Maimunah, but it also testifies to her passionate involvement with him, which he has sought to deny: 'in her own fierce, half animal, wholly passionate fashion she loved him with an intensity that subdued every other feeling in her' (SB, 259). The judgemental binary of 'saint' and 'devil' is placed upon a second, potentially complicating binary of married love and passion, but there is no serious exploration of sexual desire. Instead, there is an assertion of the stereotypical and hegemonic image of 'the angel in the house' in reaction against the sexuality and passion of Maimunah. Clifford does not allow the representation of female sexuality in the figure of Maimunah to problematise or interrogate European versions of female sexuality, but rather simply imposes the European model as superior.

The contrast between Maimunah and Cecily, and the guilty secret of Austin's sexual relationship with Maimunah which he keeps concealed from his wife, is worked out in the novel's dénouement, when Austin discovers that Maimunah has poisoned Cecily. He now takes the responsibility for the outcome ('the blood-guiltiness is mine' [SB, 280]). He sees himself as 'the slayer of his wife' (SB, 273) and the murderer of his unborn child:

> In this moment of unusual insight, he could trace, like a black line running across a chart, the little lack of strength in his character, the tiny innate weakness and want of self-control which from such small beginnings, had wrecked his whole life. (SB, 283)

And he appropriates a Malay proverb to describe this weakness as 'the drop of indigo that had discoloured a gallon of milk' (SB283). As Edmond has pointed out, one of the tropes associated with sexual relations across 'racial' lines was fear of contamination, figured as fear of venereal disease. Austin's 'blood-guiltiness', his sense of himself as the murderer of his wife and unborn child through his sexual relationship with Maimunah, and Maimunah's poisoning of the wife and child obviously draw on the same anxieties.[42]

In *A Freelance of Today*, Clifford again considers relations between Europeans and Malays.[43] More specifically, he again creates a protagonist who crosses (or attempts to cross) the boundary between Europeans and Malays. Maurice Curzon is Clifford's major study of what he termed 'de-nationalisation'.[44] As the narrator observes early in the novel, Curzon was 'a masterful son of the dominant race; yet circumstance and inclination had combined to well-nigh denationalise him' (FT, 9).[45] This process is described by the narrator as 'curiously common' among white men who have been 'thrown for long periods of time into close contact with Oriental races' and whom 'Nature has endowed with imaginations sufficiently keen to enable them to live into the life of the strange folk around them' (FT, 9). In Curzon's case, 'a clerkship in an Oriental banking-house' had taken him to Singapore, and there 'the magic of the East gripped him' (FT, 10). This 'magic' is represented objectively by 'a thousand scents, half fragrant, half repulsive, wholly enervating and voluptuous' (FT, 11), and subjectively as his consciousness of 'an unknown life underlying it all ... an unmapped country' (FT, 11). As Curzon explains later, he had 'cut himself adrift from his own people' in order to 'see the hidden life of the East' (FT, 32). Accordingly, he gives up his clerkship in order to spend two years as an interpreter 'in one of the least-known native states of the Malay Peninsula' (FT, 11). The effect of these experiences has been to produce in Curzon a 'feeling of repulsion' in relation to his countrymen 'since he had learned to look upon them through the eyes of the Oriental' (FT, 13).

The novel begins in 'a squalid street in Kampong Glam, the native quarter of Singapore' (FT, 1). Maurice's presence in this setting marks him straight away as a maverick. The political context is quickly established as the war between the Dutch and the Achinese. Curzon reads three or four books 'which concerned themselves with the history of Malaya, and especially of Sumatra' (FT, 16). Through these he comes to appreciate 'the wealth, the ships, the men, the energy, the resource, the courage of that most warlike people', the Achinese (FT, 17). He is critical of the Treaty of 1871 through which England 'shamelessly abandoned the State which had relied so long upon its sheltering strength' (FT, 20). He is, of course, even more critical of the Dutch. He is critical of the Dutch system, which he describes as based on the theory 'that colonies should support the mother-country, and that to that end indolent natives should labour ceaselessly and pay heavy taxes' (FT, 5). He is also critical of the Dutch attack on the Achinese in 1873 to add Achin to their Sumatran territories. In this telling, the Dutch, like the United States later in Vietnam, take on what looks to be an easy target, but then find themselves embroiled in an expensive war which they cannot win – and from which they cannot withdraw without a loss of face (which would also impact upon their colonial role elsewhere in the region). Curzon's decision to help run guns to the Achinese is thus explicitly support for an independence struggle against European colonisation.

In these early chapters, Curzon is presented as an 'adventurous spirit' (FT, 33) and as a romantic. His assistance to the Achinese is not, however, straightforwardly idealistic support for an independence struggle; nor, however, is it just to make money from gun-running (although he stands to make a significant profit). It is, in part, a purely selfish desire for adventure. It is also that familiar European quest to find 'the real Malay'. Since the Achinese had resisted European conquest, Curzon hopes that, in Achin, he would 'see at last the brown man as God and Nature fashioned him' (FT, 21). Achin represents for him 'the one place left upon the face of the earth in which he might find a Malay race unspoiled by European progress and vulgarity, untainted by the degeneracy which civilization seems fated to bring with it' (FT, 83).

The first hint of the likely outcome of this multiple romantic quest comes with the sense of degradation Curzon feels from his negotiations with the Jewish merchants of Penang for 'the purchase and shipping' of the weaponry (FT, 40). However, at first sight, Achin lives up to his romantic expectations: it is literally the 'unmapped country' which he had intuited, and, when he reaches the Raja's capital in the mountains, he feels that he has 'at last reached the very fountain-head of Malay life' (FT, 105).[46] His meeting with the Raja is the first step in his process of disillusionment: the Raja is stupid, and completely given over to 'women and play' (FT, 111). Curzon concludes:

> The Land of Promise had been so different from all that he had anticipated. He had looked in vain for the freedom which he had expected to find among a brown people ruled by chiefs of their own race, and he had lighted only upon misrule, oppression, ignoble tragedies and squalid, selfish vice. (FT, 141)

Curzon's experiences in Achin are like Jim's first experiences of the sea (LJ, 10): 'The reality assorted very ill with the dreams that he had dreamed', and, instead of 'romance', he finds only 'prosaic and uninspiring' dangers (FT, 141). Curzon's disillusionment with 'native rule' also, of course, implies the justification of colonial rule.[47] Curzon's disillusionment is completed when he joins the Achinese in warfare against the Dutch. First of all, in the expedition against the Dutch, he is exasperated by the inefficiency of the Achinese, their failure to mount guard at night, and their reluctance to launch an attack on the Dutch. Subsequently, when the Achinese inflict serious damage on the Dutch through guerilla warfare, Curzon is unhappy at what he sees as a lack of 'fair play':

> It had been such a one-sided business throughout. That snake-like string of men, imprisoned by hills and forest, had never had a chance of hitting back. (FT, 196)

Curzon's inability to understand the Achinese methods of fighting provides the clearest instance in the novel of the clash of cultures. The climax of this process of disillusionment comes, however, on the return from this ambush, when Curzon comes across the mutilated body of a Dutchman: 'one arm was nearly severed, and a finger was missing from the left hand; but it was not these things that brought that look of horror into Maurice's face' (FT, 197).[48] The 'horror unspeakable' (FT, 197), the emasculation of the corpse, is repeatedly hinted at but never clearly represented:

> He felt that he who looked upon it would be less a man during all his days, by reason of having witnessed that awful spectacle; that his own manhood had been contaminated, degraded ... (FT, 200)

What for Curzon is clearly a traumatic experience marks also his ultimate disillusionment with the bond he had forged with the Malay world.[49] It opens his eyes to 'the cruelty and brutal barbarism of the men with whom he had voluntarily sided' (FT, 202). As with Austin, involvement in the Malay world ends with a rejection and demonisation of that world: 'They were devils, not men' (FT, 198). In Austin's case, sexual involvement with the Malay world ended with ideas of the poisoning of white women and children. In Curzon's case, political involvement with the Malays – in the sense of support for Malay independence – ends in this traumatic image of the emasculated white male body.[50]

Curzon's involvement in the Malay world is set against a second narrative strand: that of Mabel Bellingham and her widowed sister, Etta

Burnside, touring the East Indies with their father. Curzon first encounters them in Penang (in Chapter 2), when they serve to remind him what he has denied himself by his rejection of his 'European birthright'. They also serve to produce for the reader a common trope in colonial fiction: 'the crudities, the coarseness, the barbarity of the life which he had made his own were shown to him, side by side with that delicate refinement of civilisation of which [Etta] was the complete expression' (FT, 39). As is quickly apparent to the reader, Curzon's love for Etta Burnside is as mistaken as his attachment to the Achinese cause turns out to be. Curzon thus undergoes a dual process of disillusionment in the course of the novel. It is made manifestly clear that his 'divinity' is actually a self-regarding 'flirt' (FT, 48).[51] Thus this contrast of barbarism and civilisation is not straightforward; the 'civilisation' that Etta represents is the fashionable upper-class world of drawing-rooms and country-houses, and the limitations of that 'civilisation' are apparent.[52]

In the second half of the novel, Curzon meets up with the two sisters again, when the yacht on which they are travelling with their father, accompanied by another admirer of Etta, Bertie Rundle, 'the product of an indolent and pleasure-seeking civilization' (FT, 209), runs aground on a sandbank just off the Achin coast. The possibility for an explorative comparison of fashionable metropolitan culture with either the 'barbarism' of the Achinese or the 'denationalised' position of Curzon is thus created but not fully realised. Rundle, for example, is described as considering that 'the mind of a man who knew his way about town as he did, could not conceivably stand in need of expansion' (FT, 209–10), and, when he first meets Curzon, he describes him as 'an amiable bargee' (FT, 234).[53] But Rundle's metropolitan culture becomes little more than a yearning for food, and a class-based conflict with Curzon remains undeveloped. Conrad makes much more of both in *The Rescue*. Clifford emphasises instead the capture of the Europeans by the Raja and his attempt to use them as hostages to force the Singapore Government to intervene with the Dutch.[54] He shows how this manoeuvre impacts on domestic politics in Britain and Holland, and the irony involved: 'the disconcerting fact remained that a brace of European Powers were being successfully defied and baffled by an obscure savage somewhere in the jungles at the back of beyond' (FT, 246). The Raja may not be able to defeat the Dutch militarily, but he has made an impact on both British and Dutch colonial power. However, the novel uses this situation primarily to explore relations between Curzon and the two sisters, to trace his disillusionment with Etta and his growing love for Mabel. As in *In the Beginning*, the protagonist's choice is simplified: he has to resist the 'temptation' of the former beloved, who now represents to him 'some dreaded evil' (FT, 240), while the new beloved represents a 'purity of soul' before which he stands 'infinitely humbled' (FT, 294).

A third element in the novel is represented by Pawang Uteh. Pawang Uteh ('the White Medicine Man') is 'a gentleman born' (FT, 122), who has lived as a slave in Achin. When he first appears in Curzon's hut, Curzon thinks he is a Malay and is shocked to find he is English: 'The existence of such a being, claiming kinship as a fellow white man, made the whole world seem unclean' (FT, 121). Given Curzon's own desire to identify with the Malays, there is an obvious, but unmarked irony in his response to Pawang Uteh. Pawang Uteh is successfully denationalised in terms of appearance, dress, and language. He is never given a European name; 'the vernacular ... had evidently become more familiar to him than his mother tongue' (FT, 118); and what power and position he now has derive from his skill in local magic. Pawang Uteh might almost be seen as embodying a warning to Curzon against the denationalisation he seeks. Certainly, Conrad uses the comparable figure of Jörgensen in *The Rescue* in this way. However, what stands in the way of this possibility of identification are two other aspects of Pawang Uteh's character. In the first place, in contrast to the upright and idealistic Curzon, he is servile and scheming. Secondly, although he wears Malay dress, speaks the vernacular, and knows local magic, he does not identify with the Achinese. He refers to himself in racialist idiom as 'a full-blooded white man' (FT, 125) and consistently refers to the Achinese as 'niggers'. Edmond notes how 'going native' 'turned accepted categories inside out and hierarchies on their head' (RSP, 63), but Pawang Uteh, who appears to have 'gone native', fiercely asserts those categories and hierarchies. Perhaps this is because Pawang Uteh did not choose to 'go native' but was enslaved by the Achinese after his betrayal of the Dutch to them. Perhaps Clifford could not allow himself to imagine a European in the position of Jörgensen: a European who has stayed with his 'Malay girl' and grown old with her; a European who has joined in Malay politics and continued to live in the Malay world.

In *Bodies That Matter*, Judith Butler argues that 'the construction of the human is a differential operation that produces the more and the less "human", the inhuman, the humanly unthinkable': 'These excluded sites come to bound the "human" as its constitutive outside, and to haunt those boundaries as the persistent possibility of their disruption and rearticulation' (8). In Clifford's writing of Malaysia, Malaysia provides a way of repeatedly approaching boundaries and allowing various constitutive 'outsides' to threaten where the boundaries have been drawn: the 'animal' disrupts the 'human'; the female the male; the Malay the European.

4
Cultural Diversity and Originary Identity: *Almayer's Folly* and *An Outcast of the Islands*

Traders, adventurers, pirates

The characteristics of the world of the Malay archipelago as represented in Conrad's first Malay novels, *Almayer's Folly* and *An Outcast of the Islands*, are commerce, mobility, and cultural diversity. It is a world of nomads and travellers, traders and conspirators, adventurers and pirates.[1] The novels foreground the material conditions of trade and the historical circumstance of 'piracy'.[2] Chapter 1 of *Almayer's Folly*, which describes a Macassar 'teeming with life and commerce', introduces the historical rivalry between European adventurers and Malay 'pirates':

> It was the point in the Islands where tended all those bold spirits who, fitting out schooners on the Australian coast, invaded the Malay Archipelago in search of money and adventure ... not disinclined for a brush with the pirates that were to be found on many a coast as yet ...[3]

Chester, in *Lord Jim*, is a later example of these Australian adventurers: a 'West Australian', he had been 'pearler, wrecker, trader, whaler, too, ... anything and everything a man may be at sea, but a pirate' (LJ, 161).[4] It is Lingard, however, whose entry into what is, in effect, a 'Lingard Trilogy', is anticipated in these words, and Lingard's career through the three volumes, in which he moves steadily to centre-stage, progressively problematises the initial opposition of European 'adventurers' and Malay 'pirates'. At the same time, the Lingard whose entrance these words anticipate also re-writes the adventure-hero of romance.[5]

In *Almayer's Folly*, Almayer marries Lingard's adopted daughter, 'that legacy of a boatload of pirates' (AF, 10), whom Lingard had fought and slain. Otherwise, both Lingard and piracy are largely absent from this novel. In *An Outcast of the Islands*, piracy is foregrounded through Omar and Babalatchi. Babalatchi is introduced as 'a vagabond of the seas, a true Orang Laut', who lived 'by rapine and plunder of coasts and ships' (OI, 51–2). He had been a leader of 'the Sulu rovers' and had subsequently served under Omar, 'the leader of Brunei rovers' (OI, 52). However, as the use of 'rover' rather than 'pirate' suggests, Conrad does not just reproduce the stereotype of piracy.[6] He very precisely associates Babalatchi with the groups that Brooke sought to suppress, and then offers an account of Brooke's 'war against the pirates' from the victim's perspective: 'Over the hill and over the forest … they dropped whistling fireballs into the creek where our praus took refuge' (OI, 46). Babalatchi graphically recalls 'the flames of the burning stronghold' (OI, 52), the praus 'wedged together in the narrow creek … burning fiercely', and 'the crews of the man-of-war's boats dashing to the attack of the rover's village' (OI, 53). At the same time, Lingard's reputation is linked with stories circulating in the region about his 'fight with the sea-robbers' and his 'successful recklessness in several encounters with pirates' (OI, 14).[7] However, Lingard's evocation of 'the good old days' (before the opening of the Suez Canal brought steamships into the archipelago) chimes intriguingly with Babalatchi's nostalgia for the good old days of 'throat-cutting, kidnapping, slave-dealing, and fire-raising' (OI, 152) before the arrival of Brooke. And a later survey of Lingard's career describes him as living for years 'beyond the pale of civilised laws' (OI, 235). The ambivalences present in that formulation are caught also in Lingard's memories of the wealthy sailor who 'built a house near Teignmouth': 'Made all his money somewhere out here in the good old days. People around said he had been a pirate' (OI, 196). This is the first unsettling of the opposition of adventurers and pirates. In *The Rescue*, that questioning of the opposition between adventurers and pirates is thematised through Lingard's encounter with people from home. Travers, in particular, as Lingard realises, sees him, not as the 'Rajah Laut', but as 'a fellow deep in with pirates' (Re, 160). Carter, too, views him with suspicion: he sums up Lingard's activities as 'Stopping boats, kidnapping gentlemen' (Re, 183). And, indeed, Lingard's involvement in Wajo politics has led him into an alliance with the Ilanun. However, together with this revaluation of the European adventurer, there is also, in *The Rescue*, a more sustained attempt to understand 'piracy' from the Malay perspective:

Trading, thus understood, was the occupation of ambitious men who played an occult but important part in all those national risings, religious disturbances, and also in the organized piratical movements on a large scale which, during the first half of the last century, affected the fate of more than one native dynasty and, for a few years at least, seriously endangered the Dutch rule in the East. (Re, 68)

'Piracy' is seen as part of a larger cultural practice with a political dimension that relates to both local Malay politics and resistance to European imperialism.

The sea in *Almayer's Folly* is briefly visible as the scene of a territorial contest between European adventurers and Sulus – and of a commercial contest between European adventurers, local politicians and Dutch gunboats. The land is the site of a much more complex cultural negotiation. The region has been subject to repeated incursions. Almayer himself is of Dutch extraction but was born in Java; his wife was a Sulu 'pirate' and has come to Sambir via a convent in Samarang and marriage in Batavia. Sambir is the meeting place of Sulus, Dyaks, Bugis, Dutch, Arabs, Chinese, the Siamese Taminah, Almayer's cook, the 'faithful Sumatrese Ali' (AF, 23), and the Balinese Dain Maroola.[8] But also, as the narrative proceeds, it is revealed as the site of competing commercial and political interests.[9] The opening chapters very carefully situate the action in the material world of the archipelago. Thus Almayer's decline is succinctly depicted by the contrast between Lingard's period of successful trade, when his brig carried 'his assorted cargo of Manchester goods, brass gongs, rifles and gunpowder' (AF, 8), and Almayer's present position in Sambir where the 'ruined godowns' contain 'a few brass guns covered with verdigris and only a few broken cases of mouldering Manchester goods' (AF, 28).[10] Almayer's decline is most poignantly marked when Dain first arrives seeking to trade and Almayer refers him to 'the principal traders, Arab, Chinese, and Bugis' (AF, 57). *An Outcast of the Islands* shows how Lingard and Company loses its monopoly of trade in Berau to the Arabs; *Almayer's Folly* shows the consequences of that loss. In particular, it demonstrates that 'where they [the Arabs] traded they would be masters and suffer no rival' (AF, 24). In the period in which *Almayer's Folly* is set, Almayer has become a 'much persecuted individual' (AF, 49), 'ruined and helpless under the close-meshed net' (AF, 27) of the intrigues of Lakamba and Abdulla.

Cultural diversity and cultural recoding

One simple indication of the cultural diversity of the area is Almayer's meal, in which Malayan rice and fish are combined with Dutch genever (AF, 16).[11] This diversity is also registered in the novel through its attention to different cultural codes and conventions. For example, when Dain first meets Nina, he elevated 'his joint hands above his head in a sign of respect accorded by Malays only to the great of this earth' (AF, 54). If this instance smacks of the gaze and discourse of the European travel-writer, other examples subvert such ethnocentric power-knowledge by introducing other subjectivities. Almayer, for example, is seen (and judged) at one point from the Arab perspective:

> Almayer, surprised by the great solemnity of his visitors perched himself on the corner of the table with a characteristic want of dignity quickly noted by the Arabs with grave disapproval. (AF, 44)

Almayer makes similar mistakes in *An Outcast of the Islands*. Sahamin complains to Abdulla:

> 'And ... because those white men have no understanding of any courtesy – he spoke to me as if I was a slave: "Daoud, you are a lucky man" – remark, O First amongst the Believers! that by those words he could have brought misfortune on my head – "you are a lucky man to have anything in these hard times..." And he laughed, and struck me on the shoulder with his open hand.'[12]

Almayer, like the Dutchman in 'Karain', fails to understand 'courtesy', because (perhaps assuming the superiority of his own culture) he acts as if the different behavioural codes of other cultures can be disregarded. There is a similar failure on the part of the Malays and Arabs, who also assume that only their codes are valid. At the same time, the minimal explanation of Almayer's errors assumes that the author-in-the-text and the implied reader share a superior degree of knowledge and awareness extradiegetically to either group in the novel.[13] The implied reader is generally ascribed an understanding of cultural diversity at precisely those moments when characters are most firmly mono-cultural or else when characters themselves show some consciousness of cultural diversity. *Almayer's Folly* provides an instance of the latter when Dain is introduced in Chapter 4:

He said he was from Bali, and a Brahmin, which last statement he made good by refusing all food during his often repeated visits to Lakamba's and Almayer's houses. (AF, 57–8)

This calls on a range of knowledges from the implied reader: a knowledge of the status of Hinduism in Bali in this period; the knowledge that Brahmins required their food to be cooked by Brahmins (not by other castes). But, in a region where poison is an extension of politics, there is also the suspicion that Dain (like Lingard in *An Outcast of the Islands*) might have had other reasons for refusing food. The text, in other words, assumes readers with a range of cultural knowledge, who can then appreciate how Dain, in this case, exploits cultural diversity strategically. Alternately, it might be argued that the text works to construct such readers.

Mrs Almayer embodies a different aspect of the cultural diversity of Sambir. The 'only theological outfit' that she has brought from her convent education is a little brass cross to which she attributes 'some vague talismanic properties' and 'the still more hazy but terrible notion of some bad Djinns and horrible torments invented, as she thought, for her especial punishment by the good Mother Superior in case of the loss of the above charm' (AF, 41).[14] This description clearly represents a recoding of artifacts from one culture in terms of another. However, the reader who responds to this recoding simply as an instance of narrator/reader collusion over the head of the 'primitive' Mrs Almayer is likely to miss (or be surprised by) the extent to which re-appropriation is elsewhere adopted by Mrs Almayer as a strategy of resistance. Thus, as Sobhana Kumaran notes, Mrs Almayer does not simply destroy Almayer's curtains and furniture, but she makes the western furnishings into sarongs and uses the western furniture to cook rice.[15] In Chapter 2, these actions are presented as motivated by 'unreasoning hate'; but this interpretation of her actions as 'outbursts of savage nature' against the 'signs of civilization' is focalised through Almayer (AF, 26). Chapter 7 offers a fuller account of her making over of European items to Malay uses. Significantly it describes this as occuring when Mrs Almayer is 'excited by the reminiscences of the piratical period of her life' (AF, 90).

A similar exploration of cultural recoding occurs in *An Outcast of the Islands*. Part V begins with a detailed account of the setting up of the Lingard and Company office in Sambir and the elaborate office furniture that Almayer installs: the desk, the revolving chair, the bookshelves, the safe, the books. The narrative shows the marvelling reactions of the Malays as the furniture is brought to shore, and their interpretation of these alien objects involves a cultural recoding:

> an old invalided jurumudi ... explained to a small knot of unsophisticated citizens of Sambir that those books were books of magic – of magic that guides the white men's ships over the seas, that gives them their wicked wisdom and their strength. (OI, 299–300)

Again, however, any idea of extradiegetic collusion between narrator and reader in a sense of cultural superiority over the 'jurumudi' is immediately undermined, since Almayer's own ideas about the furniture are shown to be no less 'primitive': 'he thought himself, by the virtue of that furniture, at the head of a serious business' (OI, 300). If fetishism can be defined as irrational investment in an object, then this office furniture is Almayer's fetish.[16]

Part V of *An Outcast* opens with Almayer 'alone on the verandah of his house' (OI, 291), musing and gazing on the river as the sun sets. This echoes the start of *Almayer's Folly*, where Almayer, watching the sunset on the river from the same verandah, had daydreamed his 'dream of splendid future' (AF, 3) for himself and his daughter Nina. By this dream, as *An Outcast* makes clear, the detested present environment is made 'precious' to him: 'It was the present sign of a splendid future' (OI, 292). In the same way, the office and its furniture are valued by Almayer not for themselves but for what they signified. This is stated explicitly in the account of his response to the failure of this particular plan:

> He found no successful magic in the blank pages of his ledgers; and gradually he lost his old point of view in the saner appreciation of his situation. The room known as the office became neglected then like a temple of an exploded superstition. (OI, 300)

The ledgers, which the jurumudi regarded as books of magic, are revealed to have a similar magical status for Almayer.

The most striking instance of cultural hybridity occurs at the end of Chapter 6 of *Almayer's Folly*, when the wakeful Lakamba asks for 'the box of music the white captain gave me' (AF, 88), and 'the notes of Verdi's music' float over river and forest as 'the Trovatore fitfully wept, wailed, and bade good-bye to his Leonore again and again in a mournful round of tearful and endless iteration' (AF, 89).[17] Again, the initial sense of incongruity is arresting; but the vacillation between a sense of cultural hierarchies and a relativistic idea of the equivalence of cultures comes to rest on a sense of human solidarity. Not only does Verdi's music serve the narrative function of oblique commentary on Dain and Nina, but the repeated playings of the same lament have the effect of making it into a commentary on – or emblem of – a universal human condition, as if such farewells are endlessly repeated across time and across cultures.

Hybridisation and originary identity

It is in this context of cultural diversity and hybridity that Almayer and Nina need to be considered. Almayer is described (and describes himself) as 'the only white man on the east coast' (AF, 122). He has dreams of a future in Europe, but he knows Europe only through the oral tradition of his mother's tales.[18] It is on the basis of these tales that he has constructed his dream of Amsterdam: 'his ships, his warehouses, his merchandise ... and, crowning all, ... gleamed like a fairy palace the big mansion in Amsterdam' (AF, 10).[19] As the simile suggests, it is a fictional and imaginary Amsterdam, but it is, nevertheless, the locus of his identity. For Almayer, Sambir is only a stepping stone towards Europe. The novel's title, *Almayer's Folly*, neatly encapsulates the carefully poised ambiguity of Almayer's position. Insofar as it refers to the new house he builds in expectation of the British Borneo Company's arrival, the title signifies his actual rootedness in Sambir. Insofar as it refers to his dream and the corresponding construction of identity, it signifies the fetishising of originary identity. In constructing his dream, he fails to take into account the implications of his daughter's hybridity; but also, at the moment of crisis (in Chapter 11), when he has the option of accepting the identity that Nina has found for herself, he asserts instead his identity as 'the only white man on the east coast' (AF, 122), and sacrifices his daughter to this pride in racial origins.[20]

K. S. Maniam, in his novel *The Return* (1981), addresses a similar problem of identity within the Indian community of twentieth-century Malaya.[21] The novel ends with the protagonist's father, Kannan, having retreated, like Almayer at the end of *Almayer's Folly*, into 'an intense private dream' (167). Kannan, like Almayer, is second generation.[22] Towards the end of the novel, he is driven by a desire for location – a desire to have 'house pillars' sunk 'into the clay of the land' (195) – that exactly repeats the final years of his own mother. As in his mother's case, the desire for location takes the physical form of building a new house. With his mother, the building of this house was an attempted 're-immersion' in the 'thick spiritual and domestic air she must have breathed ... back in some remote district in India' (6). For Kannan, building the house expresses simultaneously a desire to root himself in the Malayan land, the only country he knows, and a nostalgia for the culture of rural India, the culture within which he has been brought up. For the protagonist, his father has retreated into 'backward dreams' (156), and the building of the house is a refusal to come to terms with the changes in post-Independence Malaya. As a further complication, however, the protagonist has made his identity through identification with the English coloniser: the English education he has undergone puts him in a position where he can criticise his father's 'backward dreams'. Later, after experiencing his otherness within English culture, he can criticise that culture as well, but this leaves him, as the final poem suggests, 'cultureless'.

Nina's career in *Almayer's Folly* confronts similar problems of cultural identity. Her trajectory in the novel, however, actually conforms to and fulfills the pattern which Almayer sets himself. Like Almayer, Nina constructs a dream from the tales she hears from her mother: her domestic education through 'the story of deeds valorous, albeit somewhat bloodthirsty, where men of her mother's race shone far above the Orang Blanda' (AF, 42) ends in her seeing in Dain 'the creature of her dreams ... the ideal Malay chief of her mother's tradition' (AF, 64). As a result, the 'granddaughter of Rajahs' (AF, 67) becomes the mother of Rajahs. As in Almayer's case, the mother's tales produce powerful dreams, and the dreams support a myth of originary identity. Nina, however, at the end of the novel, seems to have achieved her dream and become 'Malay' (AF, 180). As Krenn observes, 'Within the frame of this fiction Nina has realized her dream' (LT, 40), yet the end of the novel must not be seen as the end of her story. Both Almayer and Mrs Almayer foretell a future beyond the time of the end of the novel – a future in which the love between Dain and Nina has faded, and Dain has taken other wives as expected in his culture. As Knowles asks: 'Is the final culmination of Nina and Dain's relationship an example of hope and desire fulfilled – or disillusion deferred?' (xxxvi).

Various critics have suggested that Nina, as someone who is both brown and white but living in a world in which brown and white are polarised, is forced to find her identity by having to choose between brown and white.[23] However it could also be argued, in the language of Homi Bhabha, that she finds her identity not through finally choosing (or being forced to choose) her mother's world rather than her father's (that is, by accepting the binaries through which identity is constructed), but rather as a constant performance of identity in the interstices between the different codes and traditions in which she is situated through 'the overlap and displacement of domains of difference'.[24] In other words, rather than privileging the end of the novel and reading it in terms of Nina's finding her identity through choosing a particular originary identity, emphasis could be placed on Nina's actual behaviour in the course of the narrative, which represents a continuous performance of identity through a constant negotiation of her own hybridity.[25] Thus, for example, Nina regularly switches between languages. Her first words in the novel, though spoken to her father, are 'in Malay' (AF, 16). Later, after Abdulla's visit with his proposal of marriage, she speaks to her father 'to his great surprise, in English' (AF, 46). Similarly, when she first meets Dain, she 'instinctively drew the lower part of the curtain across her face' (AF, 55), but later, when she searches for a 'sign of love' to give to Dain, she has recourse to 'that despised and almost forgotten' European culture (AF, 72) and kisses him. Again, during the visit from the Dutch naval officers, Nina disconcerts them by her sudden shift of cultural identity: at table, Nina 'with composed face, was answering in a low, even voice the elder officer's polite questions' (AF, 126), but, when Dain's name is mentioned, Nina responds in unexpected ways to the turns of the conversation and finally bursts out 'I hate the sight of your white faces. I hate the sound of your gentle voices' (AF, 140). In the contrasting narratives of Almayer and his daughter, Nina, the novel presents, on the one hand, the subversion of the myth of originary identity, a demonstration of 'the illusory stability of fixed identities', and, on the other, the constitution of the subject through 'a process of negotiation between layers, sedimentations, registers of speech, frameworks of enunciation'.[26]

Vagabonds

An Outcast of the Islands returns to this world of commerce, mobility, and cultural diversity. In particular, this novel emphasises the rootlessness of its central characters: Willems, Babalatchi, Lingard, Abdulla. None are native to Sambir; 'settlers of various races' (OI, 50), all are in some sense colonists of the territory. Lingard is presented as precisely one of those European adventurers who have come north from Australia to compete for the dominance of the seas – or control of trade and territory – with each other, with the Sulus, with the Arabs, and with the Dutch. Thus Lingard describes how he brought prosperity to

Sambir by settling local quarrels, even though the Dutch were technically in control of the region. He also asserts his perception of the need to 'keep the Arabs out of it' (OI, 45); ironically, Abdulla's entrance into Sambir brings even greater prosperity than was enjoyed under Lingard's control. The novel, however, is constructed around the figures of Willems and Babalatchi. Both are 'vagabonds'; both have narratives constructed as successive 'flights'.[27] Willems's two flights – from *Kosmopoliet IV* and from his disgrace in Macassar – end in parallel rescues by Lingard. The second rescue briefly enters into the oral culture:

> On the shore end the native caretaker of the wharf watched the combat, squatting behind the safe shelter of some big cases. The next day he informed his friends, with calm satisfaction, that two drunken white men had fought on the jetty. It had been a great fight. They fought without arms, like wild beasts, after the manner of white men. ... How could he know why they fought? White men have no reason when they are like that. (OI, 37)

Babalatchi, similarly, has twice had to flee. His first flight has become a legend, and the narrative of the events that occasioned his flight have something of the quality of Virgil's account of the fall of Troy:

> he stood faithfully by his chief, looked steadily at the bursting shells, was undismayed by the flames of the burning stronghold, by the death of his companions, by the shrieks of their women, the wailing of their children; ... When the end came in the explosion of the stored powder-barrels, he was ready to look for his chief. He found him half dead and totally blinded, with nobody near him but his daughter Aissa: – the sons had fallen earlier in the day, as became men of their courage. (OI, 52–3)

In both the *Aeneid* and here, we are presented with a critical moment, a turning point in an encounter between different cultures: the destruction of Troy as part of the expansion of Greek control of the Mediterranean, or the conflict between Malay maritime practices and the Europeans' attempt to control the seas around Borneo. It is significant that this heroic and epic register is used to recount the destruction of 'pirate' villages by Brooke as seen from the Malay perspective. Homeric allusions are a common feature of earlier examples of 'writing Malaysia': they attempt to negotiate the difference of Malay culture by reading it as an earlier stage of European history. Conrad's engagement with difference both draws on and problematises that discourse. Stape has commented on the use of 'familiar literary and cultural references' in *An Outcast of the Islands* and suggested that they enact 'a cultural dislocation' in the Malay context 'for they serve to recall and then immediately to deny the context they allude to'.[28] He argues that 'the cultural confrontations and struggle for hegemony occuring in the plot also take shape in the novel's literary allusions and several competing discourses and vocabularies' (Stape, xxiv). Thus the presentation of Babalatchi as a 'piratical and sonless Aeneas' (OI, 54) vacillates between ironic discrepancy and genuine equivalence.[29] The European reader's first response, given the privileged position of Roman and Greek imperial culture in European imperial culture, is to read it as ironic discrepancy. The second response is more reflective and self-reflexive: it revalues Aeneas through the equivalence. Thus Western culture begins by supplying the measure, but is then itself measured through the change of reading perspective. And Babalatchi is given his full status as 'the astute statesman' (OI, 238).[30] However, in the hesitation between these readings, this reader is placed between cultures like the writing itself.

Ultimately, Babalatchi's adaptability is set against Willems's inability to adapt, his desperate assertion (like Almayer) of an originary identity. In the same way, the atomised individualism of the adventurers and the hierarchical structures of official political agency are set against the rhizomatic networks of Abdulla:

> An uncle here – a brother there; a father-in-law in Batavia, another in Palembang; husbands of numerous sisters; cousins innumerable scattered north, south, east, and west – in every place where there was trade: the great family lay like a network over the islands. (OI, 110)

Abdulla's kinship network that is also a trading and political network corresponds structurally and organisationally to the rhizome, which Deleuze and Guattari advance as an alternative to arborescent command systems.[31] The rhizome with its transversal communication, its acentred multiplicity, its shifting directions, provides a model of alliance and flexibility that, as the novel shows, challenges, subverts, and outmanoeuvres both atomised individualism and the hierarchical structures of official political agency. It is also a model of flexibility that chimes with a fluid performance of identity.

Covert plots and hybridised political identities

As Cedric Watts has pointed out, the covert plot of *Almayer's Folly* is 'largely Syed Abdulla's plot': 'at the centre of the hidden machinations is a scheme by a trader to eliminate a rival and secure for himself the control of a commercial territory'.[32] Abdulla's plot intersects with the plot designed by Dain and his father to defend Bali against Dutch domination (and with Mrs Almayer's schemes to marry her daughter), and these intersecting plots form the matrix of local politics upon which the narrative is constructed. Almayer's dreams and domestic problems are foregrounded in the narrative, but Almayer proves to be a marginal figure even in his own household. As in Godard's *Letter for Jane*, the question of what is foreground and what is background – who is in focus and who is out of focus – is a problematic element in the encounter of East and West.[33] Chapter 3 of *Almayer's Folly* draws attention to the larger determining contexts for the novel's cross-cultural encounters. It begins by asserting that 'deliberations conducted in London have a far-reaching importance' (AF, 34). In this instance, Britain abandons its claim 'to that part of the East Coast ... leaving the Pantai river under the nominal power of Holland' (AF, 34), and Dutch flags are run up the flagpoles in the Rajah's compound. As this suggests, competition between the colonising powers of Britain and Holland produces hybridised political identities at a local level. Thus the officers of the Dutch man-of-war receive 'loyal speeches' from Lakamba and 'salaams' from Abdulla, and, in return, assure them of the 'friendship and goodwill' (AF, 34) of the Government in Batavia. The 'Dutch subject', Almayer, on the other hand, tactlessly expresses his regret at 'the non-arrival of the English "who knew how to develop a rich country"' (AF, 36). As a result, instead of the protection against the Arabs that he seeks, he receives the warning that 'Arabs were better subjects than Hollanders who dealt illegally in gunpowder with the Malays' (AF, 36). Accordingly, on the morning of the discovery of the dead body, identified as Dain's, Babalatchi visits Almayer in his 'official get up', which includes, across his breast, 'a patent leather belt bearing a brass plate with the arms of Netherlands under the inscription "Sultan of Sambir"' (AF, 93). Babalatchi is expecting a visit from the Dutch navy in relation to the gunpowder smuggling in which Lakamba, Almayer, and Dain have been involved. When the man-of-war boats arrive, the 'tricolour flag of the Netherlands' is hoisted up the flag-staff in the centre of Lakamba's courtyard, 'this emblem of Lakamba's power, that was also the mark of his servitude' (AF, 132).

In *An Outcast of the Islands*, the covert plot of *Almayer's Folly* is foregrounded. Abdulla's desire to displace Lingard in Sambir and his scheming to gain access to the river are both explicit.[34] The scheming of Lakamba and Babalatchi is similarly emphasised: the weaning of Patalolo from his allegiance to the Sultan of Koti and the subsequent removal of Patalolo by Lakamba are carefully traced (OI, 50). Early on Babalatchi outlines a policy which, in conjunction with the schemes of Abdulla, produces the political events of both novels:

> What was wanted was an alliance; somebody to set up against the white men's influence. ... Then it would be time to apply to the Orang Blanda for a flag. (OI, 57)

Babalatchi's complaint to Abdulla about Lingard's monopoly, which helps bring about these political ends, is a mirror-image of the European rhetoric of 'liberation':

> 'That unbeliever kept the Faithful panting under the weight of his senseless oppression. They had to trade with him – accept such goods as he would give – such credit as he would accord.' (OI, 115–16)

Subsequently, *An Outcast of the Islands* offers a more complex instance of hybridised political identities. At the moment of crisis, the Dutch Almayer, as Lingard's agent, runs up the Union Jack for protection, while Willems hoists the Dutch flag, 'the flag under the shadow of which there is safety' (OI, 179), over the Rajah's compound. Willems, however, is operating as Abdulla's agent, not in a personal capacity, and, as Lingard indignantly points out, 'Abdulla is British' (OI, 179). As evidence of his flexibility, Abdulla, who is a British subject, operates expediently under a Dutch flag. As if to emphasise this point, he is contrasted with the Straits Chinese Jim-Eng, similarly a British subject, who almost loses his life for asserting 'he was an Englishman, and would not take off his hat to any flag but English' (OI, 182). If the flags are signs of difference, the differences are not fixed and permanent but rather again part of a fluid performance of identity within the shifting pattern of political allegiances of the archipelago.

In *Negara*, Geertz discusses the case of Mads Lange (1807–1856), who represents a real-life instance of just such a hybridised political identity within shifting political allegiances. Lange was a Danish merchant adventurer, who shipped to the Indies at the age of 17 and began his operations in 1834 at Lombok as the *subandar* (controller of the port) to one of the two major lords there. Within the year, an Englishman, George King, was appointed *subandar* to the other major lord. The two Europeans encouraged a war between the two lords, and provided them with weapons through gun-running. With the defeat of his lord, Lange fled to Bali and set up his factory at Kuta, where it flourished from 1839 to his death in 1856. In 1840, the Nederlandsche Handelmaatschappij (NHM) rented exclusive trading rights at Kuta from the local lord. The company regarded Lange as an interloper and accordingly began to harass him. But the Dutch colonial government then decided to make Lange their agent there rather than the NHM. Thus, in 1844, Lange became a Dutch citizen and the Dutch colonial agent in Kuta. Lange was then both the agent for the Dutch government and the *subandar* for the lords of Badung. L. V. Helms, in his book, *Pioneering in the Far East* (1882), represents Lange as both a loyal representative of Dutch interests and a defender of Balinese freedom. However, as A. K. Nielsen noted, the Balinese had 1000 rifles and 25 cannon to defend their freedom, which they had presumably acquired through Lange, the Dutch agent.[35]

Common humanity

In his 'Author's Note' to *Almayer's Folly*, written by early January 1895, Conrad takes issue with Alice Meynell's criticism of colonial literature as 'decivilised' literature.[36] In an essay haunted by the spectre of degeneration (and permeated with class feelings and hatred of popular culture), Meynell addresses literature produced by Europeans in the colonies, by what she terms 'decivilised man'. For Meynell, 'colonialism is only provincialism very articulate' (190). Transplantation to the 'new soil' of the colonies has not improved the stock:

> The new air does but make old decadences seem more stale; the young soil does but set into fresh conditions the ready-made, the uncostly, the refuse feeling of a race decivilising. (190)

The essay ends with Meynell deriding the literature produced by this 'decivilised man':

> He promises the world a literature, an art, that shall be new because his forest is untracked and his town just built. (192)

Although Conrad referred to Meynell's essay as furnishing 'the impulse' for his own 'artless outpouring' – and though the Note is set up as a response to the 'lady' critic – he actually addresses a quite different issue.[37] He observes that the critic 'seems to think that in those distant lands all joy is a yell and a war dance, all pathos is a howl and a ghastly grin of filed teeth'. Conrad turns from the European colonialist to the colonial subject; from the 'vulgarity' of the colonial to the humanity of the colonised. He rejects the stereotypes of adventure fiction, the reified and purely spectacular treatment of the Other, to assert their subjectivity: 'there is a bond between us and that humanity so far away'. He concludes: 'I am content to sympathise with common mortals, no matter where they live; in houses or in huts, in the streets under a fog, or in the forests behind the dark line of dismal mangroves that fringe the vast solitude of the sea'.[38]

As well as affirming a realist credo to which George Eliot would probably have happily assented, Conrad here asserts what is essentially an Enlightenment view of mankind as 'a constant human nature, independent of time, place, and circumstance'.[39] Geertz repeats Lovejoy's citation of Mascou to illustrate this idea:

> The stage setting [in different times and places] is, indeed, altered, the actors change their garb and their appearance; but their inward motions arise from the same desires and passions of men ... (IC, 34)

Conrad explores this stage metaphor in relation to the Malay world in 'Karain' and *The Rescue*. Geertz, however, notes that this idea of 'a constant human nature' was displaced by 'the conviction that men unmodified by the customs of particular places' (IC, 35) did not (and could not) exist. In short, there is 'no backstage' where we can go to catch a glimpse of Mascou's actors as 'real persons lounging about in street clothes' (IC, 35), because mankind is 'always performing' (IC, 36).

While Conrad asserts this idea of 'common humanity', he also buys into the Enlightenment model of barbarism, savagery, and civilisation – or, at least, he makes use of this discourse (and, in particular, the savage/civilised binary) in the early chapters of *Almayer's Folly*. Thus, when Nina is introduced, her eyes are described as having 'the tender softness common to Malay women, but with a gleam of superior intelligence' (AF, 17), and it is subsequently made clear that this 'thoughtful tinge' is 'inherited from her European ancestry' (AF, 29).

Similarly, Nina's European education in Singapore is imaged (using a familiar trope) as a 'narrow mantle of civilised morality' (AF, 42), which falls away as she listens to her mother's tales. Dain's love for Nina is described as 'untrammelled by any influence of civilised self-discipline' (AF, 64), while their love for each other is 'the subtle breath of mutual understanding passing between their two savage natures' (AF, 63). In the 'Author's Note', Conrad produces a religious frame to support the idea of 'common humanity' ('their land – like ours – lies under the inscrutable eye of the Most High'); however, in *Almayer's Folly* itself, Nina provides an alternative principle to produce a 'common humanity': 'the same manifestations of love and hate and of sordid greed chasing the uncertain dollar' (AF, 43). And it is Nina's view (rather than that expressed in the 'Author's Note') that best fits the novel. For this reason, the novel's initial emphasis on the savage/civilized binary might perhaps be seen as a strategy directed against the European reader. Certainly, with the gradual revelation of the covert plot, and the movement of Malay characters from background to foreground, the savage/civilised binary is problematised. In Chapter 5, it even becomes the basis of a joke about mothers-in-law: 'There are some situations where the barbarian and the, so-called, civilised man meet upon the same ground' (AF, 67). Later the same point is made more seriously, when love is presented as having 'the same meaning for the man of the forests and the sea as for the man threading the paths of the more dangerous wilderness of houses and streets' (AF, 171). More significant, the savage/civilised binary is also transferred from the narrative to Almayer: 'What made you give yourself up to that savage?' (AF, 178) is the challenge he addresses to Nina. This way of seeing becomes part of the problem that Almayer has to face: he has to choose between his conception of duty 'to his race' (AF, 192) and his love for his daughter. His subsequent haunting by the memories of his daughter supplies an obvious judgement on the choice he makes.

An Outcast of the Islands might seem to mark a retreat from this position. The narrative combines an implicit anti-imperialism with an exploration of cross-cultural encounters that moves from a complex sense of cultural diversity to an assertion of irreducible 'racial' difference.[40] The narrative undermines ideas of the 'superiority' of Europeans (OI, 63), and it asserts a common ground 'at the bottom of all hearts, in all societies' (OI, 309). At the same time, Christians (such as Joanna) refer to the Muslims as 'heathen' (OI, 358), and Muslims (like Omar) see Christians as 'Infidels'; Willems regards Aissa as 'a complete savage' (OI, 80), and Aissa criticises European culture ('men have no mercy and women have no shame'). In this novel, rather than desire providing a common ground between different peoples, gender constructions seem to reinforce 'racial' barriers. Thus Willems's construction of masculinity ('so strong, so superior' [OI, 77]) is presented as based upon a rejection of the female constructed as Other ('contemptuously indifferent to all female influence' [OI, 77]). This manoeuvre has its counterpart in his racial attitudes: 'she, a savage. I, a civilised European' (OI, 269). But, in a movement that runs counter to *Almayer's Folly*, Willems's rejection of alterity is ultimately adopted by the narrative. Early on in the novel, there is a tendency to essentialise women, and this tendency also serves to fix a barrier of 'racial' difference. Aissa, for example, is described as having 'the unerring intuition of a primitive woman' (OI, 75). By the end of the novel, Willems and Aissa are described as 'surrounded each by the impenetrable wall of their aspirations' (OI, 333) – aspirations which are presented as both 'racial' and gendered. Generalising from Willems's racial feelings, the novel apparently accepts 'the hate of race, the hate of hopeless diversity, the hate of blood' (OI, 359) in an essentialising of 'racial' difference.[41] In 'Karain' and 'The Lagoon' Conrad explores further the inter-involvement of gender and 'race', and he arrives at a very different assertion of irreducible difference.

5

Encountering the Other: 'Race' and Gender in 'The Lagoon' and 'Karain'

Women and power

At the centre of *Almayer's Folly* is the search for identity of Nina, the child of a Dutch father and an Asian mother. In a world which is represented as polarised along racial lines, Nina chooses her mother's tradition, rather than her father's, and this decision is apparently fixed by her choice of Dain, a 'Malay chief' (AF, 64) from Bali, as her husband. Just before she leaves with Dain, however, Nina is given a quick lesson in sexual politics by her mother. To be more specific, she asks her mother what she must do to exercise 'power' (AF, 152) over Dain. In the following chapter, when she is re-united with Dain, she shows how well she has learned the lesson. She gives him what the narrator calls 'the look of woman's surrender' (AF, 172):

> She drew back her head and fastened her eyes on his in one of those long looks that are a woman's most terrible weapon; a look that is more stirring than the closest touch, and more dangerous than the thrust of a dagger, because it also whips the soul out of the body, but leaves the body alive and helpless, to be swayed here and there by the capricious tempests of passion and desire ... bringing terrible defeat in the delirious uplifting of accomplished conquest. (AF, 171)

This passage is part of the novel's extended consideration of the ambiguities of power and powerlessness (in terms of both sexuality and the complicated colonial politics of the area). It is also part of Conrad's interest in looking and seeing. In this case, Dain's 'conquest' is also his 'defeat'; his greatest feeling of pride comes from his

116

self-abasement at Nina's feet; and Nina is conscious that 'she would be his greatness and his strength; yet hidden from the eyes of all men she would be, above all, his only and lasting weakness' (AF, 172). It is worth pausing briefly on the phrase 'one of those long looks': this belongs to what Barthes calls 'reference codes', but where Barthes assigns reference codes to 'traditional human experience', this instance is clearly gendered – it posits a shared male experience as the basis of communication between narrator and reader.[1] At the same time, as Susan Jones has pointed out, the passage is also specifically western both in the highly Europeanised image of the *femme fatale* and in the method of gendering through the shared male experience of narrator and reader.[2] This provides the key to the novel's representation of women's power over men. What emerges is a male fear of 'passion and desire': sexual feelings are feared as loss of control, and the representation of sexual passion as male enslavement elides into sexual passion as demonic possession.[3]

An Outcast of the Islands takes this demonising of women further. The central character, Willems, can be seen as a precursor of 'Lord Jim': both are men with an idealised conception of their own identity, and both are faced with the situation in which their own actions have betrayed that identity. In Willems's case, this self-image explicitly involves a sense of superiority that is both individual and racial, and a crucial element in his process of self-destruction is his involvement with a young part-Arab woman, Aissa. At their first encounter, his experience is not dissimilar to Dain's: out of curiosity, Willems pursues 'a flash of white and colour, a gleam of gold like a sun-ray lost in a shadow, and a vision of blackness darker than the deepest shade of the forest' (OI, 68), but when he catches up with her, he is the one who is caught:

> He heard her rapid breathing and he felt the touch of a look darted at him from half-open eyes. It touched his brain and his heart together. It seemed to him to be something loud and stirring like a shout, silent and penetrating like an inspiration. (OI, 68–9)

When she then opens 'wide' her eyes and looks 'steadily' at him, he stares at her 'charmed with a charm that carries with it a sense of irreparable loss' (OI, 69). This is not just the loss of his 'old self' (OI, 69), but 'the fear of something unknown that had taken possession of his heart' (OI, 72). This fear of the 'unknown', which is at least as much inside himself as outside, is expressed through the inter-racial, cross-cultural encounter, an encounter in which gender and racial issues are intertwined. As he struggles against her enchantment, for example, he asserts against her his self-deluded sense of 'the unstained purity of his life, of his race, of his civilisation' (OI, 80). By contrast, he sees her as the embodiment of the 'mystery' (OI, 70) of the 'tropical life' of the surrounding forests. He experiences her as a *femme fatale*, but the sexual encounter is also inflected through familiar colonial discourses.[4] The colonial space is figured as female; the colonial landscape is figured as 'nature' rather than 'culture'; and non-Europeans are similarly situated as part of 'nature' rather than as part of 'culture'. As Joanna de Groot has noted, 'there are connections between the treatment of women and non-Europeans in the language, experience and imaginations of Western men', and the traffic in gender and racial figures moves both ways.[5]

In these two novels, then, Conrad had represented the relationship between the Malay Dain and the Eurasian Nina and between the European Willems and the part-Arab Aissa. In both cases, he had shown the women taking power over the men. In both cases, the narrative embodies male anxieties about women, passion, and sexuality, and European anxieties about the encounter with the non-European Other. In both cases, the imagery used normalises the male/female relationships in the narrative in terms of European culture. In two short stories written in the same period, 'The Lagoon' and 'Karain', male anxieties about women are presented in the explicit context of cross-cultural male-bonding.

Brotherly love

'The Lagoon' was written in August 1896 during the six months that Conrad and his wife spent in Brittany immediately after their marriage. It announces itself, at the outset, as a story of Europeans and Malays ('The white man ... said to the steersman ... The Malay only grunted ... TU, 187). The only individual named in the opening paragraph is Arsat, and, as the story proceeds, Arsat complicates what begins as a European/Malay binary opposition. The opening paragraphs describe a journey down-river to a sea-reach and then through a creek into the lagoon. The landscape resembles the now-familiar landscapes of *Almayer's Folly* and *An Outcast of the Islands*, but also anticipates that of *Heart of Darkness*:

> Here and there, near the glistening blackness of the water, a twisted root of some tall tree showed amongst the tracery of small ferns,

black and dull, writhing and motionless, like an arrested snake. ...
Darkness oozed out from between the trees, through the tangled
maze of the creepers, from behind the great fantastic and unstirring
leaves; the darkness, mysterious and invincible; the darkness
scented and poisonous of impenetrable forests. (TU, 189)

The 'darkness' this story explores is that of love, betrayal and death –
the darkness of desires and fears.

To begin with, the narrative is presented through a Malay perspective. It constructs a non-European reality of ghosts and spirits against
which the European is defined:

> White men care not for such things, being unbelievers and in league
> with the Father of Evil, who leads them unharmed through the
> invisible dangers of this world. (TU, 190)[6]

There is a nice equivocation about the 'invisible dangers': they are
'invisible' both because they belong to the spiritual rather than the
material realm and because they are unseen by these insensitive,
unbelieving Europeans with their different reality. More surprisingly,
within this Malay perspective Arsat is presented as a 'stranger' and as a
narrative enigma, 'because he who repairs a ruined house, and dwells in
it, proclaims that he is not afraid to live amongst the spirits that haunt
the places abandoned by mankind' (TU, 189). This initial blurring of the
binary opposition is reinforced when the narrative shifts to a European
perspective and is focalised through the unnamed 'white man': Arsat,
who is a 'stranger' to the Malays, is his 'Malay friend', and Arsat has
fought 'without fear by the side of his white friend' (TU, 191). Where the
opening paragraphs presented 'The white man' and 'The Malay' as a
binary opposition, this paragraph emphasises the bond between these
two individuals. However, if there is a bond of friendship, this should
not be seen as implying equality: the narrative notes that the white man
liked Arsat but 'not so much perhaps as a man likes his favourite dog'
(TU, 191).[7] That this European perspective is being objectified and not
privileged in the narrative is suggested by two subsequent manoeuvres.
First, the unnamed European is subjected to what might be termed an
'occidentalist' treatment:

> The white man gazed straight before him into the darkness with
> wide-open eyes. The fear and fascination, the inspiration and the
> wonder of death ... soothed the unrest of his race ... (TU, 193)

Secondly, the account of his thoughts that follows emphasises the psychological mechanism of projection:

> The ever-ready suspicion of evil, the gnawing suspicion that lurks in our hearts, flowed out into the stillness round him – into the stillness profound and dumb, and made it appear untrustworthy and infamous ... (TU, 193)

As a result, where the Malays are represented as inhabiting a world of ghosts and spirits, the European makes his world into 'a battlefield of phantoms': ' An unquiet and mysterious country of inextinguishable desires and fears' (TU, 194). The syntactic ambiguity about whether this 'unquiet' country is the surrounding landscape or in his own heart draws attention to this mechanism of projection. Arsat's subsequent reference to the unknowableness of the European ('you went away from my country in the pursuit of your desires, which we, men of the islands, cannot understand' [TU, 194]) both repeats the reversal of imperialist tropes and, ironically, by picking up the word 'desires', hints that the story which he tells is a displaced exploration of the white man's 'desires and fears'.

Arsat's story revolves around two motifs: the veiled lady and brotherly love. The context for the story is the power that 'the lady with the veiled face' wielded over Arsat's ruler through her 'cunning and temper' (TU, 195) and her opposition to Arsat's love for Diamelen. However, the account of Arsat's courtship of Diamelen subliminally links the two women: 'Unseeing, we spoke to one another through the scent of flowers, through the veil of leaves' (TU, 196). Similarly, Arsat's story begins by asserting his closeness to his brother ('We are two who are like one' [TU, 196]), but, from the start, this is shadowed by a similar assertion of identification with his white auditor ('We are of a people who take what they want – like you whites' [TU, 196]). As his story proceeds, it reveals how his love for Diamelen (or, more precisely, her proximity) unmans him. As soon as he and his brother have taken her into their boat, he begins to feel fear:

> 'since she was in my boat I began to think of our Ruler's many men ... I remembered the strokes of her heart against my breast and thought that two men cannot withstand a hundred.' (TU, 197)

He restrains his brother from shouting 'the cry of challenge' to the Ruler's men, and his brother responds: 'There is half a man in you now

– the other half is in that woman' (TU, 198). Similarly, when his brother outlines his plan for delaying the Ruler's men, he observes 'she is but a woman – that can neither run nor fight, but she has your heart in her weak hands' (TU, 200). When he betrays and abandons his brother, Arsat's eliptical thought ('Many men') takes us back to his fears in that first moment when Diamelen came on board the boat. Arsat's story is a story of 'desires and fears': he betrays his brother through the fear awoken in him by his desire for Diamelen. At the end of his story, Arsat asserts 'Tuan, I loved my brother' and the white man responds 'We all love our brothers' (TU, 202). Arsat has confessed and has been offered absolution, but the absolution he is offered is a complex expression of male bonding. Arsat is accepted into a male community, a community that is manifested through this assertion of brotherly love, but this assertion of brotherly love after Arsat's story might involve a recognition that brotherly love will always be likely to be subordinated to the love of women and might imply that love cannot be separated from betrayal.[8] There is a similar ambiguity about the kind of bond Arsat is being offered by the narrator: is he being offered brotherhood, or parallel and separate development? Conrad explores this kind of male-bonding further in 'Karain'.

Memory and the voice of the Other

As Mark Conroy has pointed out, the subtitle of 'Karain' ('a Memory') draws attention to the important part played by 'memory' in the story both thematically and as the agency of a chain of narrator/narratee relations.[9] At the beginning, in section I, 'memory' seems to refer to European memories of 'the East'. The opening paragraph evokes a scene of reading:

> Sunshine gleams between the lines of those short paragraphs – sunshine and the glitter of the sea. A strange name wakes up memories; the printed words scent the smoky atmosphere of today faintly, with the subtle and penetrating perfume as of land breezes breathing through the starlight of bygone nights... (TU, 3)

This scene of reading is set against the world of memory it provokes in a systematic binary opposition between the 'befogged respectability' of the metropolitan newspapers and the 'sunshine' and 'glitter' of the Eastern Archipelago, between 'the smoky atmosphere of today' and the 'subtle and penetrating perfume' of 'bygone nights'.

The narrator's memories of Karain's land and people are very clearly an outsider's view of both. They are also, as GoGwilt observes, presented in 'highly aestheticised' terms (IW, 47). Karain is represented throughout this first chapter through theatrical images: his first gesture is 'a theatrical sweep of his arm' (TU, 4); his domain is 'the stage where, dressed splendidly for his part, he strutted, incomparably dignified' (TU, 6); he is always 'word-perfect in his part' (TU, 8); and his followers seem like the bit-part players of some exotic crowd-scene:

> They thronged the narrow length of our schooner's decks with their ornamented and barbarous crowd, with the variegated colours of checkered sarongs, red turbans, white jackets, embroideries; with the gleam of scabbards, gold rings, charms, armlets, lance blades, and jewelled handles of their weapons. (TU, 4)

However, as Richard Ambrosini observes, 'the theatrical references tell us more about the frame narrator than about Karain': the narrator's 'insistence upon the dramatic quality of Karain's performance of his duties' reveals 'his own uncomprehending view of Malayan life and his inability to recognize its reality'.[10] The theatrical metaphors register the estranged Western perspective on this Eastern World at the same time as they attempt to normalise and appropriate that world: 'he was treated with a solemn respect accorded in the irreverent West only to the monarchs of the stage' (TU, 6). It is a perspective which emphasises the spectacular aspects of the Other and denies subjectivity and historical specificity. Thus, the narrator recalls how Karain's land 'appeared to us a land without memories, regrets, and hopes', a land where 'each sunrise, like a dazzling act of special creation, was disconnected from the eve and the morrow' (TU, 5). But this perspective on Karain and his people is subtly questioned by other elements in the chapter. For example, the idea of 'a land without memories' is challenged by reference to the 'soft voices' of the Malays 'speaking of battles, travels, and escapes' (TU, 4) and, above all, by the presence of Karain's bodyguard, who seems 'weary ... with the possession of a burdensome secret' (TU, 5). At the same time, the narrator's presentation of Karain as a performer on stage raises the question of what is being concealed by this performance and what is the reality that pertains to this spectacular Otherness.

Section I ends with night descending 'like a falling curtain' (TU, 9). Section II then goes backstage to reveal the actor behind the mask, and to grant subjectivity to this staged Otherness. The first surprise in the night-time world of Karain is his mysterious 'fear' (TU, 11), 'the strange obsession that wound like a black thread through the gorgeous pomp of his public life'(TU, 12).[11] This leads to the first attempts to engage with his Otherness. The narrator notes that their intimacy 'stopped short of slapping him on the back' because 'there are liberties one must not take with a Malay' (TU, 12). This recognition of different behavioural codes is followed by the narrator's attempt to enter Karain's view of Europe: 'I fancy that to the last he believed us to be emissaries of Government, darkly official persons' (TU, 12). Karain's interest in Queen Victoria indeed obliges the narrator and his colleagues to 'invent details at last to satisfy his craving curiosity' (TU, 13).[12] If this seems comfortably (or uncomfortably) patronising towards Karain, the rest of the section breaks out of this frame: it emphasises the 'quiet dignity of his bearing' and the 'ironic and melancholy shrewdness' with which he 'talked of inter-island politics' (TU, 13). Indeed, there is more than a hint of Tennyson's Ulysses about the Karain who had 'travelled much, suffered not a little', who 'knew native Courts, European Settlements, the forests, the sea' and 'had spoken in his time to many great men' (TU, 14). The effect of presenting Karain here in European heroic terms is similar to the 'cultural dislocation' enacted by Conrad's use of familiar European literary and cultural references in Malay contexts in *Almayer's Folly* and *An Outcast of the Islands*: at the same time as drawing on the resources of European culture in an attempt to represent another culture, it involves a problematising of European cultural hegemony.

In section III the narrative continues this process: the narrator vacillates between seeing Karain as a man like himself and seeing him as Other. For example, Karain is described in terms of such heroic Conradian virtues as 'fidelity' and 'steadfastness', even as the narrator states that he 'would have thought' Karain 'racially incapable' of such qualities. Similarly, he refers to Karain's 'sagacity', which is described as 'only limited by his profound ignorance of the rest of the world' (TU, 18), but this is immediately followed by the narrator's reference to Karain's 'own primitive ideas' (TU, 18). The main event in section III is the unexpected arrival of Karain on board the Europeans' ship after the death of the sword-bearer, his body-guard. This third appearance of Karain is different from both his day-time self (as seen in section I) and his night-time self (as seen in section II). At this point, there is a sense of greater individuation in the representation of Karain, which accompanies the greater individuation of the Europeans. For the first time, the Europeans are distinguished and named: 'bearded Jackson ... young Hollis and I' (TU, 20). However, the individuation of Karain has a paradoxical quality. On the one hand, there is now a sense of Karain's isolation ('And I can tell no one. No one. There is no one here faithful enough and wise enough to know' [TU, 25]), a position comparable to that of some of Conrad's European heroes (for example, 'Lord Jim' in Patusan). On the other hand, in the course of this chapter, Karain has moved from being someone who 'summed up his race, his country' (TU, 16) to being a representative of the 'loneliness of mankind' (TU, 30). He has, however, merely moved from one Orientalist discourse to another: in one case, the individual is made to represent the people or the nation; in the other, what is historically and culturally specific is universalised.[13]

In section IV, the European narrator gives way to Karain's narration, and 'the voice of the Other' (Ambrosini 76) enters the story. The scene of reading, with which the tale began, is now replaced, in this narrative recession, by a scene of oral narration, as Karain's narration replaces the European perspective with a Malay perspective. For example, it displays the Malay codes of civilised conduct by which the Dutch trader is judged and found wanting:

> he laughed aloud like a fool, and knew no courtesy in his speech. He was a big, scornful man, who looked into women's faces and put his hand on the shoulders of free men as though he had been a noble-born chief. (TU, 29)[14]

It challenges European prejudices by casually reversing the prejudiced European perspective on other peoples ('these Dutchmen are all alike' [TU, 33]). It offers a more subtle challenge to European perspectives by asserting a multiplex cultural encounter: for Karain the 'strange stone idols – carved images of devils with many arms and legs' (TU, 32) that he comes across on his travels are as alien as the Dutch trader. As in *Almayer's Folly* and *An Outcast of the Islands*, Conrad's Eastern world is not homogeneous, but an area of overlapping cultures – Islam, Hinduism, Christianity, Arab, English, Dutch, Chinese, Malay.

Karain's narration also restores the local history and politics occluded by the European narrator.[15] Karain begins his narrative: 'it was after the great trouble that broke the alliance of the four states of Wajo. We fought amongst ourselves and the Dutch watched from afar till we were weary ...' (TU, 28). Mundy noted that the southern limb of Celebes contained four kingdoms: Luwu, Wajo, Boni, Soping (NEBC, 61) and that the Dutch took sides in disputes in order to gain control (NEBC, 44).[16] Brooke, on his 1840 visit, recorded that the 1832 contested secession of Si Dendring from Boni had led to a breakdown in the system of government: 'the same cause has latterly separated Boni and Soping from Wajo, as these two sides have been inclined to side with the Dutch against the people of Wajo' (NEBC,73).[17] He goes on to observe that 'the quarrel for the Si Dendring succession has been, since 1832, the chief cause of all the agitations throughout these states' (NEBC, 79). Karain's account of his travels and adventures also includes his service with the Sultan of Sula: 'We fought the Spaniards' (TU, 42). Karain thus maps his adventures against the narrative of European colonialism in the archipelago: the Dutch involvement in the Si Dendring succession in Celebes; the Spanish expeditions against the Sulu archipelago in 1845 and 1848.[18]

The story Karain tells, however, like that told by Arsat, is a story of erotic obsession: 'I saw her! I looked at her! She had tender eyes and a ravishing face. I murmured to her in the night' (TU, 34). It is, in various ways, directly comparable to Kipling's story, 'Dray Wara Yow Dee'.[19] In 'Dray Wara Yow Dee', the Pathan narrator tells his European listener the story of his extensive travels to take revenge on the man who had cuckolded him. Kipling's story is a Browningesque dramatic monologue along the lines of 'My Last Duchess' or 'Porphyria's Lover': in this case, a story of wife-murder, vengeance, and visions of Djinns and devils. As the narrative proceeds, the European reader gradually shifts categories from 'the exotic' to 'the insane': the Pathan's narrative is implicitly judged by a normative frame supplied by the intradiegetic European listener (and the extradiegetic European reader). Conrad's story does something quite different. Karain's story discloses a reality that is different from his European audience's (and presumably different from the European reader's) but is not placed or contained by it. To begin with, when Karain concludes his story, the narrator 'looked on, surprised and moved' at 'that man, loyal to a vision, betrayed by his dream' (TU, 40). Far from rejecting Karain's narrative as 'insane', this places Karain in a category which includes the European. This is made explicit by his subsequent reference to Karain's 'obscure Odyssey of revenge' (TU, 40), which links Karain's narrative with one of the narratives at the roots of European culture. Karain's own response, however, rejects the European frame of reference: he tells how his sword-bearer's wisdom and his own courage 'are remembered where your strength, O white men, is forgotten' (TU, 42). And he leads the narrator to the 'amazing' thought that, to Karain, 'his life – that cruel mirage of love and peace – seemed as real, as undeniable, as theirs would be to any saint, philosopher, or fool of us all' (TU, 44). This relativist perception enunciated by the narrator leaves wide open the questions: what is reality?

Immediately after Karain's narration, the European narrator's own fears and inadequacies are foregrounded. For example, in the profound silence 'full of noiseless phantoms' after Karain's narration ends, he listens to the ship's chronometers 'ticking off steadily the seconds of Greenwich Time', which he experiences as 'a protection and a relief' (TU, 43).[20] This is comparable, perhaps, to Marlow's clinging to 'surface truth' as a protection against reality in *Heart of Darkness*. It might also be seen as that European fetishisation of science that Vladimir intends to attack through the bombing of the Greenwich Observatory in *The Secret Agent*. But it is also an allusion to Greenwich as the prime meridian and to the European scientific mastery of time and space that that implies. The narrator finds protection from Karain's reality in this reminder of a European reality that opens time and space to view and control. His subsequent words of comfort to Karain ('You must abide with your people. They need you. And there is forgetfulness in life. Even the dead cease to speak in time.' [TU, 43]) are, in comparison to Karain's experience, justly described by Hollis as ineffectual 'platitudes' (TU, 44).

Towards the end of section V, as the narrator contemplates Karain's story, he passes two subtly different judgements on it: he observes first that Karain had been hunted along 'the very limit of human endurance', and then he shifts from a general human to a specifically racial category as he thinks that 'very little more pressing was needed' to make Karain swerve into 'the form of madness peculiar to his race' (TU, 45). In the final section, section VI, the narrative repeatedly probes this question of sameness and difference. For example, in the ritual of exorcism that Hollis creates, the narrator is fascinated by the physical difference between Karain and Hollis: 'They were in violent contrast together – one motionless and the colour of bronze, the other dazzling white and lifting his arms' (TU, 50).[21] However, the basis of this ritual is an assertion of sameness. Hollis's first words, at the start of this section, were: 'Every one of us ... you'll admit, has been haunted by some woman' (TU, 47). In other words, the exorcism is based on male-bonding across racial divisions through positing 'woman' as the Other for both European and Malay men. This assertion of sameness is repeated in Hollis's creation of a 'charm' for Karain. The idea of creating a 'charm' to pacify Karain's fears might seem to be reproducing a common trope in colonial fiction in which the European solves a problem or takes control of a situation through a display of 'magic', which asserts the superiority of the European and the 'primitiveness' of the colonial 'Other'.[22] (A classic example is Quatermain's 'eclipse' of the sun in *King Solomon's Mines*.) In this case, however, the narrative is at pains to emphasise the source of the materials from which Hollis constructs the charm: Hollis produces a box which contains 'a bit of silk ribbon', 'a bunch of flowers', 'a narrow white glove', 'a slim packet of letters' and the photograph of a young woman. The contents are accurately described as 'Charms and talismans', as the 'Amulets of white men' (TU, 48), used in attempts to gain power over women. Hollis's mementoes are as much fetishes, as much 'primitive' and magical, as Karain's protective charm.

Difference

When Karain returns to his people and steps back 'into the glorious splendour of his stage', the narrator asks 'I wondered what they thought; what he thought; ... what the reader thinks?' (TU, 52). This unexpected direct address to the reader inscribes the reader's scene of reading into the narrative pattern of written texts and spoken narratives; it writes the reader into the chain of narratives and narratees; and it implicates the reader in the various implications of the narrative.[23] It problematises the boundary between reader and text in the same way as the narrative has problematised boundaries between cultures. This direct involvement of the reader immediately precedes the end of the story, some years later back in London, with the chance meeting in the Strand between Jackson and the narrator. Jackson seems to be haunted by Karain's story; certainly, he expresses his sense that Karain's story seems more 'real' than all the activity of the Strand that surrounds him; and the way in which the activity in the Strand is described underwrites Jackson's sense of its unreality rather than the 'befogged respectability' of the narrator.[24] The story ends, in other words, by re-asserting different realities and not subordinating the Malay world-view to the European.[25]

In 'Karain', Conrad presents radically different realities without attempting any resolution or even hierarchising of their difference. In this way he avoids what Robert Young calls 'ontological imperialism': 'the implicit violence of ontology ... in which the same constitutes itself through a form of negativity in relation to the other, producing all knowledge by appropriating and sublating the other within itself' (WM, 13). The narrator attempts to enact this gesture in the final sentence ('I think that, decidedly, he had been too long away from home', [TU, 55]), but Jackson's haunting by Karain's story marks the resurgence and insistence of an alterity that cannot be contained. The dialogue between the narrator and Jackson anticipates Paul Ricoeur's assertion: 'When we discover that there are several cultures instead of just one ... Suddenly it becomes possible that there are just others, that we ourselves are an 'other' among others'.[26] This apprehension of irreducibly different realities, however, leaves Conrad with a problem of representation, if he is to avoid the imperialism of reducing the Other to the Same. In his next Malay novels, *Lord Jim* and *Victory*, he handles this problem of representation by staying within European discourses of the Other but objectifying them. He does this, in *Lord Jim*, by foregrounding the generic affiliation to adventure fiction. He does this, in both novels, by representing the European community as an oral community and opening the European production of discourse up to critique. At the same time, in both novels, he works to register voices excluded by the hegemonic discourse.

6
Speech and Writing in *Lord Jim*

'That gossiping crowd'

It is now generally accepted that Conrad structures the narrative of *Lord Jim* by reference to light literature: in the first part of the novel, he produces a counter-version of the sea-life of romance; in the second part of the novel, in Patusan, he re-creates the colonial world of adventure romance.[1] Jim constructs his identity from 'a course of light holiday literature' (LJ, 5): Jim's image of himself is a catalogue of situations from the 'sea-life of light literature' (LJ, 6).[2] However, the experience of sea-life granted to him in the first part of the novel systematically overturns his romantic expectations: he does not 'save people from sinking ships'; he does not keep up the hearts of his companions 'in a small boat upon the ocean'; he is far from being 'an example of devotion to duty'. In addition, as Bongie notes, the places Jim visits are 'strangely barren of adventure' (LJ, 10), while the men with whom he works 'did not belong to the world of heroic adventure' (LJ, 24).[3] In the second part of the novel, in Patusan, Jim is moved into the romance world and allowed to fulfil a different heroic identity derived from popular adventure romance: the white man in the tropics. However, as Bongie suggests, the systematic overturning of romance conventions in the first part of the novel means that the romance world of Patusan has already been ruled out as a possible reality: the 'exotic space' of Patusan is an impossible, undiscovered place in the charted world of the novel.[4]

It has been less often remarked that Conrad also produces his narrative by reference to the oral forms of gossip and legend.[5] Thus, when Jim is first introduced, his own sea-life has become the subject of gossip among the oral community of the seaports of Southeast Asia;

while his subsequent flight into the interior, it is hinted from the start, has produced a different reputation among a very different oral community: 'They called him Tuan Jim' (LJ, 5). Jim's actions on the *Patna* and in Patusan circulate, to very different effect, among colonial and Malay oral communities.

The early part of the novel takes pains to establish and delineate this 'colonial' oral community – indeed, it delineates two different kinds of 'colonial' community. When Jim goes into the hospital, he is initiated into the first of these communities as the European patients 'told each other the story of their lives' (LJ, 12).[6] When he leaves the hospital to visit the town, he associates with 'men of his calling' in the port, and, again, the community creates itself through gossip:

> They talked everlastingly of turns of luck: how So-and-so got charge of a boat on the coast of China. ... how this one had an easy billet in Japan somewhere, and that one was doing well in the Siamese navy ... (LJ, 13)[7]

This is a clear instance of that kind of gossip that Spacks terms 'idle talk', but this 'idle talk' actually serves to construct and define a community.[8] Once Jim deserts the *Patna*, the action is memorialised in the gossip of this community: Jim's flight eastwards is a constantly repeated, always already doomed attempt to flee from this oral community constituted by the 'men of his calling' in the ports of the archipelago.

Marlow is the exceptional case, who also epitomises this community. As soon as he is introduced, Marlow is presented as an important agent in the transmission of Jim's tale:

> And later on, many times, in distant parts of the world, Marlow showed himself willing to remember Jim, to remember him at length, in detail and audibly. (LJ, 33)

Marlow himself describes the conditions of his re-tellings of this narrative: 'a good spread, two hundred feet above the sea-level, with a box of decent cigars handy' (LJ, 35). Marlow thus evokes a European oral community constituted through male after-dinner discourse. The narrative presented in *Lord Jim* is itself one such telling. As a result, the reader is inscribed into, and made collusive with, a male world of story-telling.[9] The 'Author's Note' refers to this world in precisely its own tones: 'Men have been known, both in the tropics and in the temperate zone, to sit up half the night "swapping yarns"' (LJ, vii). This is more than just 'idle talk'. In these after-dinner sessions, gossip 'creates its own territory'; it 'inhabits a space of intimacy, it builds on and implicitly articulates shared values' (*Gossip*, 15). The audience for these after-dinner narrative performances also, of course, gives a sense to the recurrent references to 'one of us'.[10]

However, part of the scandal of Jim's story is that it goes beyond the boundaries of this professional oral community to a much larger colonial community:

> The whole waterside talked of nothing else. First thing in the morning as I was dressing in my state-room, I would hear through the bulkhead my Parsee Dubash jabbering about the *Patna* with the steward ... you heard of it in the harbour office, at every ship-broker's, at your agent's, from whites, from natives, from half-castes, from the very boatmen squatting half-naked on the stone steps as you went up ... (LJ, 36)

The *Patna* incident cannot be confined to a gentlemanly circle of gossip: 'the tale ... was public property' (LJ, 41). It is precisely the public nature of the tale – the way it has exposed the European officer class to critical discussion by the colonised peoples – that so demor- alises Brierly: 'there he sits while all these confounded natives, serangs, lascars, quartermasters, are giving evidence that's enough to burn a man to ashes with shame' (LJ, 67). If Jim's misleading appearance raises strictly professional doubts in both Marlow and Brierly, the circulation of the *Patna* story among the larger colonial community serves to undermine the European position of authority. The *Patna* incident creates an oral community in which the diverse groups mentioned by Marlow and by Brierly are all levelled. This is the larger crisis that Jim's jump provokes.

As if in reaction to this, Marlow's inquiries within the European community continually gesture towards areas of privileged discourse, professional contexts in which oral exchanges remain confidential, outside the circuits of gossip: the confessional; lawyer-client relations; and doctor-patient relations.[11] Thus Jim's telling of his story to Marlow is compared to an act of confession: 'he confessed himself before me as though I had the power to bind and to loose' (LJ, 97). Marlow's consultation with the French lieutenant is likened, in turn, to a confession to a priest, 'one of those snuffy, quiet village priests, into whose ears are poured the sins, the sufferings, the remorse of peasant generations' (LJ, 139). It is also compared to 'taking professional opinion' from a lawyer (LJ, 145). However, in both cases, the model is simultaneously evoked and denied. Jim's confession to Marlow is not bound by the laws of the confessional. Indeed, as Marlow's narration suggests, it has become part of a tale he frequently tells. Similarly, Marlow's consultation with the French lieutenant is not bound by any professional rules of confidentiality: both parties are free to put the information exchanged into wider circulation – and, indeed, to put that act of exchange itself into circulation, as Marlow does. Marlow's invocation of these models of confidentiality can thus be seen as an attempt to deny his role in the transmission of gossip: he presents his gossip as anti-gossip through invoking models of privileged information.

Thus, for his conversation with Stein, Marlow invokes the model of doctor-patient confidentiality: 'our conference resembled so much a medical consultation' (LJ, 212). Indeed, he repeatedly summons up the idea of confidentiality: not only is Stein 'an eminently suitable person to receive my confidences about Jim's difficulties' (LJ, 203), he also 'knew how to be so generously encouraging as to make a scrupulous man hesitate on the brink of confidence' (LJ, 212). In this context of 'scrupulous' professional men, it is almost possible to forget that this confidentiality is repeatedly broken by Marlow – as it is at this moment of narration. Marlow presents himself as a scrupulous, serious-minded analytic storyteller, as the counter-type to Schomberg, 'an irrepressible retailer of all the scandalous gossip of the place' (LJ, 198).[12] In contrast to the malicious gossip of Schomberg, Marlow's gossip is of the type that 'provides opportunity for self-disclosure and for examination of moral decisions' (*Gossip*, 34). Indeed, Marlow might be said to produce that 'transformative gossip' that interprets a community to itself:

> It depends on a relatively stable group of talkers who feel themselves members of a larger collectivity. Everyone knows what a story is supposed to sound like as everyone knows what people are supposed to do, or not to do. ... The re-assurance of communal conversation counters the transgressive thrust of individual actions. (*Gossip*, 231)

Marlow is, nevertheless, subversively shadowed by Schomberg. This, after all, is the Marlow who writes 'gossipy' letters (LJ, 172) to pass the time during Jim's crisis in his hotel room.

Competing narratives, repeated narratives

After failing to convince the court of his innocence, Jim spends Chapters 7–12 telling his story to Marlow. This story is set against the counter-narrative created by the other officers of the *Patna*, which re-narrativises the events of the sinking of the *Patna* so as to exonerate themselves from blame. When the *Avondale* picks them up, they 'told their story' (LJ, 133), and Jim provides a brief narrative that serves to corroborate theirs:

> 'Shock slight. Stopped the ship. Ascertained the damage. Took measures to get the boats out without creating a panic. As the first boat was lowered ship went down in a squall. Sank like lead ...'
> (LJ, 133)

These narratives are overwhelmed by the different narrative they encounter when they reach port: 'The *Patna* ... French gunboat ... towed successfully to Aden ... Investigation' (LJ, 134). The chief clerk's brief narrative, telegraphically reported by Jim, is a digest of the expanded version supplied by the commander of the French gunboat (LJ, 137–42) that has become 'public property' (LJ, 137). This contest of narratives foreshadows the competing narratives through which Marlow constructs his narrative as well as the larger contest between the 'scandal of the Eastern seas' (LJ, 151), which is attached to Jim's name in the first part of the novel, and the 'legend of strength and prowess' that forms 'round his name' (LJ, 175), the 'Jim-myth', that develops in the second part of the novel.

These various stories circulate within the novel as part of a larger world of stories which exists beyond the limits of the novel. This larger world is gestured towards by various lost or untold stories. There are, for example, the missing tales of Tunku Allang's 'hot youth' (LJ, 249). There is the lost story of the serang on board the *Patna*: his story remains untold because the serang didn't speak French, and the French officers who boarded the *Patna* did not speak either English or Malay. More important, there is the missing story of Cornelius's wife, the 'good-looking Dutch-Malay girl' (LJ, 219) buried in Patusan:

> 'How the poor woman had come to marry the awful Malacca Portuguese – after the separation from the father of her girl – and how that separation had been brought about ... is a mystery to me.'
> (LJ, 276)

Although the details of the story are missing, it nevertheless has an important function in the novel. Indeed, Padmini Mongia suggests that the novel is haunted by 'the ghost of a woman that will not be laid to rest'.[13] These lost stories gesture towards a 'rival consciousness' or rival consciousnesses that cannot be expressed through the circulation of European male discourses in *Lord Jim*.[14]

As well as competing narratives and missing narratives, *Lord Jim* is also characterised by narratives that repeat or threaten to repeat. Indeed, these repeated narratives effectively constitute a form of male succession within the markedly masculinist focus of Marlow's narration. Thus Chapter 22 of *Lord Jim* tells how Stein was assisted by McNeil and how Stein, in turn, planned to pass on 'to a young man the help he had received in his own young days' (LJ, 230–31).[15] In opposition to this benign replication of narrative, in a male dynastic succession without recourse to women, Jewel and her mother (as Mongia has shown) suggest the malign replication of narrative for colonised women, a narrative of exploitation and desertion by European men.[16] It is significant that Jewel's fears are anticipated by Doramin. In Chapter 28, in his anxiety for his son's future, he observes to Marlow that 'The land remains where God had put it; but white men ... come to us and in a little while they go' (LJ, 274). Doramin's fears in regard to the political situation in Patusan have their parallel in Jewel's fears about her relationship with Jim. Doramin, however, seeks to establish a narrative of male succession; Jewel seeks to break a narrative of male desertion. The attempts by Stein and Doramin to replicate narratives fail; Jewel's attempt to escape the replication of narrative also fails. Nevertheless, these contrasting patterns emphasise the male inheritance of power, the female inheritance of suffering, and Marlow's subordination of non-European priorities to Jim's place among competing narratives.

The story of Jewel and Jim shows Conrad returning again to the issue of desire between Europeans and non-Europeans. Marlow begins his account of 'the story of [Jim's] love' with the observation:

> 'We have heard so many such stories, and the majority of us don't believe them to be stories of love at all ... episodes of passion at best, or perhaps only of youth and temptation ...' (LJ, 275)

Marlow acknowledges the genre to which the story of Jim and Jewel belongs, but tries to differentiate it from the standard pattern.[17]

Cornelius, of course, interprets Jim's relation with Jewel as merely the usual story: 'Every gentleman made a provision when the time came to go home' (LJ, 328).[18] Jewel too is conscious of a repeating narrative pattern ('They always leave us' [LJ, 309]). Jewel's love for Jim is set against her wish not to repeat her mother's story (LJ, 312), which turns out also to be her grandmother's story as well (LJ, 314). Mongia notes that Marlow is happy to see Jewel as a replica of her mother ('I am sure that the mother was as much of a woman as the daughter seemed to be' [LJ, 277]; and that Cornelius too sees the two women as interchangeable ('she is like her deceitful mother. Exactly. In her face, too.' [LJ, 329]); but that Jewel, while fearing mere replication, seeks to avoid it (GG7). Jewel intimates a repeated narrative for 'Malay' women who get involved with European men, which is the counter-narrative to the story familiar to Marlow and his male audience (LJ, 275). Jewel's mother's grave acts as the memory symbol for this narrative possibility (LJ, 275–6).

The formation of legends

In his book *La Formation des légendes* (1910), Arnold van Gennep observed:

> la fantaisie et l'erreur sont normales, mêmes chez nous, et ... la tendance à la deformation ... agit dès le moment de l'observation. Elle agit davantage encore lorsqu'il y a transmission par récits oraux.[19]

He accordingly set out to investigate 'les lois de la genèse, de la formation, de la transmission et de la modification des légendes'.[20] Francis Cornford, in *Thucydides Mythistoricus* (1907), was concerned with written rather than oral history, but Cornford too remarked on 'the transformation which begins to steal over all events from the moment of their occurence'.[21] In the second part of *Lord Jim*, recounting Jim's period in Patusan, Conrad had already begun to explore this 'transformation': how, in Cornford's words, 'fact shifts into legend, and legend into myth'.[22]

Chapter 16 supplies the first account of Jim's career in Patusan, and this introduction of Patusan links it firmly with the idea of legends:

> The time was coming when I should see him loved, trusted, admired, with a legend of strength and prowess forming round his name as though he had been the stuff of a hero. (LJ, 175)

When Marlow, in Chapter 24, arrives in Patusan, he begins to hear almost immediately quasi-legendary stories about Jim. The headman of the fishing-village, who acts as his pilot up the river, is Marlow's first informant:

> There was already a story that the tide had turned two hours before its time to help him on his journey up the river. (LJ, 242–3)[23]

The attack on Sherif Ali's fort is the basis for other legends. In Chapter 26, Jim provides a factual account of this episode, and then, in Chapter 27, Marlow hears how these facts have been imaginatively transformed. In the first version he encounters, 'the legend had gifted [Jim] with supernatural powers':

> Yes, it was said, there had been many ropes cunningly disposed, and a strange contrivance that turned by the efforts of many men, and each gun went up tearing slowly through the bushes, like a wild pig rooting its way in the undergrowth, but ... what is the strength of ropes and of men's arms? There is a rebellious soul in things which must be overcome by powerful charms and incantations. (LJ, 266)[24]

This version of the event is told, however, by Sura, 'a professional sorcerer,' who clearly has a professional interest in promulgating 'occult' explanations.[25] The second version he hears – which is current among 'the simple folk of outlying villages' – is itself much simpler: they believed 'that Jim had carried the guns up the hill on his back – two at a time' (LJ, 266). Jim's exploits, to his own exasperation, have been infigurated into the mould of folk-tale. In the same way, Jim's account of his attack upon the stockade is set against the 'popular story' that 'Jim with a touch of one finger had thrown down the gate' (LJ, 270). Folk-tale and legend implicitly offer an alternative narrative interpretation of Jim to Marlow's.

The story of Jewel and Jim provides the clearest example of the transformation of fact into legend. Marlow ends his account of this part of Jim's story by recounting what he calls 'this amazing Jim-myth' (LJ, 280). The Dutch 'government official' (LJ, 279) hints at the first version of this 'myth', but the hints do not make much sense until Marlow hears of the story 'travelling slowly down the coast about a mysterious white man in Patusan who had got hold of an extraordinary gem – namely, an emerald of an enormous size, and altogether priceless' (LJ, 280). The narrative makes clear that this transformation of the facts is in line with what Cornford was to call 'infiguration' (that is, 'the moulding of facts into types of myth contributed by traditional habits of thought'), when Marlow, after citing 'the famous stone of the Sultan of Succadana' as an analogue, observes that 'the story of a fabulously large emerald is as old as the arrival of the first white man in the Archipelago' (LJ, 280).[26] The second version of the story, provided by the rajah's scribe, is more sophisticated:

> Such a jewel ... he said ... is best preserved by being concealed about the person of a woman ... such a woman seemed to be actually in existence. He had been told of a tall girl, whom the white man treated with great respect and care, and who never went forth from the house unattended. (LJ, 280–1)

This version shows how the legend is able to assimilate on a second level the factual details which it originally transformed.

Conrad had already touched on such 'popular' transformations, the shifting of fact into legend, in 'The Rescuer.'[27] After his own detailed narration of Lingard's rescue of Hassim and Immada from Wajo, Conrad begins the next chapter with 'the traditional account of the last civil war' (Re, 86; Ms, 153), which is told to travellers visiting Wajo. This includes 'the legend of a chief and his sister, whose mother had been a great princess suspected of sorcery,' who escaped by magic when their enemies had them trapped 'with their backs to the sea':

> 'The chief, Hassim, was gone, and the lady who was a princess in the country – and nobody knows what became of them from that day to this. Sometimes traders from our parts talk of having heard of them here, and heard of them there, but these are the lies of men who go afar for gain. We who live in the country believe that the ship sailed back into the clouds whence the Lady's magic made her come. Did we not see the ship with our own eyes? And as to Rajah Hassim and his sister ... some men say one thing and some another, but God alone knows the truth.' (Re, 87; Ms, 153–4).

In this instance, the narrator and the European reader are confident that they also know 'the truth', and the effect is to ironise the Wajo narrator's interpretation. There is, however, a further irony about the status of evidence, which rebounds on both the narrator and this reader. Hearsay evidence, which (in European legal practices) is treated as invalid, is here probably true, while empirical evidence, which actually derives its meaning from the observer's pre-conceptions – or, more accurately, their noetic or thought world, is used to support the wrong answer.[28] In *Lord Jim*, on the other hand, Marlow concludes, 'there shall be no message, unless such as each of us can interpret for himself from the language of facts,' and facts 'are so often more enigmatic than the craftiest arrangement of words' (LJ, 340). The implication is, as Allan Simmons points out, that 'Sura's version of events – like Marlow's – is but one way of interpreting what the narrative is, ultimately, designed to leave evasive.'[29]

Myth and history

Stein has made a romantic name for himself among the oral community of Wajo through his support for Mohammed Banso in a struggle for succession ('the natives talk of that war to this day' [LJ, 206]). He has also made quite another name for himself in Europe, where he is 'known to learned persons' (LJ, 203) as a 'learned collector' of butterflies and beetles.[30] This figure at the furthest periphery of Jim's wanderings has both a local reputation and a different reputation at the metropolitan centre through the communication networks of the scientific community. Stein, with his 'cabinet of butterflies' (LJ, 203) and the 'narrow shelves filled with dark boxes of uniform shape and colour' (LJ, 204) that house his collection of beetles, is a precise embodiment of the scientific project adumbrated in *New Atlantis*, institutionalised by the Royal Society, and systematised by Linnaeus. Stein spends his time 'classing and arranging specimens, corresponding with entomologists in Europe, writing up a descriptive catalogue of his treasures' (LJ, 207).[31] At the same time, his attempt to 'annex on his own account every butterfly or beetle he could lay hands on' (LJ, 206) neatly ties the scientific into the colonial project.[32]

Stein also represents European private trade in South-east Asia: 'Stein and Co. ... had a large inter-island business, with a lot of trading posts established in the most out of the way places for collecting the produce' (LJ, 202). He even has a partner, who 'looked after the Moluccas' (LJ, 202), that historically resonant site of European trading interest. Stein's knowledge of Patusan is derived from this part of his activities:

He was as full of information about native States as an official report. ... He *had* to know. He traded in so many ... (LJ, 227)

Chapter 22 approaches Patusan through a consideration of how the place-name figures in 'collections of old voyages':

> The seventeenth-century traders went there for pepper, because the passion for pepper seemed to burn like a flame of love in the breast of Dutch and English adventurers about the time of James the First. (LJ, 226)

It then presents a series of different perspectives on these adventurers. The diminishing perspective of their motivation ('the passion for pepper') gives way to a recognition of their heroism: in particular, from the perspective of the nineteenth century, 'they appear magnified, not as agents of trade but as instruments of a recorded destiny, pushing out into the unknown' (LJ, 227). It concludes:

> They were wonderful; and ... they were ready for the wonderful. They recorded it complacently in their sufferings, in the aspect of the seas, in the customs of strange nations, in the glory of splendid rulers. (LJ, 227)

This anticipation of Conrad's account of the 'fabulous' period of geography stands in contrast with Stein's precise 'information' about the 'native States'.[33] It then becomes the context for the exploration of the factual and the wonderful, the historical and the legendary, that constitutes the narrative of events in Patusan.

So far this chapter has emphasised the legendary aspects of the narrative, but the narrative of Patusan is also firmly embedded in the material culture of the region. This is not just a matter of the historical importance of pepper, but small details such as Doramin's wearing of a folded 'head-kerchief' (LJ, 259); the use of 'small brass cannon' (LJ, 263) as currency; or the presence of body tattooing (LJ, 270).[34] The political situation it describes is also in accord with contemporary English accounts of the historical situation: here the Rajah's position is contested by a more recently arrived community of Bugis headed by Doramin, and both are challenged by a still more recent arrival, Sharif Ali, who 'on purely religious grounds, had incited the tribes in the interior' (LJ, 257).[35] However, this shades into a reproduction of the ideologically-loaded discourse of this historiographic tradition. Thus the description of the Bugis as 'intelligent, enterprising, revengeful, but with a more frank courage than the other Malays' (LJ, 256) probably derives from McNair's *Perak and the Malays*, but it repeats a view of the Bugis prevalent in Raffles and Brooke.[36] A more convincing example is perhaps the representation of the Sultan's position with his 'uncertain and beggarly revenue extorted from a miserable population and stolen from him by as many uncles' (LJ, 227). The source for the imbecile Sultan with 'two thumbs on his left hand' (LJ, 227) is Brooke (EB, I, 327). More important is the implicit view of native rule as oppressive – but also inefficient – which is the reason advanced for English intervention from Raffles to Clifford. Thus, Rajah Allang, 'the worst of the Sultan's uncles', 'ground down to the point of extinction the country-born Malays' (LJ, 228) and has ideas of trading 'indistinguishable from the commonest forms of robbery' (LJ, 257). For this reason, the fishing village, from being enslaved by the Rajah, comes under Jim's 'especial protection'. In this is audible not just Brooke but a recurrent feature of the 'anti-slavery' rhetoric of English merchants. It is no surprise to find Jim lecturing the Rajah 'upon the text that no man should be prevented from getting his food and his children's food honestly' (LJ, 250). Jim's text could be taken from the writings of Brooke: 'Piracy must be put down, slavery must be effaced, industry must be cherished and protected' (EB, I, 190).[37]

The account of Jim's rise to power in Patusan constantly plays the legendary against the historical. Jim complains about the growth of legends: 'They will sit up half the night talking bally rot' (LJ, 266). In other words the generation of legends, the Jim-myth, among the oral community of Patusan follows the same process as the proliferation of stories about Jim among the European oral community. Once again it is the very same process as Marlow himself is actively involved in at this very moment of narration. Thus what might appear as difference (between 'primitive' and 'civilised' communities) turns out to be similarity.

Furthermore, the effect of this similarity is again to produce a radical vision of endless narrative elaborations. Jim describes the problem he encountered of the old man seeking his advice about divorce. Not only was the old man's story 'impossible to fathom' (LJ, 268), but, when Jim took the story back to the old man's own community, 'Every bally idiot took sides with one family or the other' (LJ, 269). There was no privileged interpretative community for the story and no authoritative interpretation. As Jim concludes: 'The trouble was to get at the truth of anything' (LJ, 269). In other words, Jim's attempt to judge this divorce case in Patusan reflects back upon Marlow's attempt to judge Jim's own case. It also raises the possibility that Marlow's narrative as presented in *Lord Jim* is only one version of Marlow's reading of Jim's story. The fact that Marlow repeatedly tells Jim's story does not necessarily mean that he tells the same story each time.[38] Marlow's willingness to remember Jim 'at length, in detail and audibly' (LJ, 33) rather than suggesting a single narrative repeatedly reproduced, implies rather a constant re-narrativising of 'Jim's story' by Marlow at different times, in different places, for different audiences. This, in turn, suggests, the endlessness of narrative and the relativity – or even futility – of interpretation. Just as there is an infinite number of stories beyond the stories collected in *Lord Jim*, there are also, in theory at least, other Marlow versions of Jim's story that remain unrecorded.[39]

The politics of rumour

In Chapter 35, as he leaves Jim in Patusan for the last time, Marlow offers a summing up of the Patusan narrative:

> The immense and magnanimous Doramin and his little motherly witch of a wife, gazing together upon the land and nursing secretly their dreams of parental ambition; Tunku Allang, wizened and greatly perplexed; Dain Waris, intelligent and brave … the girl, absorbed in her frightened, suspicious adoration; Tamb'Itam, surly and faithful … – I am certain of them. They exist as if under an enchanter's wand. But the figure round which all these are grouped – that one lives, and I am not certain of him. No magician's wand can immobilise him under my eyes. He is one of us. (LJ, 330–1)

Through his use of the 'enchanter's wand', Marlow freezes 'Jim's people' in Patusan in a tableau around him: the implication is that these people can be summed up and fixed in this way, and that Jim alone cannot. Jim alone, it seems, has a subjectivity complex enough to make him an object of psychological or moral interest. Everyone else can apparently be characterised in a couple of adjectives: the adventures of Jim's consciousness require a book, and even then Marlow hesitates from giving the last word. This discrepancy suggests a further limitation in Marlow's perception, and a limitation to his narration: 'one of us' now marks a limit to Marlow's own awareness in terms of class, gender, and 'race'.[40] Not only does Marlow present a narrative of Patusan that is ideologically shaped by the imperialist texts that are Conrad's sources, but his account of the non-Europeans colonises and then empties out the category of the Other.[41] Thus just as Jewel struggles to set her narrative (with its different race and gender subject position) against Marlow's, so too the Malays' narrative struggles to emerge against Marlow's representations, and, where Marlow takes them out of history, their narrativising is firmly located within history. This is evident in the final part of the novel.

The final part of the novel deals with the arrival of Gentleman Brown and with Jim's death. Here, with the exception of Brown himself, all of Marlow's narrators are local: Tamb'Itam, the Bugis trader, Jewel. However, although they are trusted enough to be the source of information, nevertheless, it is noticeable that the information they supply is non-problematic – unlike the European informants earlier. They present mutually supportive narrative – not competing narratives. This suggests again the novel's incomplete realisation of the Malays: either they are not given a complex subjectivity, or the reader is not trusted sufficiently to engage with the complex subjectivity of non-Europeans.[42]

Although this final section of the narrative is presented as written rather than spoken, speech is still foregrounded – not only in the narrative method with its sequence of informers, but also in the continuing emphasis on gossip and rumour.[43] That 'busybody Schomberg' (LJ, 345) helps Marlow to find the dying Brown by 'confidentially' directing him where to look. Brown, after his first 'confidential talk' with Cornelius (LJ, 365), gains a sense of the situation in Patusan. Subsequently, Cornelius gives him 'his own version of Jim's character, ... commenting in his own fashion upon the events of the last three years' (LJ, 367). Later still, Cornelius repeats to Brown 'all that had been said in council, gossiping in an even undertone at Brown's ear' (LJ, 397). Cornelius here anticipates Schomberg's role in *Victory* as the source of information which brings disaster to others. However, it is also worth noticing that some of the substance of Cornelius's 'gossip' is the local politics of Patusan: in particular, the conflict between the Rajah and the Bugis. The arrival of another European in the settlement has the potential of undoing the balance of power established by Jim. If Brown is concerned to gather information for his ends, the Malays of the settlement are just as concerned to understand the purpose of Brown's visit – or the uses to which it might be put. As in *Almayer's Folly*, while the foreground is occupied by the problems of the Europeans, the background is full of the political life of the Bugis and the Malays. This, in turn, gives rise to the politics of rumour that replaces the Jim-myth in the final part of the novel.

Marlow's account of Jim's death begins with his return to Stein's house in Samarang and his encounter with the 'respectable petty trader', whom he had seen 'in Jim's house, amongst other Bugis men' talking 'interminably over their war reminiscences' and discussing 'State affairs' (LJ, 346). This reminder of the oral community of Patusan prepares for the final discursive encounter between the Jim-myth, Cornelius's counter-narrative of Jim, the counter-version of Jim represented by Brown ('he was always trotted out in the stories of lawless life a visitor from home is treated to' [LJ, 352]), and the rumours that begin to fly around Patusan. Brown's story is carefully situated historically: he deserts from a home ship 'in the early gold-digging days' (LJ, 352). His story is that he was 'trying to run a few guns for the insurgents' (LJ, 354) – presumably the 1870s Sulu resistance to Spanish domination. En route to Patusan, he had called at 'one of these new Spanish settlements – which never came to anything in the end' (LJ, 354).[44] And, as they cross the Java Sea, they dodge 'an English gunboat' and 'a Dutch corvette', the two colonial powers patrolling this region. Marlow even suggests that one of the attractions of Patusan might have been its remoteness from 'the ends of submarine cables' (LJ, 357).[45]

In this carefully historically-situated narrative, the 'rumours' that spread among the Malays after Brown's arrival are, unlike the 'Jim-myth', backed by an equally strong historical sense. Thus the rumour about 'a large ship at the mouth of the river with big guns and many more men' ('They were coming with many more boats to exterminate every living thing' [LJ, 363]), while, in this instance, incorrect, is nevertheless built upon historical precedents: Brooke's assault on the 'pirates', which destroyed the historical Patusan, is only one of many examples of big European ships coming with guns to 'exterminate every living thing'.[46] Tunku Allang's negotiations with Brown similarly lead to 'flying rumours' (LJ, 373). The anticipation of bloodshed, which prompts the 'poorer folk' to take to the bush and escape up river, and moves the upper class 'to go and pay their court to the Rajah' (LJ, 373), deftly sketches rational responses to the new political uncertainties occasioned by Jim's absence and the arrival of Brown.[47] It also emphasises the fragility of the 'orderly, peaceful life' (LJ, 373) which Jim has established. The adventure-romance narrative is similarly firmly rooted in nice discriminations between, for example, the readiness of the Bugis to fight and the reluctance of the non-Bugis townspeople who 'hoped that the rapacious strangers would be induced, by the sight of so many brave men making ready to fight, to go away' (LJ, 390).[48] The encounter between Jim and Brown in Patusan can usefully be approached in terms of what Marshall Sahlins calls 'the structure of the conjuncture'.[49] Sahlins uses it to explore the historical intersection of radically divergent cultural categories. Thus, in Sahlins's account of the death of Captain Cook, 'Cook fell victim to the play of Hawaiian categories, or more precisely to their interplay with his own' (xiii). The 'fatal impact' was produced by the collision between 'the Hawaiian theory of divine kingship' and 'the British practice of imperialism' (xiv).[50] Greenblatt uses this concept to discuss encounters in America between Europeans and indigenes. In Greenblatt's version, 'the structure of the conjuncture' consists of four elements: 'the operative cultural understanding of the Europeans, the historical situation in which this understanding is deployed, the operative cultural understanding of the natives, and the historical situation in which this understanding is deployed'.[51] The same approach can be used to illuminate the arrival of Brown in Patusan. The narrative supplies Jim's cultural understanding and the history in which that is deployed; Brown's cultural understanding and the history in which that is deployed; and the same for the Bugis and Malays. Where Jim had imposed a fragile peace on the rival factions, Brown's arrival re-opens the fault-lines.[52] As Greenblatt observes, 'the convergence has its own structuring force, quite apart from what any of the participants may be thinking' (NWE, x). Given that a safe outcome to this cross-cultural encounter would require 'the fortuitous convergence of fundamentally divergent expectations, understandings, and practices' (NWE, x), destruction in one form or another is almost unavoidable. In *Lord Jim*, the cross-cultural encounter is further complicated by the cultural divergences between Jim and Brown, as well as between Bugis and Malay. This is not simply a cross-cultural encounter between Europeans and indigenes; neither European culture nor indigenous culture is simple and homogenous, and the differences between Europeans and between different indigenous groups are as important for the outcome as the differences between Europeans and non-Europeans.

This is also the case in *Victory* and *The Rescue*, where the class-difference between Lingard and the yacht-people means, as Lingard observes, that the yacht-people are 'as strange' to him as the Malays are to the yacht-people (Re, 158), while the Malays too are divided into various competing groups. In *The Rescue*, as in *Lord Jim*, the narrative moves towards the construction of a complex conjuncture of radically divergent cultural categories. As in *Lord Jim*, Conrad produces a colonialist discourse but works to problematise that discourse both through objectifying it and through acknowledging the existence of other histories and other cultures. At the same time, the encounter between Jim and Gentleman Brown brings together different European cultures, and the dialogical interrogation of different European cultures is foregrounded in Conrad's next major Malay projects, *Victory* and *The Rescue.*

7
Absence and Presence in *Victory*

Said, discussing the interplay between writing, speaking and seeing in Conrad's fiction, has suggested that, characteristically, Conrad's narratives 'orginate in the hearing and telling presence of people' (95).[1] But these narratives also often assume (as Chapter 6 has demonstrated) the currency of rival versions and, indeed, are often positioned among competing narratives. Although these spoken narratives evoke a community, their existence as writing implicitly sets that evoked community against the actual isolation of the scene of writing and the scene of reading. Where gossip anticipates a community, writing produces the reader as solitary individual. Conrad's narratives circulate gossip within a community, but also, as in 'Karain' or *Lord Jim*, repeatedly return to the solitary scenes of writing and of reading.

Said argues further that writing sets the illusion of presence against the fact of 'the absence of everything but words' (WTC, 95). Conrad's narrative is grounded epistemologically in utterance 'as speech reported or spoken' (WTC, 101). Thus, in *Lord Jim*, Marlow listens to Jim and then remembers Jim 'at length, in detail and audibly' (LJ, 33) in front of other audiences. However, as Said notes, 'Jim does not speak to Marlow, but rather in front of him, just as Marlow cannot by definition speak to the reader but only in front of him' (WTC, 103). In the same way, in *Victory*, Lena has the consciousness that Heyst, when addressing her, 'was really talking to himself' (V, 196). Ironically, Lena's final words, though addressed to Heyst, are also performed in front of him rather than engaging with him in a moment of mutual understanding:

'Who else could have done this for you?' she whispered gloriously. 'No one in the world,' he answered her in a murmur of unconcealed despair. (V, 406)

What should be their moment of union, in the romantic script according to which Lena sacrifices herself, is actually marked by division and divergence. In other words, intradiegetically in both *Lord Jim* and *Victory*, speech conveys 'the presence to each other of speaker and hearer' but not necessarily 'a mutual comprehension' (WTC, 103–4). Something similar happens extradiegetically. Lena and Heyst talk in front of each other and in front of the reader. They are presented dramatically through dialogue, and the reader is left to gauge the degrees of understanding and misunderstanding, reading and misreading, involved in their interaction through her own (mis)understandings and (mis)readings. The scene of narration – with its speaker and hearer – creates the illusion of presence, if not the actuality of mutual comprehension, but the scene of writing and the scene of reading are both involved in a problematics of absence that foregrounds interpretation.[2]

Island gossip

In *Victory*, Conrad returned to many of the issues he had raised in *Lord Jim*. The most obvious of these is gossip. From the start *Victory* establishes the oral community within which Heyst has taken refuge, and returns to an exploration of gossip. Part 1 is presented by an unnamed narrator, who invokes the group ('We "out there"') to which he belongs (V, 3). He reports on Heyst's observable characteristics and recycles various attempts to interpret Heyst's behaviour made by this community. He notes that 'from the first there was some difficulty in making him out' (V, 6). This difficulty is demonstrated by the succession of labels that are attached to him ('Enchanted Heyst', 'Hard facts', 'Heyst the Spider', 'Heyst the Enemy'), each of which memorialises some incident or utterance. In the first part of *Victory*, as in the first part of *Nostromo*, various labels and public identities circulate around an absence.

The most important of the early incidents is Heyst's rescue of Morrison and the events that follow from that. The narrator introduces the incident by reference to competing narratives current in the community of gossip: 'Some said he was a partner, others said he was a sort of paying guest' (V, 10). The dominant narrative, however, is that circulated by Schomberg: 'that Heyst, having obtained some mysterious hold on Morrison, had fastened himself on him and was sucking him dry' (V, 20). Hence the label: 'Heyst the Spider'.[3] Subsequently, the Tropical Belt Coal Co. provides the stimulus for further gossip: 'Everybody in the islands was talking of the Tropical Belt Coal' (V, 24). This time, however, the gossip is prompted by the threat the Tropical Belt Coal Co. represents to the livelihood of the gossipers: 'the end of the individual trader, smothered under a great invasion of steamers' (V, 24). The beginning of the 'era of steam' (V, 21) for the islands marks the end of the era of sail.[4] Steamers keeping regular timetables render redundant the traders with their sailing-ships, dependent on wind and weather, who have constituted an important part of the oral community of Conrad's Malay novels. This gossip, in other words, is professional talk, prompted by self-interest. If the narrative is grounded epistemologically in utterance, that utterance, in turn, is grounded in the material conditions of the archipelago, though these are only seen darkly through the text's circulation of gossip and rumour.

The Tropical Belt Coal Company also generates its own form of gossip. There is, for example, Heyst's promotional talk of the 'great stride forward for these regions', which is heard by 'more than a hundred persons in the islands' (V, 6). There is the related talk of 'offices in London and Amsterdam' – though this, in practice, might amount to no more than 'one room in each' (V, 21). There is also the prospectus with its map:

On it Samburan was represented as the central spot of the Eastern Hemisphere. ... Heavy lines radiated from it in all directions through the tropics ... (V, 23)

This map is very obviously not a neutral and objective representation but an expression of value.[5] More important, as GoGwilt observes, the 'ironic failure of this map to represent a corresponding power' graphically registers the gap between 'representation and reality' (IW, 67).[6] The promotional literature that accompanies the map also produces a new label for Heyst: 'A. Heyst, manager in the East' (V, 29). The designation 'manager in the East' suggests a large concern with various managers, and again there is an obvious gap between the representation and the reality of Samburan.

Schomberg, too, is involved in this form of textual production – and to the same effect. The narrator refers to his 'famed table d'hôte dinners' and the accompanying advertising slogan 'catering "white man for white men"' (V, 97). But Schomberg's financial affairs do not match up to his rhetoric: indeed, they 'had never been so unpromising since he came out East directly after the Franco-Prussian War' (V, 96).

In 'Falk', Schomberg made a promotional speech to the narrator: 'I only charge a dollar for the tiffin, and one dollar and fifty cents for the dinner. Show me anything cheaper. Why am I doing it? ... I do it for the sake of a lot of young white fellows here that hadn't a place where they could get a decent meal and eat it decently in good company' (Ty, 174). The narrator had undermined this speech by observing that the 'convinced way he surveyed the empty chairs made me feel as if I had intruded upon a tiffin of ghostly Presences' (Ty, 174). Again, the effect is to emphasise the gap between representation and reality.

It is Schomberg who keeps Heyst's name current in island gossip. He is Conrad's anatomy of gossip: 'asking everybody about everything, and arranging the information into the most scandalous shape his imagination could invent' (V, 30).[7] Part I ends with Schomberg's narrative of Heyst, in which Heyst's actions are interpreted in line with this rule (V, 61). Heyst's rescue of Lena gives Schomberg an even stronger motive to make Heyst the object of his gossip. Part II describes how it became 'a recognised entertainment to go and hear his abuse of Heyst' (V, 95). If Schomberg has a 'genius' for catering, he also has granted to himself a licence for 'the inventing, elaborating and retailing of scandalous gossip' (V, 97). Schomberg's gossip has become commodified. For his audience, it is no longer primarily a communicative act but rather a performance. Like Jim, Schomberg speaks 'in front of' rather than 'to' his audience. Nevertheless, it is Schomberg's version of Heyst – 'a Heyst fattened by years of private and public rapines, the murderer of Morrison, the swindler of many shareholders' (V, 156) – which circulates and will direct Ricardo and Jones to Heyst's island in Part III.[8]

Victory effectively equates gossip with exile. At least, it is the condition of exile that underlies the construction of this particular European community through gossip. Schomberg's successive hotels are the emblem of this rootless society, and it is no accident that they are a centre for the production and distribution of gossip. However, Schomberg's production of gossip does not protect him from becoming himself the subject of gossip. With Lena's escape, for example, he briefly becomes a character in others' gossip. Davidson is told about Schomberg's fight with Zangiacomo when he arrives at Schomberg's hotel, and that story opens onto other story-telling:

> The captains of vessels, coming on shore later in the day, brought tales of a strange invasion, and wanted to know who were the two

offensive lunatics in a steam-launch, apparently after a man and a girl, and telling a story of which one could make neither head nor tail. (V, 49)[9]

These stories are subsequently re-circulated by Davidson to Heyst ('the story of the violent proceedings following on the discovery of his flight' [V, 56]). It is also gossip about Schomberg that has brought Ricardo and Jones to his hotel. When Schomberg discovers from Jones that he has been the subject of talk rather than the source of talk, he is 'astounded' (V, 101) – a response that prefigures Heyst's, when Lena reveals to him that she had heard talk about his partner: 'The idea of being talked about was always novel to Heyst's simplified conception of himself' (V, 206). Discovering that you are the subject of talk risks encountering others' objectification of you. Thus Heyst is forced to realise that he is not 'above the level of island gossip' (V, 206), as he had imagined. But that objectification of himself through gossip also intrudes into his relationship with Lena. It reinforces Lena's sense of insecurity; it also affects how Heyst regards himself. Lena repeats the story she has heard – how Morrison's partner 'first got all there was to get out of him' and then 'sent him out to die somewhere' (V, 208). She tells Heyst how she heard that 'everybody in these parts knew the story' (V, 208), and Heyst considers, for the first time, 'how the business looked from outside' (V, 208). In the privacy and isolation of Samburan the oral community catches up with Heyst: first, through Lena; subsequently, through Jones and Ricardo.

When they arrive on the island, Jones tells Heyst that he is 'a much talked-about man' (V, 377). For Ricardo, the 'Schombergian theory of Heyst' becomes 'a profound conviction' (V, 264). It is a conviction that has prompted their voyage to Samburan and will end in the death of all the Europeans on the island. The awareness of these 'ugly lies' (V, 381) also has an impact on Heyst's ability to defend himself against Ricardo and Jones. Thus he writes his own possible responses to their presence into the Schombergian script: 'after luring my friend and partner to his death from mere greed of money', he would now be said to have 'murdered these unoffending shipwrecked strangers from mere funk' (V, 361). However, despite the influence of Schomberg's gossip in the narrative, gossip is actually a sign of powerlessness rather than of power. As Spacks suggests, 'gossip gets its power by the illusion of mastery gained through taking imaginative possession of another's experience' (*Gossip*, 22). Schomberg's gossip thus becomes the measure of his powerlessness: if 'verbal acts' are designed to 'extend our control over a world that is not naturally disposed to serve our interests', then gossip both epitomises that desire for control and, by the same measure, declares the lack from which that desire springs.[10]

The privileged reader

In *Lord Jim*, for much of the novel the written text aspires to the condition of orality – with the recovery of the immediacy, community and presence of oral storytelling. The last part of the novel, however, complicates this picture. Although, as Chapter 6 demonstrated, the narrative is still presented as oral testimony from a variety of sources, that oral testimony has not been reproduced orally by Marlow, but has been sent as writing to the 'privileged man' (LJ, 337). The introduction of the 'privileged man' emphasises distance, isolation, and absence as components of the scene of reading – just as immediacy, community, and presence, were the characteristics of oral narration. One of the problems, however, is why this particular individual was chosen as the privileged reader.[11] As Marlow emphasises, this man is, on the surface, the least likely to be receptive to Jim's narrative. He is, after all, the member of the audience for Marlow's oral story-telling who believed that 'giving your life up to them … was like selling your soul to a brute'; he insisted, instead, that 'we must fight in the ranks' (LJ, 339).

When Marlow's narration ends, the temporary community constituted by the act of narration disperses, and each returns to the condition of being separate individuals ('Each of them seemed to carry away his own impression [LJ, 337]). Unlike the end of 'Karain', where the narrator's encounter with Jackson on the Strand reconvenes a version of the European group that had featured in the tale, the end of *Lord Jim* emphasises separateness. It does this by turning from oral narration to written texts, from the collectivity of an audience to the isolation of the scenes of writing and reading. The privileged man, whom Marlow contacts some two years later, is presented with a packet containing four texts: a letter to Jim from his father; 'a good many pages closely blackened and pinned together'; 'a loose square sheet of greyish paper'; and 'an explanatory letter from Marlow' (LJ, 338). The novel insists not just on the written sources of the final stage of the narrative but also on the materiality of that writing. At the same time, each of these texts asserts a sense of isolation, exclusion, and absence. The 'loose square sheet of greyish paper', for example, contains Jim's attempt to write after the catastrophe, but the attempt is unsuccessful – and it is not clear even who is addressed.[12] The letter from Jim's father is the last letter Jim received from home – received just before he joined the *Patna* (LJ, 341). This letter, full of 'mild gossip' about his family (LJ, 342), four pages of 'family news' offering him the possibility of 'converse' (LJ, 342), represents that family circle from which his actions on the *Patna* have excluded him. The final document, the many closely-written pages of text, is the narrative assembled by Marlow – a substitute for the unavailable narrative which Marlow invokes: 'the story in [Jim's] own words, in his careless yet feeling voice' (LJ, 343). Marlow's invocation of Jim's voice emphasises Jim's absence. Jim's voice is displaced by writing, and these documents are all that is left to gesture towards the life that has passed. However, while Jim's voice is unavailable, the written nature of Marlow's final narrative is de-emphasised: there is no marked stylistic difference between Marlow's oral narration that occupies most of the novel and the written text with which it ends. If Jim's voice is unavailable, Marlow's voice apparently 'cannot be silenced' (Y, 97). Marlow's written text resurrects Marlow's speaking voice and produces the illusion of Marlow's presence. However, the condition for that 'speaking' remains the irremediable absence of Jim and the temporary absence of Marlow.

Magic books

In *Victory*, Heyst is the 'privileged man' insofar as he is the privileged reader of his father's texts. In Part 3, as he contemplates his own uprootedness, he consults his father's book, *Storm and Dust*. The text is supplemented by the icon of his father's scene of writing, the portrait of his father 'with the quill pen in his hand' (V, 195), the primal textual scene. It is also supplemented by Heyst's memories of his father's voice. As he said earlier, 'They read his books, but I have heard his living word' (V, 196). Now, as he reads, 'it seemed to him that he was hearing his father's voice' (V, 219): 'He abandoned himself to the half-belief that something of his father dwelt yet on earth – a ghostly voice, audible to the ear of his own flesh and blood' (V, 219). Despite the emphasis on writing, the bond between Heyst and his father is founded on presence – or the illusion of presence – and presence as signified by speech. The absent father is present in the text through Heyst's memory; he is, above all, present in his shaping influence on Heyst's life. This is the marvellous irony of the scene in which Ricardo enters Heyst's house in search of 'clues', sees the room full of books and the portrait, but can't see the clue that stares him in the face. He has the key to Heyst in front of him, but does not realise it: 'what guess could one make out of a multitude of books' (V, 286). Heyst's father is the determining absence for the scheme of drifting that has been Heyst's life. Heyst invokes his father's voice as prior to his father's writing; but his father's writing, in the broader sense, has determined Heyst's own speaking. Where Heyst hears his father's voice authorising his texts, Heyst's own existence has been programmed by his father.

Heyst has taken refuge in the oral community of the archipelago from the metropolitan print community associated with his father. After leaving school at eighteen, he had spent three years living in London with his father, who was then 'writing his last book' (V, 91). Heyst's mourning for his father has a similar textual aspect: his tears are prompted by the reading of 'a few obituary notices generally insignificant and some grossly abusive' (V, 175). This textual reference is maintained in the relics of his father Heyst brings to Samburan: his father's books and the portrait of his father in the act of writing 'pen in hand above a white sheet of paper' (V, 189). For Heyst, the portrait of his father is 'a wonderful presence in its heavy frame on the flimsy wall' (V, 218). This icon of writing has, however, an ambiguous status.[13] The portrait is described as 'looking exiled and at home, out of place and masterful' (V, 219). The figure in the portrait is represented as 'looking at home' and 'masterful', but the portrait shares with Heyst the sense of being displaced, 'transplanted', with the consequent problematising of its 'mastery'. Furthermore, insofar as the portrait is a copy of the father, the father is also displaced. From Heyst's perspective, the portrait represents two versions of origin: the father and the father's writing. However, the 'wonderful presence' of the father is in fact the mark of his absence. In addition, as Barthes has argued, 'writing is the destruction of every voice, of every point of origin'.[14] With writing, 'the voice loses its origin, the author enters into his own death' (IMT, 141). Or, as Derrida puts it, against the self-presence of the father in speech, writing is the 'miserable son' orphaned and wandering the world.[15] The condition of being 'exiled and at home, out of place and masterful' thus corresponds to the ambiguities of presence and absence, apartness and power that the novel explores in relation to spoken and written language.

Intertextuality plays a part in that exploration. The Heyst who 'had plunged himself into an abyss of meditation over books' (V, 180) in

Samburan is also a re-enactment of Prospero. His existence on Samburan is a version of Shakespeare's *The Tempest* – with Lena as Miranda; Wang as Ariel; Mr Jones as Duke Ferdinand; Pedro as Caliban.[16] As Jerry Brotton has observed, the power of books and the power of possession of books is an important feature of *The Tempest*.[17] Prospero's 'immersion in "the liberal arts" (I.ii.73)' allows him 'unprecedented access to the arcane mysteries of the elements most feared and respected by early modern cosmographers and travellers – the sea and the stars' (TT, 29). Brotton notes how Prospero's involvement in books is constantly emphasised. He was banished from Milan for neglecting 'worldly ends' (I.ii.89) by treating his library as 'dukedom enough' (I.ii, 109–10). In the conspiracy to overthrow Prospero, Caliban admonishes Stephano and Trinculo: 'Remember/ First to possess his books' (III.ii.89–90) (TT, 29). In *Almayer's Folly*, Almayer's office was imaged as a 'temple' and his ledgers were perceived as 'magic books'. *Victory*, too, is concerned with books, but the power of books is much more problematic. In Part III, Heyst comes to appreciate the power of words, but this appreciation comes as a result of the calumnies of Schomberg. He then reads one of his father's books, but his father's written words are experienced by him through the evocation of his father's voice. The text is used by him to produce the illusion of presence, but that illusion is based on the assumed priority of speech to writing. However, speech and presence also cause him problems. Indeed, where he converts text into the illusion of presence, when confronted with Otherness he converts presence into text. Thus, when he turns to Lena, she becomes reduced to a script, but, unlike his father's text, Lena is 'a script in an unknown language' or 'like any writing to the illiterate' (V, 222).[18] The magic does not work: this text does not give a comforting illusion of presence, but insists instead on its opacity – its Otherness. Heyst's scheme of drifting has been a way of avoiding contact with Otherness. It has also been a way of avoiding the strangeness of exile. In Kristeva's words, 'as he chooses a program he allows himself a respite or a residence' (SO, 6). Lena's presence on the island forces Heyst to engage in an interrogation of Otherness. He is 'intensely aware of her personality' (V, 192), but, if he tries to go beyond primary sense data, he runs into difficulties. Thus, 'in the intimacy of their life her grey, unabashed gaze forced upon him the sensation of something inexplicable reposing within her' (V, 192). If he tries to explore this Otherness, presence immediately turns into its opposite: 'something inexplicable' under the pressure of his interrogation becomes 'simply an abysmal emptiness' (V, 192).

Metropolitan problems

Paul Brown has pointed out that *The Tempest* 'bears traces of the contemporary British investment in colonial expansion'.[19] More recently, Peter Hulme has written on the dual location of *The Tempest*: how it fuses the Mediterranean and the West Indies.[20] Conrad transplants that hybrid to a third location: the East Indies. Here the South American, Pedro, is a Caliban out of his element, and none of the characters (with the possible exception of the almost invisible Alfuros) are native to the island.[21] Hulme notes how class-conflict was an aspect of the Bermuda narrative and how Shakespeare re-figures that class-conflict in the Stephano/Trinculo sub-plot, the conspiracy of the lower orders against the nobles. In *Victory*, this re-surfaces as a component of the sexual relationship between Ricardo and Lena: their similar class background is emphasised, and Ricardo indeed sees their relationship as a conspiracy against the two 'gentlemen'. This concern for the metropolitan experience is signalled by Ricardo's nostalgia for the West India Docks (V, 127) and the life of 'walking the pavement and cracking jokes and standing drinks to chums' (V, 129).[22] It is signalled also by Lena's memories of 'poor lodging-houses' (V, 78) in North London (V, 191). It is confirmed by the account of Heyst's years in London with his father and by Jones's world of gentlemen's clubs and 1890s sexual scandal. In the colonial setting of *Victory*, it is not the colonial encounter that is foregrounded but rather metropolitan problems.[23]

However, if metropolitan problems are foregrounded, the colonial encounter is not ignored. The introduction of the 'privileged man' at the end of *Lord Jim* raised questions about English views of colonised peoples that were not resolved. *Victory* addresses some of those questions. Although the colonial encounter is kept in the background – and the cross-cultural encounter that is foregrounded in *Victory* is between different English cultures rather than European and non-European cultures – this is another case where the background gradually comes to the fore. English attitudes towards colonised peoples are thematised from early on along with the intrusion of metropolitan concerns into Heyst's Samburan retreat. From the start, there is Heyst's general tendency to disregard Wang: Heyst is represented (and represents himself) as living alone on Samburan. Lena shares this attitude: 'There is no one here to think any thing of us good or bad' (V, 188). Wang is like the invisible servants in Austen novels, or like the slave-girl, Taminah, in *Almayer's Folly*.[24] In Chapter 8 of *Almayer's Folly*, Reshid tries to make use of Taminah, 'an apparition of daily recurrence and of no importance whatever' (AF, 110), to spy on Almayer's household. Ironically, the powerless and disregarded Taminah is already in possession of the important information that Reshid seeks. In *Victory*, however, this is not just an issue of class. Chapter 20 of *Lord Jim* provides an instructive comparison. Here Marlow is guided to Stein's study by a Javanese servant who, after throwing open the study door, 'vanished in a mysterious way as though he had been a ghost only momentrarily embodied for that particular service' (LJ, 204). This figure of the ghostly, disembodied servant that appears briefly as an embellishment in *Lord Jim* is built into *Victory* as one of its constituent parts. Conrad's translation of *The Tempest* to the archipelago casts Wang in the role of Ariel, and, if Conrad does not make much space for their voices, he at least makes visible the invisibility of servants and subject peoples.[25] When Schomberg and Ricardo are considering obstacles in the way of a visit to Samburan, both agree that 'native craft' can be ignored:

> Both these white men looked on native life as a mere play of shadows. A play of shadows the dominant race could walk through unaffected and disregarded in the pursuit of its incomprehensible aims and needs. (V, 167)

Later, discussing Wang, Ricardo and Jones agree that he can safely be disregarded, 'a Chink was neither here nor there' (V, 268). In addition to the manifestation of these racist attitudes, the idea of 'race' itself is explicitly articulated in the narrative. There is, for example, the casual working-class racism of Lena: she and Heyst, discussing Wang, seem to agree that 'One Chinaman looks very much like another' (V, 182). Later still, when Lena realises that Heyst had planned to send her to the Alfuros' village for safety, she protests: 'That was a strange notion of yours, to send me away. ... To these savages, too! ... You can do what you like with me – but not that, not that!' (V, 349). For Mr Jones, racism is not casual but a conscious ideology. He asks Heyst 'Do you believe in racial superiority, Mr Heyst?' and, without waiting for a reply, adds ' I do, firmly' (V, 382).

Wang, for obvious reasons, becomes the focus of English attitudes towards non-Europeans. Wang, first of all, represents the Chinese community of the archipelago, making visible this group which is glimpsed at the edges of Conrad's Malay world. They are most prominent in the form of the Chinese coolies on board the *Nan-Shan* in 'Typhoon'. They are pervasive in the Macassar of *An Outcast* as servants in the Sunda Hotel; billiard markers; tellers in Hudig's office; shipowners; serangs and pirates. They are also present as the shopkeepers in Patusan; as Davidson's shipowners in *Victory*; as the silent servants in Schomberg's hotels in *Lord Jim* and *Victory*. Wang's own career also produces a catalogue of Chinese roles in the archipelago through his transition from miner to cultivator, from coolie labour to entrepreneur, as he cultivates his patch of ground and markets his produce to Heyst. Where Ariel's magic powers perhaps explain Wang's mysterious ability to appear and disappear, Ariel's invisibility becomes the 'invisibility' of servants and the colonised. Wang as a version of Ariel foregrounds the notion of invisible agency, of work which is done 'magically' – in other words, the mystification and occlusion of labour by class and imperial ideologies. At the same time, through the narrative, Wang also asserts his agency. Wang, in a noticeable reversal of colonial positions, 'annexes' both Heyst's keys and his gun (V, 180, 314). Wang similarly annexes the ground next to his hut and turns it over to cultivation (V, 181). More significantly, Wang is disregarded by Jones and Ricardo, but is instrumental in their defeat: he shoots Pedro and shoves off their boat. Finally, when all the Europeans are dead, it is Wang and his Alfuro wife who remain in possession of the Diamond Bay settlement.

In the final act of *The Tempest*, Prospero shows Alonzo his 'cell' and 'discovers' Ferdinand and Miranda playing at chess. In the equivalent moment in *Victory*, Mr Jones makes Heyst return to his bungalow and discovers Ricardo and Lena engaged in a much less innocent game: 'Behold the simple Acis kissing the sandals of the nymph' (V, 393). In the following chapter, Ricardo's rhetoric ('What you want is a man, a master that will let you put the heel of your shoe on his neck' [397]) and his actions ('She advanced her foot forward a little from under the hem of her skirt; and he threw himself on it greedily' [V, 400]) continue this notion of foot fetishism. Fetishism – like 'racial superiority' – is thematised in the novel.[26] Early on, Morrison's 'famous notebook' is described as 'the fetish of his hopes' (V, 18). Later on, when Ricardo is reflecting on Jones's fear of women, the narrator suggests that 'there is no real religion without a little fetichism' (V, 161). If the logic of fetishism involves the over-valuation of objects, then fetishism recurs throughout the novel. Heyst has made a fetish of his father's books and portrait. Lena makes a fetish out of Ricardo's knife. Indeed, as this last example suggests, various objects are fetishised by the narrative: Heyst's keys; Heyst's revolver; Ricardo's knife. The revolver that Wang takes from Heyst leaves him 'a man disarmed'. In the same way, Lena's acquisition of Ricardo's knife similarly disarms him, even while her purpose is to empower Heyst.[27] The narrative focus on the capturing of Ricardo's knife might itself be seen as a kind of narrative fetishising of it. These instances call out for a psychoanalytic decoding. More important, however, fetishism can also be related to the invisibility (or concealment) of labour. As McClintock notes, Marx's account of commodity fetishism hinges on the over-valuation of commodity exchange and the undervaluation of labour. The reverse side of fetishism, in other words, is the disregarded labour of the colonial subject, the making invisible of the colonised people. *Victory* shows how colonised peoples can be made invisible, and, in foregrounding that 'making invisible', points towards the realm that it cannot represent.

Exchange

If the narrative method of *Victory* engages with the problem of representation by foregrounding the circulation of discourses among the European community of the archipelago, the narrative itself, like that of Conrad's earliest Malay fiction, is firmly grounded in the material conditions of the archipelago: commodities, trade, technological developments. Thus Willems, in *An Outcast*, recalls a successful period of trade as Hudig's agent, when he was involved in 'ponies' from Lombok; opium; 'the illegal traffic in gunpowder'; 'the great affair of smuggled firearms' (OI, 8). Lingard, too, with his monopoly of trade in Sambir has access to an 'inexhaustible' supply of 'guttah and rattans' (OI, 43), and, when Willems arrives in Sambir, he watches 'the up-country canoes discharging guttah or rattans, and loading rice or European goods' (OI, 52) on the wharf of Lingard and Company. In *Victory*, however, as part of the novel's sense of belatedness, 'exchange' also seems to have broken down. In Part I, Chapter 2, the narrator describes Morrison's 'trade':

> He was the dearly beloved friend of a quantity of God-forsaken villages up dark creeks and obscure bays, where he traded for 'produce'. He would often sail through awfully dangerous channels up to some miserable settlement, only to find a very hungry population clamorous for rice, and without so much 'produce' between them as would have filled Morrison's suitcase. (V, 10)

Morrison is equally unlucky in his dealings with the local colonial powers. When Heyst rescues him, he has fallen foul of 'the Portuguese authorities' in Dilli, who, 'on some pretence of irregularity in his papers, had inflicted a fine upon him and had arrested his brig' (V, 12). Heyst's attempt at imperial capitalism, the Tropical Belt Coal Company, is no more successful, producing little more than a lot of 'island gossip' and the prospectus with its proleptic map of the triumph of commodities. Schomberg seems little more successful as a hotel-keeper. He has been a hotel-keeper 'first in Bangkok, then somewhere else, and ultimately in Sourabaya' (V, 20). Whatever his reasons for moving, his hotel in Sourabaya (to judge by his actions in the novel) is hardly a major success: through Zangiacomo, he is effectively involved in prostitution; while through Jones and Ricardo, he becomes involved in gambling. Wang alone sets up a successful (though small-scale) commercial venture – selling vegetables to Heyst. The oral community of island traders is just waiting to be put out of business by steam.

Lena's attempt to exploit her transplantation to a new environment is equally unsuccessful. In Part III, Chapter 9, she appears in 'a hand-woven cotton sarong' (V, 252). She is described as 'exotic yet familiar' with her 'white woman's face and shoulders above the Malay sarong' (V, 253). Lena's change of dress registers her new life in Samburan. It suggests her attempt to find a new identity for herself outside of European models.[28] As she tells Heyst, she is 'not what they call a good girl' (V, 198). But here, on Samburan, 'There's no-one ... to think anything of us, good or bad' (V, 188). Heyst's rescue of Lena from Schomberg can thus be seen also as an escape from European terms of reference. The arrival of Jones and Ricardo, however, checks that exploration of other possibilities. Henricksen observes:

> Narrative knowledge ... is a powerful constituent in the lives of individuals, where it creates a sense of selfhood and identity while at the same time creating subject positions that people can and often must occupy in the narrative of a community's values and actions. (NV, 13)

Ricardo, in particular, brings back to Lena the working-class culture of her London childhood. To deal with Ricardo, Lena draws on the 'narrative knowledge' of that childhood – specifically, Sunday School narratives of guilt and redemption and cultural constructions of self-sacrificing womanhood. She writes a script for herself rooted in the metropolitan culture of her childhood, and the sarong is finally exchanged for a black dress (V, 371) that she had brought with her from her former life.

In *The Rescue*, Conrad returns to the exploration of metropolitan conflicts in the colonial context. The cross-cultural encounter is again both that of Europeans and non-Europeans and also that of different kinds of European. Again, he uses performance and theatricality as a focus. However, where the main theatrical elements in *Victory* are the dramatic handling of dialogue and the use of a Shakespearean intertext, in *The Rescue* the scenic method is supplemented by a pro-liferation of theatrical imagery and a closer attention to cultural cross-dressing.

8
Dialogue and Cross-Dressing in *The Rescue*

History and desire

GoGwilt has suggested that, despite his career-long engagement with the Malay Archipelago, 'the full importance of that historical setting' seemed increasingly to elude Conrad (IW, 69). Thus, for example, *Almayer's Folly* presents a Sambir dependent 'on a whole set of contingent economic and political interests' (IW, 84); it gives a sense of 'Malay resistance to European colonialism' (IW, 84) through the figures of Babalatchi and Mrs Almayer; and it 'articulates the historical process of decolonisation' through the problem of Nina's split identification. In *Lord Jim*, by contrast, Marlow's rhetorical manoeuvres refuse the possibilities he glimpses in the cross-cultural encounter: 'Such beings', he affirms of Dain Maroola, 'open to the Western eye ... the hidden possibilities of races and lands over which hangs the mystery of unrecorded ages' (LJ, 262), but the language of revelation actually marks the limits of Marlow's vision. As GoGwilt observes: 'What such possibilities *are* ... interests Marlow even less than the light this discovery casts on Jim' (IW, 101). They remain 'hidden possibilities'. GoGwilt might also have pointed to Marlow's response to his first conversation with Jewel. Her account of her mother's death, he notes, 'had the power to drive me out of my conception of existence', but this effect lasts only a moment ('I went back into my shell directly' [LJ, 313]). A safely-defended Marlow can then sum up the encounter in a way that shows how little he has allowed his 'conception of existence' to be challenged: 'To discover that she had a voice at all was enough to strike awe into the heart' (LJ, 315). As Chapter 6 has tried to show, however, *Lord Jim* attempts to mark and escape from the limits of Marlow's narration by setting it among competing narratives and by indicating various narratives that Marlow marginalises or suppresses.

In *The Rescue*, GoGwilt sees Conrad as trying at last 'to give specific political representation' (IW, 77) to the Bugis who have appeared throughout his major Malay fictions. The 'precarious balance of conflicting political interests that hold the Europeans hostage' (IW, 77) registers 'the inter-island politics' of the 'ethnically-diverse populations' (IW, 78) of the archipelago. However, in this attempt, Conrad's Malays 'became more stereotyped' and 'the political perspective' was lost: 'The Wajo political romance is forgotten, in a carefully staged forgetting' (IW, 77). GoGwilt is particularly critical of what he sees as the misogynistic attempt to blame Mrs Travers 'for the collapse of the Wajo project' (IW, 80). The novel uses her ignorance 'to exaggerate the stereotyped Orientalism with which [it] increasingly presents its tale' (IW, 80). GoGwilt claims that the 'effect of *The Rescue*'s crossing of gender, nation and race' produces 'a stereotyped doubling of Edith Travers and Immada in a contrast that seems designed to authenticate an imaginary native identity by displaying an ignorant European reading' (IW, 80–1). Above all, he claims, the novel enforces 'an absolute division between knowledge and ignorance of Malays, on the model of Edith Travers's ignorance of the Malay language' (IW, 81).

GoGwilt, in other words, registers the novel's strategy of ignorance, but he sees it merely as part of a failure to represent Malay culture and politics.[1] This chapter will argue that Conrad's strategy of ignorance is an ethical response to the problem of representing another culture. GoGwilt plays down the fact that it is not just Mrs Travers, but d'Alcacer, Travers, and the whole range of European characters who manifest their ignorance to varying degrees. As previous chapters have shown, after 'The Lagoon' and 'Karain', Conrad moved away from attempts to represent Malay realities to an engagement instead with the problematics of representing another culture. From *Lord Jim* onwards he simultaneously uses and problematises particular European modes of representation. In *The Rescue* this becomes a strategy of representation through situated misrepresentation.

The Rescue, like *Lord Jim*, engages with the issue of European commitment to Malays. Lingard, like Jim, involves himself in local politics – more specifically, Lingard aims to influence the Wajo succession as part of a dream of re-forming the Wajo confederacy: 'The four states welded together, by his hand; the land awakened, living, breathing; growing strong enough not to be meddled with .... And if he once went in he would not come out – never'.[2] *The Rescue*, however, makes it clear (as *Lord Jim* does not) that this political involvement is a challenge to Dutch colonial interests.[3] At the same time, the nature of Lingard's political ambitions is more ambiguous. Is this renegade behaviour (as in Clifford's *A Freelance of Today*), or one-man imperialism on the model of Brooke? In a letter to Blackwood (6 September 1897), Conrad refers to 'an Englishman called Wyndham' who had been 'living for many years with the Sultan of Sulu' and was 'the general purveyor of arms and gunpowder' and to William Lingard's 'great if occult influence with the Rajah of Bali' (CL1, 383) as sources for the novel; both cases suggesting the renegade. In this context, Lingard's 'planned war' might be read, as Krenn suggests, as 'a conscious revolt against the consolidation of European powers in the East' (LT, 105). However, Lingard's commitment to Wajo politics actually springs from his bond with Hassim.

With the arrival of the yacht people, that bond is betrayed. Hassim's presence in key scenes is then used to mark the successive stages of that betrayal. In Part IV, Chapter 3, Hassim's 'loyalty was shaken', and he began to doubt Lingard's constancy (Re, 221–2). In the following chapter, when Lingard decides to leave his brig, Hassim fully understands the significance of the decision:

> He smiled at his white friend. There was something subtle in the smile and afterwards an added firmness in the repose of the lips.
> (Re, 234)

Hassim is, effectively, silenced by the combination of Lingard's choice and his own cultural practices. He understands that he is being betrayed, but also, as Krenn notes, he responds with a mixture of resignation and generosity. In this scene, Lingard's decision-making is foregrounded, but the narrative provides subtle hints as to Hassim's responses, and the indirectness of this method provides an escape from the mastering discourse of ethnographic representation. As in *Lord Jim*, the foreground is occupied by the European's dilemma – in this case, the process by which Lingard is drawn to betray his commitment to Hassim. In the background, Hassim and Immada repeat the narrative of Doramin and Jewel – the political and personal betrayal of Malays by Europeans. From this point on, the narrative focuses on Lingard's new commitment to Mrs Travers – his chivalric articulation of desire – while, in the background, the complex structure of the conjuncture of the heterogenous peoples brought together by Lingard and the chance arrival of the yacht people drives on towards its catastrophic conclusion.

The narrative focus of *The Rescue* thus becomes Lingard and Lingard's desire. As Harpham has argued, the narrative of the realisation of that desire moves from Lingard's identification with his ship to his commitment to Hassim and Immada, and then finally to his passion for Edith Travers.[4] Lingard is wrenched from the 'narcissistic security' of his involvement with the brig, and his desire sends him 'out in the wide world, the world of Wajo and women' (OU, 107). In this narrative movement, the Malays and Wajo politics move into the centre of his attention, but are then displaced by Mrs Travers. Lingard's polymorphously sexualised involvement with his ship leads to the male-male bond with Hassim, but both give way before the much more dangerous passion for Mrs Travers. This progressive reconfiguration of Lingard's desire leads to the marginalisation of Immada, in particular. To begin with, she is introduced as part of a dyad with Hassim, in which she acts as his feminised double. However, Lingard's bond is primarily with Hassim and only secondarily with Immada. Hassim is shown independently of Immada, but Immada has no role independent of Hassim. Heterosexual desire appears only through Lingard's encounter with Mrs Travers. Although this is a much younger Lingard than in *Almayer's Folly* and *An Outcast of the Islands*, his response to Immada is to treat her as a daughter – as he did Mrs Almayer. It is through the encounter with Mrs Travers that Lingard confronts woman as Other, and, as in 'Karain', this encounter is more problematic than the encounter with the non-European Other with which the novel begins.[5]

Cross-cultural negotiations

The first part of *The Rescue* introduces Lingard and creates a sense of various mysteries surrounding him partly through the ignorance of his new mate, Shaw, and partly through the ignorance of Carter, the second officer of the yacht, stranded off the Borneo coast. The novel thus foregrounds different kinds of ignorance from the start. The second part goes some way to dispelling these mysteries. It describes, in particular, the development of Lingard's relationship with the Bugis prince and princess, Hassim and Immada, and his involvement, through that relationship, in Wajo politics. Part II provides a precise and economical account of Wajo politics in the mid-century. It also presents a careful depiction of the complexities and subtleties of cross-cultural encounter through its attention to Lingard and Hassim and their reactions to each other.

The account of Lingard's experiences emphasises the 'responsive sensitiveness' (Re, 74) which generally allows him to negotiate cross-cultural situations, but it also presents occasions where he misreads the situation as well. Lingard's responsiveness to the 'appeal' of events is often a positive element in the cross-cultural encounter. For example, when he arranges for one of the ship's guns to be fired for the sea-burial of the member of the crew killed protecting him in New Guinea, this demonstration of respect wins approval from Hassim and his followers.[6] Similarly, his gift of three barrels of gunpowder to Hassim – to repay the three bullets fired by Hassim in his rescue of Lingard – is a much-appreciated act of generosity.[7] Lingard's imaginative responsiveness and his generosity can, however, also lead him astray. Thus his ministering personally to Hassim's loyal follower, Jaffir, after Jaffir has swum out to the *Lightning*, temporarily 'lowered' (Re, 84) him in Jaffir's eyes. This small example instances the treacherous channels of cross-cultural encounter – as difficult to navigate as the approach to 'The Shore of Refuge'.

Lingard's major errors recorded in Part II are, however, first of all, his reckless behaviour in New Guinea, which leads to the beginnings of his friendship with Hassim, and, secondly, his misreading of the impassivity of Hassim and his followers, after Lingard's rescue of them from Wajo. In the first case, Lingard's arrival on shore in New Guinea is focalised through Hassim, and Hassim's view of Lingard provides a measure of Lingard's carelessness.[8] Where Hassim is cautious about going ashore – and finally goes ashore 'well escorted and armed' (Re, 69), Lingard goes to meet the 'coast-savages' (Re, 69) without weapons and with only four Malays from the brig's crew as escort. The incident which follows from the Papuan's explorative spear-jab would have been disastrous, if it hadn't been for Hassim's intervention. Lingard's subsequent relationship with Hassim and his Bugis followers is a complex mixture of sensitivity and misreadings. Lingard begins his relationship with Hassim through a misconception. The narrative notes how, on board the *Lightning* after this rescue, Lingard treats Hassim and his followers with 'hearty friendship', whereas their response to him is merely 'discreet courtesy' (Re, 74). This disjunction is comparable to that between Heyst and Lena, where Heyst responds to Lena with 'simple courtesy' (V, 79), but Lena, from her working-class background and hard life with the Zangiacomo orchestra, reads his courtesy as more than courtesy – as friendship, concern, special regard. Lingard's closer involvement with Hassim's political cause also comes about through a misreading, when he responds to the impassivity of the Bugis survivors whom he takes away from Wajo in the *Lightning*.

Through his egotism, he reads their impassivity as trust, as an appeal to him to involve himself in their plight.

At the same time, the narrative also shows how the political situation in Wajo also leads to attempts by Hassim to read Lingard. The dialogue between Hassim and Lingard is modelled on that of Brooke's encounter with the Wajo chiefs in the 1830s.[9] In both cases, there is an attempt by the Wajo chief to understand this phenomenon of the private Englishman with his ship. In a sense, it can be seen as an encounter between the *kerajaan* of the archipelago and the economic individualism of Victorian capitalism. Hassim's questions very clearly try to fit Lingard into Wajo categories – or, more generally, the categories prevalent in the Malay culture of the archipelago. Thus he inquires about Lingard's relation to the dead Lascar: 'was this man your debtor – a slave?' (Re, 73). From Lingard's response, he decides that Lingard's own status is comparable to that of a Malay chief (Re, 73). Similarly, he inquires (for obvious reasons) about the relative strengths of Holland and England, and, on Lingard's assurances of England's superior strength, asks about the payment of tribute (Re, 75). Again, Hassim draws on the political practices of the archipelago to attempt to understand the European situation. Lingard's assertion that paying tribute is 'not the custom of white men' (Re, 75) provokes Hassim's sardonic response: 'They are stronger than we are and they want tribute from us' (Re, 75–6). Hassim thus undermines Lingard's confident assertion by foregrounding colonial relations and the very different practices current between colonising power and colonised in the archipelago from those in operation between colonising powers at home in Europe.[10] Hassim emphasises asymmetries of power and the different codes Europeans follow in European and colonial political situations.[11]

Travers and d'Alcacer are similarly the object of local analysis. To Hassim they are 'two powerful Rajahs – probably relatives of the Ruler of the land of the English whom he knew to be a woman' (Re, 242). Daman and the Ilanun come closer to the truth, drawing on their different experience of Europeans in the archipelago: 'They were such men as are sent by rulers to examine the aspects of far-off countries and talk of peace and make treaties. Such is the beginning of great sorrows' (Re, 223). Travers and d'Alcacer are, indeed, very carefully placed by the narrative as members of the ruling class: Travers as an ex-MP; d'Alcacer as the former Spanish cultural attaché to London and nephew of the Governor-General of Manila. The cross-cultural encounters foregrounded in the novel thus begin with Lingard's encounter with the Bugis viewed from both sides. But this is followed (and complicated) by the second encounter (for both groups) with the metropolitan culture of the yacht people. Conrad explores this new situation through the staging of dialogue – in this case, the objective presentation of encounters in which different languages are spoken by different participants.[12]

The staging of languages

Conrad had used this device in his earliest Malay fictions. In Part IV Chapter 4 of *An Outcast of the Islands*, for example, when Lingard meets up with Willems for the first time since Willems betrayed his secret, there is a heated exchange between Lingard and Willems in Aissa's presence, but it is only some way into the dialogue that Conrad reveals that Aissa is linguistically excluded:

> At the sound of their rapidly exchanged words, Aissa had got up from the ground where she had been sitting ... and approached the two men. She stood on one side and looked on eagerly ... with the quick and distracted eyes of a person trying for her life to penetrate the meaning of sentences uttered in a foreign tongue: the meaning portentous and fateful that lurks in the sounds of mysterious words ... (OI, 264)

Aissa's exclusion from the dialogue adds an additional element of suspense to these exchanges in which Lingard will reveal what he has decided to do with Willems, and what Aissa's fate will be. Aissa's attempt to 'penetrate the meaning' of these incomprehensible sounds also repeats Lingard's own attempt to make sense of Willems's actions, to square Willems's betrayal of him with his sense of himself and his sense of the world. This had been the central concern of Part III: Lingard is convinced that 'In life – as in seamanship – there were only two ways of doing a thing: the right way and the wrong way' (OI, 199), but Willems's betrayal challenges his confidence in the moral simplicity of existence.

In Chapter 5, as the dialogue continues, Willems gives an account of Aissa and his relations with Aissa, which Aissa hears but cannot understand. The deliberate exclusion of Aissa allows Willems to present his version of events, while his use of English as the linguistic medium enacts and underlines his assertion of his 'whiteness'. Even in his choice of language he attempts to assert his bond with Lingard and his distance from Aissa (and from the Willems who was involved with Aissa). At the end of the chapter, when Willems and Aissa have been left alone with each other, Willems still refuses to drop his linguistic guard:

> 'It is all your doing. You ...'
> She did not understand him – not a word. He spoke in the language of his people. ... And he was angry. Alas! he was always angry now, and always speaking words that she could not understand. ... She did not move. What need to understand the words when they are spoken in such a voice? In that voice which did not seem to be his voice – his voice when he spoke by the brook, when he was never angry and always smiling! (OI, 285–6)

This linking of different languages with different identities is repeated in the final section of the novel, when Willems's wife arrives at the island. Joanna's arrival offers him an escape from the imprisonment with Aissa that was Lingard's punishment for him, while her forgiveness also offers the prospect of a return to the identity he lost at the start of the novel. This return to a lost identity is signalled by his use of Dutch with Joanna, while the struggle between the two women for Willems (and between Willems's different identities) is enacted through his alternate conversations with Joanna and with Aissa, in Dutch and Malay respectively, from which one or other of the women is always linguistically excluded.

In these attempts to interpret and 'make sense', the characters of the novel clearly replicate the action of the reader, while, as John Stape has suggested, the narrative's switching between languages and the self-consciousness about language operate as alienation-devices and serve to break down 'the illusions of complicity and common cultural identity' between writer and reader.[13] In particular, the emphasis on the characters' use of, and switches between, different languages economically points to the presence in the novel of what Stape terms 'self-coherent worlds radically different from but equally valid to the reader's own'.[14] The linguistic system is a synecdoche for the cultural system. The reader is thus made aware both of the constructedness of culture and of cultures as signifying systems.

Cultural difference

From the start, *The Rescue* foregrounds cultural difference and different cultural systems. The first dialogue between Lingard and Shaw in the opening chapters of the novel brings in Lingard's story of the 'French skipper in Ampanam' who 'had an affair with a Bali girl' (Re, 250).[15] As Florence Clemens pointed out long ago, Conrad found the story in Wallace's *Malay Archipelago*, but he subjects it to a more complex cultural analysis than is found in Wallace.[16] Wallace uses the story to illustrate (with some inappropriateness) a generalisation about the men of Lombock as 'very jealous and strict with their wives'.[17] When Lingard finishes the story, the following exchange occurs:

'Would those savages kill a woman for that?' asked Shaw, incredulously.
'Aye! They are pretty moral there. ...' (Re, 21)

Lingard's response challenges Shaw's term 'savages' by asserting the fact of a different culture with a different moral code. The word 'savages' thus comes to be revealing of the speaker rather than of the referent, just as, later, Mr Travers's repeated use of the term 'natives' becomes a sign of his ideological preconceptions. In addition, Lingard's version of this story ends with the European making a fetish out of the flower, which, after the girl's death, he 'wore under his shirt, hung round his neck in a small box' (Re, 21). As in 'Karain' (which was written in the same period as the early part of *The Rescue*), Conrad displays a Frazerian awareness of cross-cultural analogues: he draws attention to 'the amulets of white men', white men's 'charms and talismans' (TU, 48), as part of a relativistic presentation of different cultures.[18]

The story of the French skipper and the 'Bali girl' is also contextualised by the prior representation of Shaw, which emphasises the cultural differences between the two Europeans. Where Lingard is an adventurer, with a 'responsive sensitiveness to the shadowy appeals made by life and death' (Re, 74) and a ready sympathy for the Malays, Shaw is attached to the 'little house with a tiny front garden, lost in a maze of riverside streets in the east end of London', where his wife and child live, and feels himself 'immeasurably superior to the Malay seamen whom he had to handle' (Re, 12). Shaw denies his own failings and inadequacies through an assertion of racial superiority and a mechanism of projection and blame, and he uses the power-structure of the ship to deploy these strategies. For example, after he catches himself nodding off for a moment, he accuses the Malay helmsman of sleeping and allowing the ship to get 'stern way on her' (Re, 7). He then asserts his power by making the helmsman undertake unnecessary manoeuvres to remedy this non-existent error. The narrative notes that 'The white man looked at the impassive Malay with disgust' (Re, 7), but it also explores that impassivity to reveal the Malay's 'disdainful obedience' (Re, 8).

Another incident in this opening chapter explores that impassivity further. After Shaw has scanned the horizon with the telescope and reported to Lingard 'nothing in sight' (Re, 15), the Malay seamen discuss the boat between the islands, which Shaw has failed to see. The passage begins with the impassivity of the *serang*: 'very straight and stiff by the side of the compass stand' with his face 'as inexpressive as the door of a safe' (Re, 15). However, when the seacannie insists that he saw a boat and asks 'Have you seen her too?', the serang snaps back 'Am I a fat white man?' and reminds the other 'The order is to keep silence and mind the rudder' (Re, 16). Impassivity is not allowed to be read as absence of subjectivity: the Malay seamen are shown to have a critical attitude towards the European officer; and their impassivity is disclosed, not as an essential characteristic, but as a mode of behaviour adopted within an appreciation of the power structure of their relations with the Europeans. Subsequently, when Lingard questions the *serang* about his failure to report the sighting, he answers:

> 'He said "Nothing there," while I could see. How could I know what was in his mind or yours, Tuan?' (Re, 27–8)

It is instructive to make comparison with the Malay helmsman on the *Patna*, who stayed at the helm because 'there had been no order':

> [He] declared it never came into his mind then that the white men were about to leave the ship through fear of death. He did not believe it now. There might have been secret reasons. He wagged his old chin knowingly. (LJ, 98)

In both cases European behaviour and thinking is presented as the object of Malay knowledge, and there is a perception of the incomprehensibility, the otherness, of the European to the Malay. However, where the *Patna* helmsman has made this otherness an object of respect and admiration, the crew of the *Lightning* have a more critical and politic attitude. The impassivity of the Malay also lies behind Lingard's commitment to the political cause of Hassim and Immada. The possibility of cross-cultural misunderstanding is implicit in the description of Lingard's first forming a bond with Hassim:

> The talk conducted with hearty friendship on Lingard's part, and on the part of the Malays with the well-bred air of discreet courtesy, which is natural to the better class of that people. (Re, 74–5)

In the contrast between Lingard's 'hearty friendship' and the 'discreet courtesy' of the Malays, it is interesting (given the novels concern with the 'primitive' and the 'sophisticated') that the more 'sophisticated' behaviour is manifested by the Malays. After Lingard rescues Hassim and his party from Wajo, the process by which Lingard persuades himself that this is 'a life calling to him distinctly for interference' is carefully delineated:

> But what appealed to him most was the silent, the complete, unquestioning, and apparently uncurious, trust of these people. They came away from death straight into his arms as it were, and remained in them passive as though there had been no such thing as doubt or hope or desire. This amazing unconcern seemed to put him under a heavy load of obligation. (Re, 88)

In Lingard's reasoning, it is precisely because they 'did not ask' that he feels this burden of obligation. The perceived passivity and impassivity of the Malays creates a blank onto which Lingard projects his desire to interfere and control.

Dialogue and the stage

Part III features the exploration of cultural difference through the staging of different languages. It begins with the confrontation between Travers and Lingard. This confrontation, at first glance, is merely the clash of two men who are used to having their importance recognised in their own worlds, but the narrative goes beyond this to appraise the two separate worlds subtended by these two men, that confront each other in this encounter, and two versions of colonial discourse. Travers produces a familiar political rhetoric: he talks of 'progress' and 'the duty to civilise' and asserts that 'if the inferior race must perish, it is a gain, a step toward the perfecting of society' (Re, 147–8). Lingard represents a romantic paternalism; although, at the same time, as Benita Parry points out, he seeks to dominate the area through technological superiority, embodied in the *Lightning*. The dialogue juxtaposes the 'benign adventurer' Lingard to the 'sordid reality of his colonial successor', Travers.[19] More importantly, for Lingard, the yacht-people have entered his world at the very moment when 'he had wandered beyond that circle which race, memories, early associations, all the essential conditions of one's origin, trace round every man's life' (Re, 121–2). As Parry shows, the yacht places metropolitan culture (and its conflicts) at the heart of Lingard's colonial adventure: as Lingard puts it later, it was 'like home coming' to him, when he 'wasn't thinking of it' (Re, 155).

While d'Alcacer and Mrs Travers look on like spectators at a drama, Lingard and Travers play out their comedy of misrecognition:

> 'I don't see my way to utilize your services', he said, with cold finality.
> Lingard, grasping his beard, looked down at him thoughtfully for a short time.
> 'Perhaps it's just as well,' he said very slowly 'because I did not offer my services. I've offered to take you on board my brig for a few days, as your only chance of safety.' (Re, 129)

Travers's presence brings out the class conflicts of metropolitan society: Lingard tells him 'if I hadn't been an adventurer, I would have had to starve or work at home for such people as you' (Re, 134). The arrival of Hassim and Immada then leads into the staging of simultaneous conversations in different languages. Their conversation with Lingard takes place in Malay, but this is only revealed later through the responses of others. Mr Travers's angry ' What is this new intrusion?' (Re, 135) is the first indication. The sailing-master's reply makes the linguistic situation clear:

> 'These are the fisher-folk, sir ... Hey! Johnnie! Hab got fish? Fish! One peecee fish! Eh? ...' He gave it up suddenly to say in a deferential tone – 'Can't make them savages understand anything, sir ...'
> (Re, 135–6)

The misrecognition of Hassim and Immada through pre-conceptions about non-Europeans is emphasised by the dignified exchange between Hassim and Lingard that follows:

> 'Why did the little white man make that outcry', he asked, anxiously.
> 'Their desire is to eat fish' said Lingard ... (Re, 136)

The sailing-master's use of pidgin is also a reminder of Shaw's behaviour earlier. Shaw, in the opening scene with the Malay crew, had used pidgin as a put-down, playing derisively with the helmsman's observation 'No catch wind – no get way' (Re, 7). Later on, Shaw similarly displays his inability (or unwillingness) to discriminate one kind of non-European from another in his description of Hassim and Immada as 'Niggers' (Re, 239). (The narrator wryly notes the 'proper feeling of racial pride in the primitive soul of the mate' [Re, 240] in another of the novel's reversals of the conventional discourse of the 'primitive'.) The sailing-master's alternation between degrading the Malays and degrading himself before Travers also repeats Shaw's alternation between disdain for the Malays and superficially deferential behaviour towards his captain.

This scenic method is then developed through a carefully constructed montage of voices. First, Travers and Lingard continue their fierce quarrel:

> 'How long is this performance going to last? I have desired you to go.'
> 'Think of these poor devils,' whispered Lingard with a quick glance at the crew huddled up near by. (Re, 138)

Then Mrs Travers and Immada are juxtaposed in a conventional trope:

> Fair-haired and white she asserted herself before the girl of olive face and raven locks with the maturity of perfection, with the superiority of the flower over the leaf, of the phrase that contains a thought over the cry that can only express an emotion. Immense spaces and countless centuries stretched between them: and she looked at her as when one looks into one's own heart with absorbed curiosity, with still wonder, with an immense compassion. (Re, 140)

This passage seems to assert a very simple evolutionary model of racial difference quite at odds with what elsewhere is a much more relativistic and cultural approach. In particular, the image of 'the phrase that contains a thought' in opposition to 'the cry that can only express an emotion' seems to instate an image of the eastern woman that deprives her of thought and articulation which conflicts with the representation of Immada elsewhere. However, the key is provided at the start of the chapter: 'D'Alcacer, standing back, surveyed them all with a profound and alert attention' (Re, 138). In the previous chapter, d'Alcacer and Mrs Travers acted as both audience and chorus for the dramatic action taking place on the stage provided by the yacht's deck. In this chapter, as Mrs Travers leaves her chair to enter the action, d'Alcacer is left alone as audience and chorus, and the choric function is fulfilled through narrative focalisation.[20] The chapter accordingly presents d'Alcacer's view of Mrs Travers and, in particular, his interpretation of her encounter with Immada. The deprivation of Immada of thought and language is to be explained by d'Alcacer's lack of Malay, in the same way as Marlow's iconic presentation of Kurtz's African mistress is to be explained by Marlow's lack of knowledge of Bantu languages.[21] Immada for d'Alcacer, like the African woman for Marlow, has a purely spectacular and iconic value. This is borne out by the similar presentation, through d'Alcacer's eyes, of Lingard's later encounter with the Ilanun: 'D'Alcacer, uncomprehending, watched the scene' (Re, 441). This introduces a tableau of staged figures: 'the Man of Fate puzzled and fierce like a disturbed lion, the white-robed Moors, the multitude of half-naked barbarians, squatting by the guns, standing by the loopholes in the immobility of an arranged display' (Re, 441). This is not just focalised through d'Alcacer, it also represents his way of seeing. D'Alcacer (for explicable historical reasons) consistently sees the Arabs as 'Moors'; and d'Alcacer's eyes produce the scene as an ethnographic tableau. This is a clear instance of Conrad's strategy of ignorance: representing through situated misrepresentation.

Juliet McLauchlan noted that 'When Conrad returned to the abandoned MS', he shaped its final form partly through 'drastic excisions', partly through 'the immensely impressive introduction of imagery associated with acting and the stage' (216).[22] However, it is not just drama but also opera that lies behind Conrad's representation of the Malay world in *The Rescue* and elsewhere. As early as 2 May 1894, in a letter to Marguerite Poradowska about the writing of *Almayer's Folly*, Conrad had implied the conscious adoption of an operatic model in his Malay fiction:

I shall soon send you the last chapter. It begins with a *trio* – Nina, Dain, Almayer – and ends with a long *solo* for Almayer which is almost as long as the *solo* in Wagner's *Tristan*. (CL1, 156)

In this chapter, the dialogue is again constructed like an operatic trio. In this trio, Lingard alternates between Malay dialogue with Immada and English dialogue with Mrs Travers. A particular feature of this exchange is that Mrs Travers's comments on Immada are challenged by Lingard's responses but repeatedly surmount the challenge. Mrs Travers's patronising approach to Immada, which objectifies and aestheticises her ('Almost a child! And so pretty!' [Re, 140]), is directly challenged by Lingard: 'She knows war … And hunger, too, and thirst, and unhappiness; things you have only heard about' [Re, 141]. Her resistance to this challenge ('That child!') is, in turn, subverted by the narrative: 'the glances of the two women, their dissimilar and inquiring glances, met, seemed to touch, clasp, hold each other with the grip of an intimate contact' (Re, 141). Her insistence on her original attitude ('Poor girl. … Are they all so pretty?' [Re, 141]) is again directly challenged by Lingard ('Who – all? … There isn't another one like her if you were to ransack the islands all round the compass' [Re, 141–2]) and indirectly by the nature of Immada's own questions to Lingard ('What are they come for? Why did you show them the way to this place?' [Re, 141]). Mrs Travers's eventual triumph is foreshadowed not only in her resistance (even at the end of the scene, she is still using the same patronising formula: 'I hope … that this poor girl will know happier days' [Re, 143]) but also by the gradually muted responses of the other two: at the end of this scene, Immada asks her questions 'faintly', while Lingard 'mumbled' his (Re, 141).

Parry has suggested that Mrs Travers is 'the fiction's unseeing eye, rejecting the unknown as unknowable and defending her innermost self from any incursions' (Parry, 56). One way in which she does this is by constructing an image of Immada through her own dissatisfactions with European upper-class life, much as d'Alcacer constructed an opposition between Mrs Travers and Immada based on his admiration for Mrs Travers:

She envied, for a moment, the lot of that humble and obscure sister. Nothing stood between that girl and the truth of her sensations. She could be sincerely courageous, and tender and passionate and – well – ferocious. (Re, 153)

This is not veridic but derives from Mrs Travers's projections. It is that use of the oriental as the Other that Said described in *Orientalism*: 'European culture gained in strength and identity by setting itself off against the Orient as a sort of surrogate and even underground self' (3). As Said says, 'the imaginative examination of things Oriental was based more or less exclusively upon a sovereign Western consciousness ... according to a detailed logic governed not simply by empirical reality but by a battery of desires, repressions, investments, and projections'. To put it in other terms: while the novel's use of focalisation can be read as a reduction of the Other to the Same, its use of staged dialogue can be seen as a way of resisting that reduction.

Print culture and the picturesque

Part III of *The Rescue* begins with Lingard's observation that 'Some people ... go about the world with their eyes shut' (Re, 121). This blindness is then associated with the print-culture of the Europeans. Travers's voyage, for example, is itself in part motivated by ideas of textual production. He decides to use the time lost by being stranded on the sandbank 'putting in order the notes collected during the year's travel in the East' (Re, 126). The sailing-master of the yacht relies on just such textual production as an authoritative guide. Thus he insists: 'My book says "Natives friendly all along this coast!"' (Re, 134). (By comparison, Lingard's anxieties about the safety of the yacht-people suggests a much less comfortable reality.) Similarly, Mr Travers's indignant assertion that 'This coast ... has been placed under the sole protection of Holland by the Treaty of 1820. The Treaty of 1820 creates special rights and obligations ...' (Re, 147) reveals a touching trust in the power of the written word. If 'sophisticated' Europeans have their doubts about the reliability of oral traditions, these instances point to the problematic nature of writing: its detachment from experience, its abstraction.

It is textuality, too, which influences Travers's reading of Lingard. For Travers, Lingard looks 'as if he had stepped out from an engraving in a book about buccaneers' (Re, 126). D'Alcacer and Mrs Travers, for their part, respond to Lingard through the category of the picturesque. Reina Lewis notes that 'the greater experience of travel outside Western Europe' in the late nineteenth century 'blurred the differences between conventions of the picturesque and Orientalism, leading to an overlap between the two areas of representation'.[23]

When Lingard first boards the yacht, d'Alcacer observes to Mrs Travers that 'the picturesque man is angry' (Re, 131), reducing him to a visual and aesthetic category. Mrs Travers's response to this argument between Lingard and her husband is similarly aesthetic: 'this is – such – such a fresh experience for me to hear – to see something – genuine and human' (Re, 132). This first glimpse behind Mrs Travers's veil reveals a spectator – someone who treats others as spectacle, as objects. With d'Alcacer and Mrs Travers, the upper-class eye reduces Lingard to an aesthetic experience. There is an homology between the English upper-class eye in relation to the lower classes and the same eye in relation to other peoples. As McClintock puts it, this 'high point of view – the panoptical stance – is enjoyed by those in privileged positions in the social structure, to whom the world appears as a spectacle, stage, performance' (IL, 122). In both cases, the Other can be reduced to an aesthetic category, and the aesthetic category above all asserts distance between the viewer and the viewed. Indeed, it fixes what is viewed at a distance and strives to prevent it from questioning or disrupting the viewer. Thus, in Chapter 6, as Mrs Travers reflects on 'the occurrences of the afternoon', her thoughts return to Lingard and Immada: 'what struck her artistic sense was the vigour of their presentation' (Re, 152). Mrs Travers responds to both the lower-class Lingard and the Wajo princess, Immada, through her 'artistic sense'. This stands in contrast to the 'faculty of affection' (Re, 162), which Hassim and Immada aroused in Lingard. Similarly, when Lingard explains the situation to her, Mrs Travers responds to his 'picturesque speech', and the narrator observes: 'She forgot that she was personally close to that tale which she saw detached, far away from her' (Re, 163).

Conrad's own narrative replicates this aesthetic vision. The introduction of Malay characters is often the verbal equivalent of the plates used to illustrate Raffles's *History of Java*. Thus the introduction of Hassim can be read as grounded in the material culture of the Bugis:

> From the twist of threadbare *sarong* wound tightly on the hips protruded outward to the left the ivory hilt, ringed with six bands of gold, of a weapon that would not have disgraced a ruler. Silver glittered about the flintlock and the hardwood stock of his gun. The red and gold handkerchief folded round his head was of costly stuff, such as is woven by the high-born women in the households of chiefs ... (Re, 65)

However, the subsequent description of Immada is already moving towards the static pictorialism of the ethnographic plate:

> Her *sarong*, the kilt-like garment which both sexes wear, had the national check of grey and red, but she had not completed her attire by the belt, scarves, the loose upper wrappings, and the head-coverings of a woman. (Re, 65–6)

In both these examples, the contradictory signs and the incompleteness of the costume tend to individualise the portrait. By the time Conrad returned to *The Rescue*, the essentialising ethnographic pictorial mode has taken over. Thus in Part IV, Chapter 3, the Ilanun chiefs are introduced as a static image:

> Their ample cloaks fell from their shoulders, and lay behind them on the sand in which their four long lances were planted upright, each supporting a small oblong shield of wood, carved on the edges and stained a dull purple. (Re, 222)

Daman in Belarab's courtyard is subject to similar treatment:

> A white cloth was fastened round his head by a yellow cord. Its pointed ends fell on his shoulders, framing a thin dark face with large eyes, a silk cloak striped black and white fell to his feet ... (Re, 289)

It might be argued that this last example is focalised through Mrs Travers; that Mrs Travers cannot understand the language in which the debates take place and thus is forced to emphasise the visual. The narrative's pictorial representation of the Ilanun then becomes Mrs Travers's recourse to the textual tradition – in this case, the textual tradition of ethnographic illustration. Part iv would support such a reading.

Cross-dressing and the aestheticisation of the Other

Iain Sinclair, in *Lights out for the Territory*, in Conrad's metropolitan territory of the Kingsland Road, reads the signs of what might be called post-colonial political struggle brought from the peripheries of empire to its metropolitan heart.[24] Conrad in *The Rescue* traces an opposite movement and takes the political struggle of the metropolitan centre to the edges of empire. Thus Part iv stages the encounter of these two worlds: London metropolitan society and the political and cultural world of the Malays. To begin with, Chapter 3 presents the struggle for Lingard's allegiance as a psychomachia between different linguistic communities:

> Mrs Travers felt as though she were engaged in a contest with them; in a struggle for the possession of that man's strength and of that man's devotion. (Re, 217)

Mrs Travers's triumph in this contest leads to her accompanying Lingard to the Settlement, an entry into the Malay world which takes her, as far as she is concerned, 'beyond the limits of the conceivable' (Re, 214).

Parry has commented on Mrs Travers's aestheticising tendency as one of the ways in which she protects herself from this experience. For example, she conceives of herself as like 'some woman in a ballad, who has to beg for the lives of innocent captives' (Re, 216). Her first glimpse of one of the inhabitants of the Settlement she expresses in terms of 'an enigmatical figure in an Oriental tale' (Re, 260), quite clearly using the categories supplied by literary experience to contain the unknown and render it manageable. This is most apparent in her response to the dangerous Daman, who delighted her 'not as a living being but like a clever sketch in colours, a vivid rendering of an artist's vision of some soul, delicate and fierce' (Re, 297). In short, Daman is encountered not as 'a living being' but as an aesthetically rendered simulacrum of himself. Mrs Travers's refusal of the encounter with alterity in the person of Daman is also a refusal of dialogue with the political Other.

It is also significant that, for the purposes of this encounter with the Malays, Mrs Travers has changed from European to Malay clothes:

> She was wearing a Malay thin cotton jacket, cut low in the neck without a collar and fastened with wrought silver clasps from the throat downward. She had replaced her yachting skirt by a blue check *sarong* embroidered with threads of gold. (Re, 264–5)

A context for this cultural cross-dressing is supplied by the ritual dressing of Lingard in preparation for this expedition:

> 'How many changes of clothes shall I put up, sir?' asked the steward, while Lingard took the pistols from him and eased the hammers after

putting on fresh caps. – 'I will take nothing this time, steward.' He received in turn from the mulatto's hands a red silk handkerchief, a pocket book, a cigar-case. He knotted the handkerchief loosely round his throat; it was evident he was going through the routine of every departure for the shore ... (Re, 235–6)[25]

Besides using the ritual as a way of routinising this exceptional experience, the careful process of preparation also suggests the performative aspect of power. However, in Mrs Travers's case, the costume clearly has a different significance. In the first place, it signals her victory over Immada: on a literal level, she has deprived Immada of a costume that was destined for her. Secondly, having set up the Oriental as Other, she now appropriates the external trappings of the Other. Simon During has described a process of constructing a new identity 'by appropriating elements of another's identity'.[26] This, however, is not what Mrs Travers is doing. In joining Lingard for this journey, Mrs Travers is venturing 'beyond the limits of the conceivable' (Re, 214), but the costume-change is not so much opening herself to that experience through identifying with the Other – or opening herself to the Other through a relation with it – as a way of protecting herself through aestheticising the Other and then appropriating an aes-theticised version of the Other through role-playing. Her husband's sardonic comment, 'Indulging your taste for fancy dress' (Re, 264), is telling. Lingard, for his part, coaches her in the role. He persuades her, for example, to cover her face with a veil and to cover her hands with the edge of the scarf to shake Daman's hand:

> Mrs Travers ... felt extremely Oriental herself when, with her face muffled to the eyes, she encountered the lustrous black stare of the sea-robbers' leader. (Re, 293)

But her frame of reference is always strictly aesthetic: with 'her hand resting lightly on Lingard's arm', she 'had the sensation of acting in a gorgeously got up play on the brilliantly lighted stage of an exotic opera' (Re, 295).[27] Mrs Travers's dress is not an acceptance of Otherness, but rather deprives Otherness of its subjectivity and sub-stantiality; and this masquerade ends in the sacrifice not only of Lingard's political schemes against Dutch hegemony in the region but also of his allies, Hassim and Immada. As Parry points out, Mrs Travers sails through these experiences supported by an unshaken conviction of cultural superiority; as a result, her actions put into effect the political rhetoric of her husband. The 'inferior race' perishes so that she can save her husband and herself.

In *Culture and Imperialism*, Said commented upon the effect of such 'distancing and aestheticising cultural practices' that 'they split and then anaesthetise the metropolitan consciousness' (157). Mrs Travers's aestheticising of her experience represents precisely this anaesthetising of the metropolitan consciousness. Mrs Travers's reduction of the Malay world to imperial spectacle – and her insistence on viewing Lingard as 'picturesque' and the Malays as 'exotic' – allows her to ignore the disastrous effects of her own private and domestic agenda on both Lingard and the Malays. Mrs Travers's cultural cross-dressing crystallises the novel's concern with the encounter with Otherness. Shaw and Travers assert an Englishness that refuses any encounter with Otherness. Mrs Travers aestheticises Otherness and makes it part of a play that effectively defuses it. Lingard, who thought he had gone beyond 'that circle which race, memories, early associations ... trace round every man's life' (Re, 121), is faced with an unexpected 'homecoming' and forced to re-examine his relation to 'the essential conditions' of his origin. Even Jörgensen, whom Parry singles out as the 'unacknowledged hero' of the novel, because he remains 'loyal to his aged Malayan girl' (Parry, 50), is not able to escape his Europeanness. He presents himself to Lingard as someone who has lost his connection with 'the essential conditions' of his origin:

'I can speak English, I can speak Dutch, I can speak every cursed lingo of these islands ... but I have forgotten the language of my own country.' (Re, 103)

In contrast to the practice of much contemporary fiction, Jörgensen's 'going native' appears as a sign of 'moral strength rather than of deterioration' (LT, 111). However, the advice he gives to Lingard (to 'drop' his plan) is spoken from a European subject position: 'you don't get me to meddle in their infernal affairs' (Re, 104). Jörgensen apparently occupies a liminal position between Europeanness and Otherness, but even Jörgensen is not able to reach a complete surrender to Otherness.

9
Homecoming

If Conrad was 'annexing' Borneo for English literature, he was also writing in the context of a textual tradition relating to Malaysia. Conrad's first novels derive from his own experiences in the region and the stories that he heard there. They attempt to represent the place and its peoples in terms of a common humanity. This attempt ends, in 'Karain', with the recognition of the irreducible alterity of the Malay reality. Conrad then has recourse to the textual tradition as a textual tradition. In other words, he is subsequently not so much concerned with representing the cross-cultural encounter as engaged with the problems of representation. If, as Bongie suggests, Conrad was unable to complete 'The Rescuer' in the 1890s because of the unresolved problem of Lingard's belatedness, the hollowing out of Brookean imperialism, Conrad found a solution in *Lord Jim* by using Brooke material for the construction of an impossible adventure-romance world. *Lord Jim* foregrounds the production of narrative, and Brooke material is incorporated into the novel's self-conscious and critical attention to the production of narrative. The Malay world that is annexed is (in *Lord Jim*, at least) always already a fiction. It is 'like something you read of in books' (LJ, 233–34).

In *Lord Jim*, as in *Heart of Darkness*, there is also a consciousness of the return home and of the need to render an account on returning. This involves the problem of reporting the colonial encounter to the metropolitan audience, which Conrad himself repeatedly confronts in writing his fiction. Conrad's solution, as James Clifford noted, was to represent the activity as 'a contextually limited practice of storytelling'.[1] Hence the fiction, too, repeatedly returns to the scene of writing and the scene of reading, to the production of narrative and the reception of narrative. The introduction of the 'privileged man' as the recipient of the final part of Marlow's narrative in *Lord Jim* is the most obvious acknowledgement of this need to render an account to the metropolitan audience. It also raises the issue of 'service in the ranks' or 'straying from the path', the issue of commitment to the metropolis or to the peoples of the periphery. Conrad, like Hugh Clifford, repeatedly engaged with this in his Malay fictions. It is the central dilemma in *The Rescue*. It is the problem that is constantly faced by any author who needs to render one world in terms of another.

In his later Malay fiction, the cross-cultural encounter that is foregrounded takes place between different kinds of European. Metropolitan problems involving class, gender, and sexual orientation are acted out upon the colonial stage. For Lena and Heyst in *Victory*, as for Lingard in *The Rescue*, the arrival of other Europeans is 'like home coming' when they were not thinking of it (Re, 155).

Death in exile

Before he introduces the story of Jim's experiences in Patusan, Marlow devotes much of Chapter 22 to an extended meditation on home-coming. Marlow himself is about to return home: 'for each of us going home must be like going to render an account' (LJ, 221), he says. Nostalgia is a recurrent motif in *Lord Jim*. When Marlow first involved himself in Jim's case, he explained his sense of responsibility for Jim in terms of the brotherhood of the sea, but he invokes that sense of brotherhood by creating a scenario involving meeting again back at home one of the young men he has trained for the sea: 'Were I to go home tomorrow, I bet that before two days passed over my head some sunburnt young chief mate would overtake me at some dock gateway or other' (LJ, 44). In Chapter 21, he summons up the negative version of that scene to the same effect: 'The earth is so small that I was afraid of, some day, being waylaid by a blear-eyed, swollen-faced, besmirched loafer, with no soles to his canvas shoes, and with a flutter of rags about the elbows, who, on the strength of old acquaintance, would ask for a loan of five dollars' (LJ, 223–4). In this counter-narra-tive, the encounter does not take place at home. Part of the poignancy of Jim's situation is that he 'could never go home now', because his father will have read of the *Patna* incident 'in the home papers' (LJ, 79). At the Sailors' Home, Jim had already become 'like a ghost without a home to haunt' (LJ, 104). The Inquiry's decision about Jim is, as Marlow says, effectively 'a sentence of exile' (LJ, 159). Signifi-cantly, one of the documents in the packet of papers sent to the privileged man at the end is 'the last letter he ever had from home'

(LJ, 294), which Jim has carried round with him. Enforced exile is a link between Jim and Stein. Stein has built up his career in the archipelago because, after his involvement in revolutionary politics in 1848, he had 'no home to go to' (LJ, 193). He came out East as the assistant to a Dutch naturalist, but, when the naturalist 'went home', Stein had to remain.

In *Almayer's Folly*, Almayer effectively lives and dies 'in exile': exiled from the Europe that he has never known except through his mother's stories, but which he has made the basis for his identity.[2] Rivetted 'to an elsewhere', seeking 'that country that does not exist but that he bears in his dreams' (SO, 5), he has created for himself the conditions of exile almost independently of his move from Batavia to Sambir. In *An Outcast of the Islands*, Willems, too, dies 'in exile'. But, long before his death, he had already contemplated the irretrievable loss of home. At the end of Chapter 3, when his thoughts 'wandered home', he recalls the architecture of Rotterdam and his father's efforts to earn 'bread for the children that waited for him in a dingy home'. But he ends this retrospection by being forced to recognise that 'it would never come back': 'He had cut himself adrift from that home many years ago' (OI, 31). If Almayer, Willems, Jim, and Heyst face death in exile, homecoming, in Conrad's Malay fiction, is not without its problems. Morrison, in *Victory*, for example, goes home 'to push the magnificent coal idea personally in London', but finds himself 'as lonely as a crow in a strange country' (V, 22). When he visits his family in Dorset, he catches a cold and dies (V, 22). Lingard, in *Almayer's Folly*, similarly returns to Europe 'to raise money for the great enterprise' of gold- and diamond-mining 'in the interior of the island' (AF, 24). Subsequently, Almayer receives only one letter from him in England 'saying he was ill' and 'had found no relation living' (AF, 28). After that 'a complete silence': 'Europe had swallowed up the Rajah Laut apparently' (AF, 28). For Lingard as for Morrison, 'Going to Europe was nearly as final as going to Heaven' (V, 20).[3] If *Lord Jim* is permeated by nostalgia and the exile's longing for home, *Almayer's Folly* and *Victory* express anxieties not only about possible feelings of estrangement on returning home but also that returning home might be equivalent to dying.

The return of the stranger

Two other works by Conrad explore these anxieties about homecoming from the perspective of the return to Europe. The early short story 'Amy Foster' presents a complicated exploration of home and exile.[4]

The inset story of 'Yanko Gooral', shipwrecked off the English coast, presents the nightmare of exile. His arrival on shore is described in the language of narratives of exploration: 'England was an undiscovered country ... for all I know he might have expected to find wild beasts or wild men here' (Ty, 112). This reversal of the direction of discovery sets the tone for this early part of the narrative. In effect, his story is a captivity narrative with England as the place of capture. The narrative emphasises his isolation and his sense of alienation from the world he finds himself in. This begins with the estranged account of Yanko's journey from Carpathia to England:

> There was a roof over him, which seemed made of glass, and was so high that the tallest mountain-pine he had ever seen would have had room to grow under it. Steam-machines rolled in at one end and out at the other. (Ty, 114–5)

The defamiliarisation is produced partly through attending to Yanko's linguistic isolation, partly through foregrounding Yanko's attempt to make sense of this new world by drawing on the terms and experiences of his former life. Yanko's departure from home produces the first of the story's encounters with 'the incomprehensible': the narrative emphasises both his 'utter aloneness' and his translation 'out of his knowledge' (Ty, 118). This characterises also his response to England. Thus, he 'could talk to no-one, and had no hope of ever understanding anybody' (Ty, 129). To make things worse, there was 'nothing here the same as in his country' (Ty, 129). Even when he settles in England, he feels himself 'separated by an immense space from his past and by an immense ignorance fom his future' (Ty, 132). As Kristeva would confirm, all of these are key components of the experience of exile.[5] At the same time, in moving to England, Yanko also becomes 'the incomprehensible' to other people. The story emphasises violence and hostility as the natives' response to 'the incomprehensible' as embodied by Yanko ('the dread of an inexplicable strangeness' [Ty, 120]). The one exception is Amy Foster. Amy's 'act of impulsive pity' brings Yanko 'back again within the pale of human relations' (Ty, 125). However, once they have a child, the cultural differences between Yanko and Amy become crucial. Yanko's desire to bring up his son speaking his language and according to the customs of his own country asserts a difference that Amy finds increasingly frightening.[6] Finally, in the ultimate nightmare for exiles, Yanko in his fever speaks in his own language, when he thinks he is speaking English, and Amy, overcome with 'the terror, the unreasonable terror, of that man she could not understand' (Ty, 139), deserts him to flee home to her parents. Thus Yanko experiences that 'death in exile' that featured in the epigraph to Conrad's first novel.

However, if Yanko presents a nightmare version of death in exile, Dr Kennedy, who narrates his story, subtly encodes some of the problems of returning home. The 'country doctor', Dr Kennedy, has returned home to England after living abroad:

> He had begun life as a surgeon in the Navy, and afterwards had been the companion of a famous traveller, in the days when there were continents with unexplored interiors. His papers on the flora and fauna made him known to scientific societies. (Ty, 106)

Kennedy is a version of a familiar tropical figure glimpsed in *Almayer's Folly* and *An Outcast of the Islands* and most fully embodied in Stein. Kennedy, however, has returned home, but his account of Yanko Gooral raises questions about that 'return home'. In the first place, there is his projection into Yanko's experience of exile as evidenced by the story he tells. More significant, however, is the contrast that Kennedy's narrative sets up between Yanko's 'lithe and striding figure' and the dullness of the natives, 'uncouth in body and as leaden of gait as if their very hearts were loaded with chains' (Ty, 111). This contrast is reinforced by the observations of the unnamed, primary narrator, who has also returned 'from abroad':

> The men we met walked past, slow, unsmiling, with downcast eyes, as if the melancholy of an over-burdened earth had weighted their feet, bowed their shoulders, borne down their glances. (Ty, 110)[7]

Kennedy and the narrator, although both have returned home from abroad, are almost as alien as Yanko. They express the perception of the native that Kristeva assigns to the foreigner: 'his scornfull hosts lack the perspective he himself has in order to see himself and to see them' (SO, 6–7). Kennedy and the narrator, like Yanko, have a sense of distance from the natives who have never left home. Through Kennedy and the narrator, the story anticipates Kristeva's injunction: 'to appreciate ourselves as strange in order better to appreciate the foreigners outside us instead of striving to bend them to the norms of our own repression'.[8]

In *The Rover*, the return of the native to the home territory is again used by Conrad to explore this idea of a home that is no longer home.

Peyrol has spent more than forty years in 'the Eastern seas' as a member of the piratical 'Brotherhood of the Coast' (Ro4). As a result, he has 'grown into a stranger to his native country', and, when he sets foot again on his native soil, 'he felt like a navigator about to land on a newly discovered shore' (Ro2). As with 'Amy Foster', the direction of exploration is reversed: Peyrol's scene of arrival takes place on the European shore from which he originally started. Peyrol has obviously changed through this lengthy period of absence. This has a subjective dimension: 'the memories of his native country' have been 'overlaid by other memories, with a multitude of impressions of endless oceans' (Ro8). His experiences away from home are fuller and more vibrant than his earliest memories of home. In addition, as Peyrol realises, his years away from home have made him a stranger: 'Nobody could know what his forty years or more of sea-life had been, unless he told them himself' (Ro5). But he is also a stranger in another sense: he has been away so long that home itself has changed. Although he inhabits a familiar landscape, 'well known to him from his boyhood's days' (Ro6), there is nobody there who remembers him. There is also a further sense in which he feels a stranger: when he encounters local people, he has repeatedly impressed upon him what he would have been like if he had remained. He is simultaneously aware of them and of how he has become different, something else. Peyrol's position stands in sharp contrast to Arlette's. She is succinctly introduced in the following terms: 'She belongs to the place. She was born on it. We know all about her' (Ro18).

Strangers to ourselves

'Homo duplex has in my case more than one meaning', Conrad wrote to Kazimierz Waliszewski (CL3, 89). As Harpham observes, Polishness was already 'an insistently multiple identity': 'If to be Polish at that time was to be defined by such oppositions as East and West, it was not necessarily to choose or to be able to choose one or the other' (OU, 11–12).[9] As a result, Harpham concludes, Conrad's 'relation to contexts in general is unclarified and insecure' so that, while Marlow or the narrator of *Victory* asserts his identity as 'one of us', there is something that marks Conrad 'as one of them as well' (OU, 12). Thus, Harpham continues, Conrad seems to occupy the position that Bhabha theorises as the 'Third Space of enunciation': 'a position of "hybridity" outside of and beneath the dualism of Same and Other, a nonposition founded on discontinuity, heterogeneity, and non-fixity' which 'underlies all positive articulations of cultural difference' (OU, 50).[10] Harpham, however, rejects this idea to suggest, less convincingly, that Conrad was 'both Same and Other, a thoroughly English gentleman who was also an oppressed Pole' (OU, 50). Harpham has already argued the 'multiple identity' marked by the term 'Pole'; he fails to have observed that Conrad's 'Englishness' was never other than mimicry: Conrad playfully described himself, in a letter to Karol Zagorski, as 'A Polish nobleman, cased in British tar' (CL1, 52). Harpham also ignores Conrad's other lives. Frederick Karl subtitled his biography 'The Three Lives'; Bernard Meyer went even further and begins his biography with a reference to Conrad's 'five separate and distinct lives': a 'Polish gentleman-student; a sea-faring adventurer on French ships out of Marseilles; a British sailor who, by dint of his labors, attained the rank of Captain in the Merchant Navy; a Congo River boatman caught in the sordid history of Belgian cupidity; and a lyrical master of English prose, the novelist Joseph Conrad'.[11] However, even if one were to demonstrate that Conrad had more lives than a cat, this would be approaching the issue from the wrong angle. In *Strangers to Ourselves*, Kristeva refers to 'the moment when the citizen-individual ceases to consider himself as unitary and glorious but discovers his incoherences and abysses, in short his "strangenesses"' (SO, 2). To be even briefer, 'the foreigner lives within us: he is the hidden face of our identity' (SO, 1).

Strangers to Ourselves begins with the actual experience of exile. Kristeva asserts that 'the foreigner keeps feeling threatened by the former territory, caught up in the memory of a happiness or a disaster' (SO, 4). At the same time, he is driven to wandering: 'he seeks that invisible and promised territory, that country that does not exist but that he bears in his dreams, and that must indeed be called a beyond' (SO, 5). While the exile's life of 'multiplying masks' means that 'he is never completely true nor completely false' (SO, 8), the logic of exile is 'an elsewhere that is always pushed back, unfulfilled, out of reach' (SO, 6). In *The Mirror of the Sea*, Conrad affirms: 'Happy he who, like Ulysses, has made an adventurous voyage, and there is no such sea for adventurous voyages as the Mediterranean' (MS, 151). Conrad then recalls how his own 'adventurous voyage' took him out of the 'inland sea' of the Mediterranean: 'this spirit found the way to the Indies, discovered the coasts of a new continent, and traversed at last the immensity of the great Pacific' (MS, 152). Conrad thus maps his own experience onto the narrative of European maritime exploration of the oceans beyond the Cape, but, in doing so, he evades the issue of return which the reference to Ulysses inescapably evokes. Levinas asserts against Ulysses another model of exile: 'To the myth of Ulysses return-ing to Ithaca, we would like to oppose the story of Abraham leaving his country for ever to go to a still unknown land'.[12] As Davis observes: 'The biblical Abraham, opposed to the Hellenic Ulysses, appears repeat-edly as the privileged figure for Levinas's philosophical project as he leaves behind his home (ontology) to explore an unknown world (alterity) without expectation of return' (Davis, 94). This figure marks 'a movement of the Same unto the Other which never returns to the Same'; indeed, it replaces the return with an emphasis on the endlessly open horizon.[13] Kristeva too rejects the idea of the return, but she finds her analogue in the figure of Io and the 'madness that leads a woman not on a journey back to the self, as with Ulysses', but rather 'towards a land of exile' (SO, 43). Accordingly, she advocates 'a cultivation of strangeness to the very end, without finish or conclusion' (SO, 138), 'a consciousness on the move that becomes estranged to itself in order to have another meaning come forth' (SO, 136).

Conrad, in his writing practice, is closer to Kristeva than to Ulysses. He is, in Andrew Gibson's words, 'not one thing nor the other', but rather 'displaced, modified by context, caught between identities, always suspended somewhere between origin and alien context'.[14] In addition to his literal nomadism, the radical scepticism that permeates his work produces the effect in his writing that Braidotti describes figuratively as nomadism: 'the kind of critical consciousness that resists settling into socially coded modes of thought and behaviour' (NS, 5). Conrad's fictions can be seen as 'a technique of strategic re-location in order to rescue what we need of the past in order to trace paths of transformation of our lives here and now' (NS, 6). It is 'a reterritorial-ization' that has 'passed through several versions of deterritorializa-tion'.[15] At the same time, as this work has tried to show, each fiction is precisely situated in contingency, history and change.

Notes

Introduction

1. 'The Rescuer', 61. 'The Rescuer' is in the British Library Manuscript Collection, Ashley 4787.
2. Arthur Waugh, 'London Letter', *Critic*, xxvi (11 May 1895), 349; reprinted in Norman Sherry, *Conrad: the Critical Heritage* (London: Routledge & Kegan Paul, 1973), 50–1; hereafter cited as CH. Compare Edward Garnett's manifesto for *The Overseas Library*: 'Mr Kipling arrived and discovered modern India to the English imagination'.
3. Arthur Waugh, 'Reticence in Literature', *The Yellow Book*, vol. I, 1894, 212.
4. *Almayer's Folly* was published by Fisher Unwin on 29 April 1895.
5. Unsigned review, *Spectator* (19 October 1895), 530; unsigned review, *Nation*, lxi (17 October 1895), 278; reprinted CH, 61, CH, 60.
6. Unsigned review, *Scotsman* (29 April 1895), 3; unsigned review, *Athenaeum*, 3526 (25 May 1895), 671; unsigned review, *Literary News*, xvi (September 1895), 268–9; reprinted in CH, 48, CH, 52, CH, 59. Frank Swettenham (1850–1946) arrived in Singapore in 1871 and, after a career as Collector and Resident in various parts of peninsular Malaya, was Resident General (1896–1901) and subsequently High Commissioner (1901–1904) of the Federation of Malay States. He was also the author of many books about Malaysia.
7. Joseph Conrad, 'A Glance at Two Books', *Last Essays*, 197. The essay was written in 1904, but was first printed in *T.P.'s and Cassell's Weekly* (1 August 1925).
8. It is a perhaps unconscious attempt to suggest the innocence of European colonisers in this process that leads to the irresistibility of progress being represented by the Hindu Juggernaut. The gendering of the Malay as male is part of that presumption of the male as normative that Rosi Braidotti (among others) has discussed.
9. D. J. M. Tate, *Rajah Brooke's Borneo* (Hong Kong: John Nicholson, 1988). Tate concentrates on the reporting of Brooke's activities in the *Illustrated London News*. A fuller account of Borneo's annexation for the popular imagination would also have to consider the representation of Borneo in both educational and adventure books for children. That 'enslaver of youth', F. S. Marryat, had published his *Borneo and the Indian Archipelago* in 1848 ('Tales of the Sea', NLL, 53). More relevantly, James Greenwood had published *The Adventures of Reuben Davidger; Seventeen Years and Four Months Captive Among the Dyaks of Borneo* (London: S. O. Beeton, 1865). Greenwood's captivity narrative (with its self-conscious glance back at *Robinson Crusoe*) epitomises the kind of novel Conrad does not write, as its narrative successively works through the popular tropes about Borneo: pirates (Chapter 4); headhunters (Chapter 5); orangutan (Chapter 5).

10. Conrad had professional contacts with the ILN. In June 1898, Clement Shorter, the editor, agreed to serialise 'The Rescuer', but dropped this plan in February 1900. Gordan suggests that Conrad's problems writing 'The Rescuer' might have arisen from the attempt to write more of an adventure story. Certainly the novel involves pirates, captivity, and Lingard's rescue of kidnapped Europeans. In June 1914, Conrad's article 'Protection of Ocean Liners' was published in the ILN.

11. The Malaysia of headhunters and orangutan is less relevant to Conrad. This work will focus rather on 'pirates' and Sir James Brooke.

12. Unfortunately, the account failed to conceal that what had taken place was a massacre rather than a battle: the 'pirate' fleet had been taken by surprise and annihilated. The report led to public meetings in London; questions in the Houses of Parliament; and eventually an official Inquiry.

13. There might have been other factors involved in Burns's death. Spenser St. John describes Burns as 'a disreputable adventurer'; he also notes the accusation that Brooke had 'bribed the pirates to murder Mr Burns' (*The Life of Sir James Brooke* [Edinburgh: William Blackwood, 1879], 239).

14. The attitude taken here to the 'insurrection' against Brooke's predecessors is very different to that taken the previous month in the account of the Chinese 'insurrection' against Brooke. 'The Insurrection at Sarawak' (ILN, 2 May 1857) reproduced Brooke's 'thrilling account' of the incident from a letter 'written to a friend'. That this letter had already been printed in *The Times* suggests an acute sense of the importance of news management on the part of Brooke and/or his supporters.

15. It is no surprise that Brooke features in W. H. Davenport Adams, *'In Perils Oft': Romantic Biographies Illustrative of the Romantic Life* (London: John Hogg, 1885), which makes much of Brooke '"putting down" head-hunting' and trying to 'extirpate the Dyak pirates' (308). It does, however, note that, in deciding to help the Raja Muda Hassim, Brooke was acting as a 'soldier of fortune' (303), fighting for the side that would pay him best.

16. Henry Keppel, *The Expedition to Borneo of H.M.S. Dido for the suppression of piracy* (London: Chapman & Hall, 1846), 2 vols; hereafter cited as EB. Rodney Mundy, *Narrative of Events in Borneo and Celebes* (London: John Murray, 1848), 2 vols; hereafter cited as NEBC. Brooke's precursor here was Captain James Cook. See Rod Edmond, *Representing the South Pacific: Colonial Discourse from Cook to Gauguin* (Cambridge: Cambridge University Press, 1997); hereafter cited as RSP. Edmond discusses the mythologising of Cook through the production and circulation of official and unofficial narratives of his voyages, and, in particular, through the production and circulation of prints and etchings of his death.

17. In the same way, stories of Cook's arrival in Hawaii emphasised how he was received as a god. Edmond notes 'the long history of a myth of white gods that has served European interests' (RSP, 58): whether the Haiwaiians regarded Cook as a god is contested, but there was certainly a need in Europe for 'a godly Cook' (RSP, 40). Edmond interrogates this narrative and also draws attention to the way in which it forms the basis for the evangelical counter-narrative, in which Cook's death is not a martyrdom but rather punishment for his allowing himself to be worshipped as a god (RSP, 28).

18. The review of *Tales of Unrest* in the *Academy* (14 January 1899) can thus be seen to make an interesting slip. It describes Conrad as 'one of the notable literary colonists,' and then adds 'He has annexed the Malay Peninsula for us' (CH, 110). Conrad's tales are set in the archipelago not the peninsula, but the peninsula was, indeed, the focus of British colonial interest.

19. CL2, 129–30.

20. Lloyd Fernando, 'Conrad's Eastern Expatriates', reprinted in Keith Carabine (ed.), *Joseph Conrad: Critical Assessments* (Helm Information, 1992), II, 51–70; 52, 52–3.

21. Hugh Clifford, 'The Genius of Mr. Joseph Conrad', *North American Review*, 178 (June 1904), 842–52.

22. Joseph Conrad, *Youth, and two other stories*, 27.

23. The term 'arrival scene' is taken from Mary Louise Pratt, *Imperial Eyes: Travel Writing and Transculturation* (London: Routledge, 1992), 78; hereafter cited in the text as Pratt. Pratt describes 'arrival scenes' as 'potent sites for framing relations of contact and setting the terms of its representation' (Pratt, 78). See also M. L. Pratt, 'Field Work in Common Places' in James Clifford and George Marcus (eds), *Writing Culture* (Berkeley: California University Press, 1987).

24. As GoGwilt suggests, the ship's name and origin ('Judea. London') succinctly marks this disjunctive cultural origin: the construction of 'Western' identity is based on this suppressed 'East'/'West' split (IW, 23).

25. Pratt quotes a comparable moment from Mungo Park's *Travels in the Interior of Africa* (Edinburgh: Adam & Charles Black, 1860), 104–5: 'I was surrounded by so great a crowd as made it necessary for me to satisfy their curiosity by sitting still' (Pratt, 80). Pratt describes Park's narrative as marked by 'the desire to achieve reciprocity' (Pratt, 80). Park, of course, was one of the explorers Conrad praises in 'Geography and Some Explorers'. His recognition of African agency and critical self-questioning is perhaps one of the models for Conrad's colonial fiction.

26. See Douglas Kerr, 'Crowds, Colonialism and *Lord Jim*', *The Conradian*, 18.2 (Autumn, 1994), 49–64, which notes how the western imagination of the orient is marked by a sense of its enormous populations. Kerr comments on this passage from 'Youth': 'The Asian crowd is an essential part of the first impressions of all travellers who have set out to see the east and find their gaze returned' (51).

27. As GoGwilt points out, young Marlow's enthusiasm for the exotic names 'Bangkok', 'Java', and 'Singapore' homogenises politically distinct locations: 'The difference between Java, the central island of the Dutch East Indies, and Bangkok, capital of Siam, marks a difference between the most highly organised system of colonial rule and exploitation ... and virtually the only nation in the region to sustain its independence from European colonial aggression' (IW, 21). Singapore, of course, is 'the seat of British hegemony in Southeast Asia' (IW, 21). By supplying these names Conrad marks an historical and political context which remains invisible to the youthful Marlow.

28. Conrad had visited the region briefly in 1885: in April 1885, he had signed on as second mate on the *Tilkhurst* (bound for Singapore and arriving there in September).

29. G. J. Resink, 'The Eastern Archipelago Under Joseph Conrad's Western Eyes', *Indonesia's History Between the Myths* (The Hague: W. van Hoeve, 1968), 307–87; 308. Hans van Marle had noted that Conrad could have read the books of Wallace, McNair, Multatuli, and books by and about James Brooke, in the library of the Raffles Museum, Singapore, during his visits of 1883 and 1887.
30. Jerry Allen, *The Sea Years of Joseph Conrad* (London: Methuen, 1967), 190.
31. Norman Sherry, *Conrad's Eastern World* (Cambridge: Cambridge University Press, 1966), 175–94; hereafter cited as CEW.
32. Conrad's efforts to provide this understated historical dimension to the cross-cultural encounter in the archipelago undermine and challenge his European characters' regular attempts to de-historicise the Malay world.
33. Sir Frederick Weld was Governor of Singapore from 1880 to 1887. He was Hugh Clifford's uncle and had been responsible for bringing Clifford out to serve in Malaya. Bonham was Governor of Singapore from 1837 to 1843. In 'The End of the Tether', Massy recalls Carlo Mariani, 'the Maltese hotel-keeper at the slummy end of Denham Street' (Y, 269). The fictional 'Denham Street' is named after Denham, just as the non-fictional Bonham Street was named after Bonham. In *Lord Jim*, the chief engineer of the *Patna* takes refuge in 'Mariani's billiard-room and grog-shop near the bazaar'. Antonio Mariani had 'ministered to his vices in one or two other places' (LJ, 49), just as 'Charley' Mariani 'made his living by ministering to various abject vices' (Y, 269).
34 *The Rescue* was laid aside in 1899; it was worked at intermittently between 1899 and 1915; it was taken up seriously early in 1915 and completed in May 1919.
35. See the World's Classics edition of *An Outcast of the Islands* (Oxford: Oxford University Press, 1992), 373.
36. Conrad letter to William Blackwood, 6 September 1897, (CL1, 382).
37. See J. H. Stape and Owen Knowles (eds), *A Portrait in Letters: Correspondence to and About Conrad* (Amsterdam: Rodopi, 1996), 66–8.
38. Achin is in Northern Sumatra. The Dutch Government in Batavia declared war on Achin in 1873. Achin fell in January 1874, but the Achinese maintained a guerilla war through to 1878 and again from 1881 through to 1905. Gun-running to the Achinese features in Clifford's novel, *A Freelance of Today* (discussed in Chapter 3), and gun-running generally is a recurrent motif in Conrad's Malay fiction.
39. *A Portrait in Letters*, 69–70.
40. See Letter to Perceval Gibbon, [11 September 1909], CL4, 272–3. Laurence Davies dates this letter [11 or 18 September?], but Marris gives September 14 as the day of departure, and the letter is written prior to meeting Marris. Conrad described him to Clifford as 'A soft-eyed black-bearded man married to a Patani girl of good family', and noted that they had talked of Clifford and his books (Letter to Sir Hugh Clifford, 19 May 1910, CL4, 330–1).
41. Letter to J. B. Pinker, [11 October 1909], CL4, 276–8. Marris died shortly after his return to Penang.
42. Conrad wrote 'The Secret Sharer' immediately after Marris's visit in November/December 1909, and 'Freya of the Seven Isles' between

November 1910 and February 1911 using information supplied by Marris. Conrad, in his letter to Pinker, described Marris's visit as 'a visit from a man out of the Malay Seas', CL4, 277. In a letter to Edward Garnett, [4 August 1911], Conrad relates the origins of 'Freya of the Seven Isles' to Marris's visit, CL4, 469–70.

43. He began work on *Victory* in May 1912, and the novel was completed in June 1914.

44. Conrad received a copy of *My Life in Sarawak* (London: Methuen, 1913) in January 1914. He resumed work on *The Rescue* in 1918 and finished it in 1919. He wrote to Lady Margaret Brooke (15 July 1920), acknowledging his use of her autobiography in *The Rescue*. See C. T. Watts (ed.), *Joseph Conrad's Letters to Cunninghame Graham* (Cambridge: Cambridge University Press, 1969), 210–11.

45. Andrea White, *Joseph Conrad and the Adventure Tradition* (Cambridge: Cambridge University Press, 1993), 103–4. See also John Gordan, *Joseph Conrad: The Making of a Novelist* (Cambridge, MA: Harvard University Press, 1940) and Watts, *Joseph Conrad's Letters to Cunninghame Graham*, 209–11.

46. Rod Edmond addresses a similar problem in *Representing the South Pacific*. He notes that 'Polynesia', for example, would be a problematic term, since it is 'a nineteenth-century colonial construct ... heavily implicated in the hierarchies of race produced by Pacific colonial discourse', but that twentieth-century terms only raise different problems through their association with 'forms of cultural nationalism of an essentialist kind' (RSP, 15). He settles upon using nineteenth-century terms while remembering their historical and ideological provenance.

47. Paul Wheatley, *Impressions of the Malay Peninsula in Ancient Times* (Singapore: Eastern University Press, 1964), 2; hereafter cited as IMP.

48. C. Mary Turnbull, *A Short History of Malaysia, Singapore and Brunei* (Singapore: Graham Brash, 1981), 4; hereafter cited as SH.

49. Peter Bellwood, *Prehistory of the IndoMalaysian Archipelago* (Academic Press Australia, 1985), 142; hereafter cited as PIMA.

50. A. C. Milner, *The Invention of Politics in Colonial Malaya* (Cambridge: Cambridge University Press, 1995), 12; hereafter cited as IPCM. Zawiah Yahya, however, paints a quite different picture: she suggests that the 'small community of mixed parentage (Malay-Indian; Malay-Arab)' were defined as 'not-Malay' (*Resisting Colonialist Discourse* [Kuala Lumpur: Universiti Kebangsaan Malaysia, 1994], 54). Mahathir bin Mohamad, on the other hand, distinguishes between 'rural Malays', with customs of endogamous marriage, and 'town Malays' described as 'of mixed Malay-Indian or Malay-Arab descent' (*The Malay Dilemma* [Kuala Lumpur: Times Books International, 1970], 26.

51. This recalls Alexander Dalrymple's promotion of Balambangan, an island off the coast of North Borneo, to the East India Company. Dalrymple obtained the cession of Balambangan from Sultan Bantilan (Muizz ud-Din) of Sulu in September 1762. He thought the small island an ideal location for the important trade with China as well as for trade with the surrounding islands: 'if a circle of 2,000 miles be drawn round the East Indies the middle point will be found at Balambangan' (Quoted by James Francis Warren, *The Sulu Zone 1768–1898* [Singapore: Singapore University Press,

1981], p.18). See Howard Fry, *Alexander Dalrymple and the Expansion of British Trade* (London: Cass, 1970).

52. Christopher GoGwilt, *The Invention of the West: Joseph Conrad and the Double-Mapping of Europe and Empire* (Stanford: Stanford University Press, 1995), 67; hereafter cited in the text as IW. I will return to some of the issues raised here in Chapter 1. According to Jim Warren, Conrad's first two novels accurately describe 'the transformation that occurred in trade along the southern periphery of the Sulu zone' ('Joseph Conrad's Fiction as Southeast Asian History: Trade and Politics in East Borneo in the late-nineteenth Century', *Brunei Museum Journal*, 4.1 [1977], 21–34, 21–2).

53. Joseph Conrad, 'Geography and Some Explorers', *Last Essays* (London: J. M. Dent, 1926), 12. In this essay, Conrad divides geography into three historical phases: fabulous, militant, and scientific.

54. According to Jerry Allen, *The Sea Years of Joseph Conrad*, the names Babalatchi and Lakamba belonged to two Buginese traders in Berau, while the name Dain Marola belonged to a Buginese clerk there (233).

55. As Ian Watt notes in his Introduction to the Cambridge Edition of *Almayer's Folly* (Cambridge: Cambridge University Press, 1994): the historical Olmeijer was of mixed Dutch and Malay ancestry; he was a respected and successful trader on the Pantai River; and he died back home in Sourabaya in 1900 – five years after Almayer's death in *Almayer's Folly*.

56. Warren, 23.

57. See Norman Sherry, *Conrad's Eastern World* (Cambridge: Cambridge University Press, 1966), 90–116.

58. However, the rivalry between the British Borneo Company and the Dutch for Sambir, which is the context in which Almayer builds his new house, seems to have no historical basis. Ian Watt suggests that, by Lingard's time, Britain had no serious interest in 'annexing parts of Eastern Borneo as far south as Tanjung Redeb' (xxv).

59. After helping the Sultan of Brunei, Brooke was made Rajah of Sarawak in 1841. See N. Tarling, *Britain, the Brookes, and Brunei* (Oxford: Oxford University Press, 1971); hereafter cited as BBB.

60. In the opening chapter, Shaw refers to 'the Crimea five years ago' (20). The Crimean War began in 1854.

61. The Padri movement began in 1803 as a movement of social reform among Mainangkabau pilgrims in Sumatra. It became a *jihad* to implement the Islamic code and, from 1821 to 1838, a war with the Dutch. See C. Dobbin, *Islamic Revivalism in a Changing Peasant Economy: Central Sumatra 1784–1847* (London & Malmo: Scandinavian Institute of Asian Studies, 1983).

62. Peter Hulme and Ludmilla Jordanova (eds), *The Enlightenment and Its Shadows* (London: Routledge & Kegan Paul, 1990), 7.

63. ibid.

64. Neil Rennie, *Far-Fetched Facts: the Literature of Travel and the Idea of the South Seas* (Oxford: Clarendon Press, 1995), 39.

65. Francis Bacon, *The Advancement of Learning and New Atlantis* (London: Oxford University Press, 1966), 78; hereafter cited as AL.

66. Boorstin, 97. I am indebted to Daniel Boorstin for much of what follows.

67. Boorstin, 98. Ptolemy awaited rediscovery in the early 15th century.

68. There is not space here to describe how Prince Henry brought together books and charts; sea-captains and pilots; map-makers and instrument-makers; compass-makers and ship-builders. For a fuller account, see Boorstin, 158ff. More recently, Jerry Brotton has argued for the cultural importance of the opening of the Indian Ocean and has argued against the overshadowing of trade with the East by over-emphasis on the discovery of the 'New World'.

69. Judith Butler, in *Bodies That Matter*, (London: Routledge, 1993) suggests that 'the figuring of nature as the blank and lifeless page ... is decidedly modern, linked perhaps to the emergence of technological means of domination' (4).

70. See D. L. Higdon, 'Conrad's Clocks', *The Conradian* 16.1 (September 1991), 1–18 for an earlier exploration of clocks and Greenwich Mean Time in relation to Conrad's fiction.

71. PR, 112–21.

72. Joseph Conrad, 'Travel', *Last Essays*. The essay was first published as the Introduction to Richard Curle's *Into the East: Notes on Burma and Malaya* (1923).

73. In my first book on Conrad, *Joseph Conrad: Betrayal and Identity* (London: Macmillan, 1993), I argued that the 'achievement and decline' paradigm had resulted in the neglect of Conrad's early and late fiction.The present volume, while quite different in emphasis and approach, builds on that earlier argument. I have excluded from consideration fictions (such as *The Shadow-Line* and 'The Secret Sharer') set in the waters of the region that do not primarily involve encounters with non-Europeans.

74. The present work does not examine the adventure romance tradition. Andrea White, Richard Ruppell, and Linda Dryden have already worked in this area. Nor does it examine the version of 'writing Malaysia' produced by women such as Isabella Bird and Emily Innes, since Conrad does not refer to this (although he does make use of the autobiography of Lady Margaret Brooke). This will be the subject of a subsequent study.

75. Florence Clemens, 'Conrad's Favorite Bedside Book', *South Atlantic Quarterly* XXXVII (1939), 305–15.

76. John D. Gordan, *Joseph Conrad: the Making of a Novelist* (Cambridge, Ma.: Harvard University Press, 1941).

77. Heliéna Krenn, *Conrad's Lingard Trilogy: Empire, Race, and Women in the Malay Novels* (New York: Garland Publishing, 1990); hereafter cited as LT.

78. Benita Parry, *Conrad and Imperialism: Ideological Boundaries and Visionary Frontiers* (London: Macmillan, 1983); Andrea White, *Joseph Conrad and the Adventure Tradition: Constructing and Deconstructing the Imperial Subject* Cambridge: Cambridge University Press, 1993); hereafter cited in the text as JCAT.

79. Parry's reading of *Heart of Darkness, The Rescue, The Nigger of the 'Narcissus', Lord Jim* and *Nostromo* examined imperialism across a range of locations – Africa, South America, as well as the archipelago.

80. Henry Louis Gates (Jr), 'Critical Fanonism', *Critical Inquiry*, 17 (Spring 1991), 462; quoted by Edmond, 11.

81. See Aijaz Ahmad, *In Theory: Classes, Nations, Literatures* (London: Verso, 1992), 171–2.

82. Laura Chrisman, 'The Imperial Unconscious? Representations of Imperial Discourse', *Critical Quarterly*, 32, 3 (1990), 38.
83. Homi Bhabha, 'Signs taken for Wonders', *The Location of Culture* (London: Routledge, 1994), 112. Young has challenged the term 'hybridity', but Bhabha touches here on precisely the anxiety Clifford explores in his first two novels: how the coloniser can be 'denationalised' through contact with the culture of the colonised.
84. Conrad read Wallace's *Malay Archipelago*, Clifford's fiction, and materials relating to Brooke. Conrad and Clifford were friends for almost all Conrad's writing career.
85. As Gordan points out, Conrad 'created his fictional Arabs by moving the actual Arabs forward one generation' (JCMN, 47). Thus Syed Moshin appears in *Almayer's Folly* under the name of his son, Abdulla, while the fictional nephew Reshid is modelled on the historical Abdulla.
86. See Mark Conroy, 'Ghostwriting (in) "Karain"', *The Conradian*, 18.2 (Autumn, 1994), 1–16.
87. Julia Kristeva, *Strangers to Ourselves* (London: Harvester Wheatsheaf, 1991), 3.

1   Problems of Historiography

1. J. D. Legge, 'The Writing of Southeast Asian History' in N. Tarling (ed.), *The Cambridge History of Southeast Asia*, vol.1 (Cambridge: Cambridge University Press, 1992), 1ff.
2. See Thomas Stamford Raffles, *The History of Java*, which begins in precisely this way.
3. Vasco da Gama's 1498 voyage around the Cape of Good Hope had established a sea-route to the East. This immediately replaced the overland route with its heavy duties. This led to a fall in the price of spice in Europe; it cut out the Venetian merchants; and it produced Portuguese domination of the European pepper trade. See Lisa Jardine, *Worldly Goods* (Macmillan, 1996), 288–301.
4. As Jardine notes, Spain and Portugal came to Saragossa with rival maps and rival cartographers. In the end, Pedro Reinel's map of the region was rejected and Dogo Ribeiro's was attached to the settlement. In Jardine's words: 'Charles V's cartographers at Saragossa spuriously established that the Moluccas Islands lay within the Spanish sphere of influence on the map' (WG, 288). For a detailed discussion of the Moluccas, see Jerry Brotton, *Trading Territories: Mapping the Early Modern World* (London: Reaktion Books, 1997), 119–50.
5. Malacca had actually been under Spanish control for some time: in 1580, Philip II of Spain had annexed Portugal, and Portugal was under Spanish rule until 1640.
6. The Vereenigde Oost-Indische Compagnie (VOC), described by Benedict Anderson as 'the greatest "transnational" corporation' of the first half of the seventeenth century, was liquidated, in bankruptcy, in 1799; the colony of the Netherlands Indies dates from 1815, when the independence of the Netherlands was restored, Benedict Anderson, *Imagined Communities* (London: Verso, 1996), 166, 180.

7. The East India Company survived until the Indian Mutiny/First War of Indian Independence in 1857.

8. Penang, for example, came into existence as a freeport through the activities of a 'country trader', Francis Light, acting for the East India Company. See: H. P. Clodd, *Malaya's First British Pioneer: the Life of Francis Light* (London, 1948). The East India Company needed a naval base in Malaya or Siam to improve its control over the Bay of Bengal. In 1770 Sultan Muhammad of Keddah sought assistance against Siam and the Bugis. The Company's intervention in Keddah led to the establishment of an English base on the island of Penang. Francis Light formally took possession of Penang in August 1786.

9. Until 1833 most of this trade was monopolised by the East India Company. In 1833 the East India Company monopoly was broken; in 1858 the British Government took over the East India Company's administrative role.

10. N. Tarling, 'British Policy in the Malay Peninsula and Archipelago 1824–1871', *Journal of the Malayan Branch of the Royal Asiatic Society*, vol.xxx, pt.1 (October 1957), 10; cited hereafter as Tarling (1957). The journal will be cited hereafter as JMBRAS.

11. Tarling, BBB, 9.

12. At the same time, the British were anxious to avoid conflict with the Siamese on the peninsula or with the Chinese authorities more generally.

13. For Conrad's response to this development and the Spanish-American War generally, see his correspondence with Cora Crane (27 June 1898) and R. B. Cunninghame Graham (30 July 1898); CL2, 72–4; 80–1. By the Treaty of Paris, December 1898, the United States acquired Guam and Puerto Rico and bought the Philippines.

14. Paul Wheatley, *Impressions of the Malay Peninsula in Ancient Times* (Singapore: Eastern University Press, 1964).

15. See Legge, 7–9.

16. Tarling is referring specifically to Brunei, but the observation can be generalised, as the later part of this chapter will show. The *Sejarah Melayu*, the earliest written account of the history of peninsular Malaya, which recounts events from legendary times to the arrival of the Portuguese, includes, in one chapter, genealogies from Sri Maharaja, the Bandahara of Johore, down to Mansur Shah, Sultan Muda of Perak, clearly designed to legitimate the Perak Sultans through displaying their descent from the Bandaharas. See R. O. Winstedt (ed.), *The Malay Annals or Sejarah Melayu*, JMBRAS, XVI.iii (1938).

17. See Robert Young, *White Mythologies: Writing History and the West* (Routledge, 1990), 45–7.

18. J. C. van Leur, *Indonesian Trade and Society* (The Hague: Van Hoeve, 1955), 261. D. G. E. Hall's *A History of South-East Asia* (London: Macmillan, 1955) prompted an extended debate on Eurocentric history. For 'studying Malaya from within, looking outwards', see the preface to K. G. Tregonning (ed.), *Papers in Malayan History* (Singapore: University of Malaya Press, 1962).

19. For this model, and for information in this paragraph, I am indebted to N. Tarling, *A Concise History of Southeast Asia* (New York/London: Frederick A. Praeger, 1966).

20. The traditional silk and spice routes overland, over which Marco Polo had travelled to China in the thirteenth century, had become insecure. At the same time, the expansion of Siam posed a growing threat. China looked to Malacca in order to establish an alternative route to Arabia and to form an alliance against Siam. See Wang Gungwu, 'The Opening of Relations Between China and Malacca, 1403–5' in J. Bastin (ed.), *Malayan and Indonesian Studies* (Oxford: Clarendon, 1964), 87–104.

21. The Kelantan shadow-play provides another instance. This exists in two forms: a popular form, derived from Cambodia via Thailand, based on the Indian epic, the *Ramayana*; and the Jawa form, introduced in 1835 by a Malay puppet-master trained in Java, which is based either on the Indian *Mahabarata* or the Javanese *Panji* tales. Performances still begin with a Hindu blessing, even though the performers are all Muslims, and this *puja* is performed in Thai. Southeast Asian culture, like British culture, draws together elements from a range of cultural and ethno-linguistic backgrounds.

22. Tarling, *A Concise History*, Ch. 5.

23. Note that the Padri War (1803–38), the Java War (1825–30), and the Achin War (1873–1912) were all fought as religious revolts against colonial expansion, while the religious 'fanatic' is a recurrent figure in European writings about Malaysia.

24. Quoted in Lady Sophia Raffles, *Memoir of the Life and Public Services of Sir Thomas Stamford Raffles FRS etc* (London: John Murray, 1830). See Hugh Clifford, *Further India*, 53; hereafter cited as FI. Raffles's collection of manuscripts included a copy of the *Sejarah Melayu*, which offers a different account of the capture of Malacca. This was translated by his friend John Leyden and published in *Malay Annals* (London: 1821).

25. Clifford notes that this is the stratagem adopted in similar circumstances by 'the Pious Aeneas' (FI, 53).

26. Curiously, in his *The History of Java*, Raffles re-tells the story of Europeans gaining land by this trick using an animal skin, but this time he gives his source as 'Javan historians'; the Europeans are the Dutch rather than the Portuguese; the location is Jakarta rather than Malacca; and the date is 1620 rather than 1511 (HJ, II. 153–4).

27. Compare Richard Price, *First-Time: the Historical Vision of an Afro-American People* (Baltimore: Johns Hopkins University Press, 1980). Price handles the problem of conflicting Dutch written sources and local oral tradition, where both are clearly interested accounts, by dividing his page horizontally and offering parallel, alternative narratives. One of the dangers for non-Malay speakers in attempting to use Malay sources is made evident in Syed Hussein Alatas, *Thomas Stamford Raffles 1781–1826: Schemer or Reformer* (Sydney: Angus and Robertson, 1971). Alatas's account of Raffles's responsibility for the massacre of 24 Dutch and 63 Javanese at Palembang in 1811 (7–12) hinges on the translation of the phrase 'buang habiskan sekali-kali' in Raffles's letter, sent in Malay, to Mahmud Badruddin, the Sultan of Palembang. Alatas makes short work of Wurtzburg's attempted defence of Raffles despite his ignorance of either Dutch or Malay and his consequent dangerous reliance on translations.

28. Clifford also notes d'Albuquerque's numerous acts of piracy on the way to Malacca (FI, 56–60).

29. Lloyd Fernando, *Scorpion Orchid* (Singapore/Kuala Lumpur: Times Books International, 1992), 144; hereafter cited as SO.
30. Anderson, 167.
31. Bellwood, for example, suggests that Srivijaya was an interlocked group of trading towns rather than an 'empire' (*Prehistory*, 137).
32. Clifford Geertz, *Negara: the Theatre State in Nineteenth-Century Bali* (Princeton: Princeton University Press, 1980).
33. Hildred Geertz and Clifford Geertz, *Kinship in Bali* (Chicago: University of Chicago Press, 1975), 23; hereafter cited as *Kinship*.
34. Milner, *Kerajaan: Malay Political Culture on the Eve of Colonial Rule* (Tucson: University of Arizona Press, 1982), viii. He develops this work further in *The Invention of Politics in Colonial Malaya* (Cambridge: Cambridge University Press, 1995).
35. His obvious target here is Geertz's *Negara*.
36. As Milner notes, although Munshi Abdulla was indigenous to the peninsula, he was not an 'insider' (IPCM12). He was a subject of the Straits Settlements (not of a Malay sultanate), and his family background was Indian/Arabic. Like his father and grandfather before him, he lived in the colonial settlement of Malacca and served the European community as translator and language teacher.
37. It was only with the decline of Dutch power that the Dutch made a strategic withdrawal to concentrate on territorial control in Java.
38. Raffles to the Supreme Government, 7 June 1823; quoted in Charles Buckley, *An Anecdotal History of Old Times in Singapore* (Singapore: Fraser and Neave, 1902), 120–1.
39. Carl Trocki, *Prince of Pirates: The Temenggongs and the Development of Johor and Singapore, 1784–1885* (Singapore: Singapore University Press, 1979), 51.
40. N. Tarling, *Sulu and Sabah* (Kuala Lumpur: Oxford University Press, 1978), 8. Similarly, the Bajow, the 'Sea-Dyaks' or 'Sea-gypsies', were an entirely nomadic, sea-going people, without any sense of homeland beyond their ships.
41. Tarling (1957), 14.
42. N. Tarling, *Piracy and Politics in the Malay World: a Study of British Imperialism in Nineteenth-century South-east Asia*, (Melbourne: F. W. Cheshire, 1963), 113; hereafter cited in the text as PP.
43. D. K. Bassett, 'British Commercial and Strategic Interests in the Malay Peninsula during the Late Eighteenth Century', in J. Bastin and R. Roolvink (eds), *Malaysian and Indonesian Studies* (Oxford: Oxford University Press, 1964).
44. Raffles seems to have been the source for this theory of 'piracy' as a result of political disintegration. In a letter to Lord Minto, Raffles uses this to explain Sulu involvement in piracy: 'About fifty years ago they were much devoted to commerce. ... Since that time, it has been subject to constant civil commotions, and the breaking down of the government has covered the Sulu seas with fleets of formidable pirates' (Quoted in *Memoir of the Life*, 63). Tarling (1957) also suggests that declining 'empires' could produce piracy. Using the example of Johore, Tarling writes: 'the decline of an empire would leave at its centres an aristocracy and its followers that, deprived of

imperial revenues, resorted to piratical means of subsistence' (15). This 'decay theory' of piracy has been challenged by J. F. Warren (see the Sulu Zone).

45. Tarling notes that the subsequent Inquiry confirmed neither of these allegations. This emotionally-charged motif of the captured European female recurs: it is part of the initial motivation of Lingard in *The Rescue*.

46. Quoted by Tarling (PP, 114). Dalton's papers are published in J. H. Moor (ed.), *Notices of the Indian Archipelago and Adjacent Countries* (London: Cass, 1967). Pappas has examined in detail the trope of 'piracy' in nineteenth-century writings about Malaya. See P. A. Pappas, 'The Hallucination of the Malay Archipelago: Critical Contexts for Joseph Conrad's Asian Fiction', Unpublished Ph.D. Thesis, University of Essex, 1997.

47. In *Worldly Goods*, Lisa Jardine draws attention to European maritime practices from the Renaissance onwards as a necessary context for European accusations of piracy by others. She notes, for example, the attitude of the Portuguese after da Gama had opened the Indian Ocean to European trade: 'since there were only "infidels" in the region, they were entitled to seize the trade they desired by force, in the name of Christendom' (WG, 368).

48. Warren draws attention to a sarcastic letter by William Lingard to the *Makassarsch Handelsblad* (4 January 1876), in which he criticises Dutch 'laxness' towards piracy, by citing the trading activities of his own ships. See James Francis Warren, 'Joseph Conrad's Fiction as Southeast Asian History: Trade and Politics in East Borneo in the Late Nineteenth Century,' *The Brunei Museum Journal* (1977), 21–34, 27.

49. Consider, for example, relations with Achin, where accusations of piracy derived from the refusal to recognise the 'imperial' claims of Achin – 'the claims of Acheh over its dependencies, which members of the Sultan's family, anxious for revenue, tried to enforce' (Tarling, 1957, 132).

50. James Francis Warren, *The Sulu Zone 1768–1898: the Dynamics of External Trade, Slavery and Ethnicity in the Transformation of a Southeast Asian Maritime State* (Singapore: Singapore University Press, 1981).

51. Warren notes, of the Tirun district of Borneo, 'Until the end of the nineteenth century, all groups were labelled Dayak in official Dutch despatches and occasional travel accounts, whether they were actually Tidong of the Sibuco and Sambakong, Bahau, Wahau, Long Wai, and Tring of the middle Mahakan river, or Segai-i of the upper reaches of the Berau' (84–5).

52. English commercial interests chimed with the evolving role of the Sultanate in the late eighteenth century, and the Sultanate became important to Britain again in the 1860s for commercial and strategic reasons.

53. After 1820 this trade was taken over by North Americans. Raffles was warning Minto as early as June 1811 about the North Americans in the archipelago: 'The Americans, wherever they go, as they have no object but commercial adventure, and as fire-arms are in the highest request ... these would be considered as the most profitable articles' (*Memoir*, 74). Note also the 'New England' arms-dealer with his shot-guns, rifles, and Colt pistols in *The Rescue* (Re, 96).

54. For an account of William Lingard, on whom Conrad seems to have based his Tom Lingard, see Sherry, CEW, 89–118.

55. C. A. Majul makes the point that the Sultanate of Sulu did not fit the model of 'Oriental despotism': the pyramidic structure of sultan, *panglimas* and *datus* with the sultan as the highest political authority, the *panglimas* as his representatives on the various islands of the sultanate, and the *datus* as the local chiefs was more complicated in practice. The *panglimas* could not perform their official duties without the cooperation of the *datus*, and the richest and most powerful *datus* advised the sultan in his council. See C. A. Majul, 'Political and Historical Notes on the old Sulu Sultanate', JMBRAS, XXXVIII, 1 (July 1965).

2 The Advancement of Learning

1. Marco Polo's *Travels* records the 17 years he spent at the court of the great Khan, Kublai. In 1292 he set sail from Zaitun in Fokien province to return to Venice. The fleet sailed down the Chinese coast, crossed the Gulf of Tonking to Champa in Cambodia, and then probably sailed directly to the island of Bintang at the mouth of the Strait of Malacca. They were subsequently delayed for five months on the north-east coast of Sumatra by the monsoon before they could continue their journey by Nicobar and the Andaman Islands in the Indian Ocean. Marsden produced a translation of *The Travels of Marco Polo* (London: Longman, Hurst, Rees, Orme & Brown, 1818).
2. Raffles's *The History of Java*, for example, consciously looks back to it as a model. Bastin, however, is misleading: Marsden's work is not so much a matter of system as a matter of method.
3. According to a footnote in *Memoirs of a Malayan Family* (London: J.Murray, 1830), which Marsden translated, he was introduced to Banks by Captain Thomas Forrest in January 1780 (51). Banks (1743–1820) had been elected President of the Royal Society in 1778 – a position he held until his death in 1820.
4. He became Sub-secretary (1773) and then Secretary (1776) of the Presidency Government.
5. John Gascoigne, *Joseph Banks and the English Enlightenment: Useful Knowledge and Polite Culture* (Cambridge: Cambridge University Press, 1994); hereafter cited as JBEE.
6. Banks's collection, which he started in 1763, became the basis of the British Museum of Natural History.
7. Officially, the Botanic Gardens at Kew belonged to George III.
8. Banks's close friendship with the Earl of Sandwich played an important part in the development of his career. Sandwich seems to have had a hand in Banks's election as President of the Royal Society; he also facilitated Banks's voyage with Cook.
9. The Admiralty had a key role in the linkage of science and empire, and here Marsden could help Banks: Marsden was Second Secretary at the Admiralty (1795–1804) and then First Secretary (1804–1807).
10. In *Science in the Service of Empire: Joseph Banks, the British State and the Uses of Science in the Age of Revolution* (Cambridge: Cambridge University Press, 1998), Gascoigne notes the symbiosis between 'the growth of commerce

and the exploitation of science', drawing particular attention to 'the imperial use of botany' (12); hereafter citied as SSE.

11. Banks was also later to be the recipient of half of Raffles's natural history collection, put together while he was in Sumatra (1818–1823). The other half was lost in the fire on board the *Fame* (1823). Banks and Raffles were also instrumental in the establishment of the London Zoo: on his visit to England in 1817, Raffles was keen to set up a Zoological Society of London on the model of the Jardin des Plantes in Paris. On his return to London in 1826, Raffles put this project into effect.

12. Banks was accompanied on the *Endeavour* by Daniel Carl Solander (1733–1782), a protégé of Linnaeus at the University of Uppsala. In 1763, Dr Solander had joined the staff of the British Museum as a Keeper of the Natural History collections with the task of classifying, describing, and cataloguing its collection of plants, insects, mammals, birds, fishes, and reptiles. Solander worked closely with Banks until his death: he worked with him on the *Flora Kewensis*, the catalogue of Kew Gardens, and on Banks's major botanical work, the unpublished *Florilegium*. Like Banks – and like Linnaeus and Buffon – Solander was a Fellow of the Royal Society.

13. Linnaeus's disciple, Solander, also took part in the voyage of the *Endeavour*. Pratt takes the publication of Linnaeus's *The System of Nature* in 1735 as the starting point for 'the new knowledge-building project of natural history' (Pratt, 24). She notes how 'Linnaeus' students ... began turning up everywhere collecting plants and insects, measuring, annotating, preserving, making drawings, and trying desperately to get it all home intact' (Pratt, 25). However, as my account makes clear, this activity had started in England in the Renaissance. Linnaeus initiated a 'totalising, classificatory project' (Pratt, 28), but the start of such a project is already implicit in Bacon.

14. On the other hand, as Julie R. Solomon points out, there were arguments in the Renaissance that painters and men of scientific and technological expertise should be taken on voyages: painters 'to bring the descriptions of all beasts, birds, fishes, trees, townes, etc.' (Hakluyt, 338) and geographers 'to make description of the landes discovered'. As she points out, Raleigh's 1585 voyage to establish a permanent English settlement in the 'new world' took John White, a painter, and Thomas Harriot, a mathematician, to create 'maps that provided strategic geographical information' and to supply 'visual and verbal descriptions of native culture, climate, and commodities' (529). See Julie R. Solomon, '"To Know, To Fly, To Conjure": Situating Baconian Science at the Juncture of Early Modern Modes of Reading', *Renaissance Quarterly*, vol. 44 (1991), 513–58. I am grateful to Eliane Glaser for drawing this article to my attention.

15. I am grateful to Judith Hawley for pointing out to me the danger, in statements such as this, of colonising the past through imposing twentieth-century concepts, categories, and disciplinary divisions on a quite different scientific practice.

16. J. C. Beaglehole (ed.), *The Endeavour Journal of Joseph Banks 1768–1771*, 2 vols (Sydney: Angus & Robertson, 1962); hereafter cited as EJ. Hawkesworth's account of Cook's first voyage was based on Banks's journal. Banks also helped prepare the edition of Cook's journals of the third voyage.

17. M. Foucault, *The Archeology of Knowledge*, trans. A. M. Sheridan Smith (London: Routledge, 1997), 33–4.

18. Antonio Pérez-Ramos, 'Bacon's Legacy', in Markku Pettonen (ed.), *The Cambridge Companion to Bacon* (Cambridge: Cambridge University Press, 1996), 311–34, 316; hereafter cited in the text as CCB.

19. Thomas Sprat, *History of the Royal Society* (1667; reprinted London: Routledge and Kegan Paul, 1959), 35–6. Sprat was not alone in claiming Bacon as a precursor for the Royal Society. Joseph Glanvill, for example, had asserted that 'Salomon's House in the NEW ATLANTIS was a Prophetick Scheam of the ROYAL SOCIETY'. See R. S. Woolhouse, *The Empiricists* (Oxford: Oxford University Press, 1988).

20. This frontispiece seems to have been originally intended for a work by John Beale.

21. It could be argued that Bacon's presence and invocation by Sprat is strategic: through Bacon, Sprat is able to assert a courtly tradition, affirming the loyalty of experimental science to the restored monarchy, occluding the scientific achievements of the republican period by asserting a dynastic connection to Bacon. Michael Hunter, in *Science and Society in Restoration England* (Cambridge University Press, 1981), hereafter cited as SSRE, argues that the frontispiece was originally intended for a work by John Beale, which was overtaken by Sprat's *History*; he notes Beale's assertion that 'our way to support our owne Enterprise is to devise all wayes to revive Lord Bacons lustre', and accordingly the frontispiece was designed as 'a pictorial celebration of Francis Bacon and the Stuart monarchy' (SSRE, 195–6).

22. The compass was introduced into Europe by the Arabs, but was probably invented by the Chinese – as, of course, were printing and gunpowder.

23. Michel Malherbe, 'Bacon's Method of Science', CCB, 75–98, 75. Malherbe has argued that 'as far as the method of science' was concerned, Bacon's *instauratio* was a dead end as early as the seventeenth century. Antonio Pérez-Ramos has similarly argued that it is a misconception to see Bacon as 'the father of British empiricism' because 'British' empiricists in fact derive from Descartes and continental philosophy (CCB, 113). Lisa Jardine has suggested that the inductive method is less important than Bacon's 'actual involvement in the intellectual and technological ferment of emerging 17th-century science', 'A Cogitative Courtier', THES (9 October 1998), 27.

24. However, it is important not to over-identify the Royal Society with Baconianism, just as it is important not to identify Restoration science with the Royal Society. Hunter states that the vitality of the former and the existence of the latter are purely coincidental.

25. See also 'Of Tribute', B. Vickers, (ed.), *Francis Bacon* (Oxford: Oxford University Press, 1996), 34–6.

26. AL, 256. Rawley originally published this translation in the same volume as *Sylva Sylvarum: or A Natural Historie*.

27. In 'Geography and Some Explorers', Conrad similarly affirms a Baconian model of science: 'Descriptive geography, like any other kind of science, has been built on the experience of certain phenomena and on experiments prompted by that unappeasable curiosity of men which their intelligence has elevated into a quite respectable passion for acquiring knowledge' (LE, 2).

28. It is no surprise, therefore, that the only 'inventor' named among the 'principal inventors' honoured by statues in the College is Christopher Columbus.

29. Joseph Acosta, *The Naturall and Morall Historie of the East and West Indies* (London: Edward Blount & William Aspley, 1604). I am grateful to Martin Dzelzainis for drawing my attention to Acosta's work (and for other advice relating to Bacon).

30. On Cook's second voyage, Banks was replaced by the German naturalist, Johann Reinhold Forster. Although Banks's journal wasn't published until 1962, it is interesting to note that Forster, in his *Observations Made during a Voyage round the World* (1778), uses similar categories for his account of the people of the South Seas: food; dress; ornaments; language; marriage; cultivation; cloth-making; basket-making; houses; boat-building; dance, music, poetry, and dramatic performances; disease and medicine; religion; mythology; cosmogony; worship.

31. Peter Hulme and Ludmilla Jordanova (eds), *The Enlightenment and Its Shadows*, 4.

32. Rosi Braidotti, *Nomadic Subjects* (New York: Columbia University Press, 1994), 49; hereafter cited as NS.

33. In this context, it is significant that Salomon's House is described as 'the very eye of this kingdom' (AL, 267).

34. Edward Said, *Orientalism* (1978; New York: Vintage Books, 1979), 6, 7.

35. Kenneth R. Andrews, *Trade, plunder and settlement: Maritime enterprise and the genesis of the British Empire, 1480–1630* (Cambridge University Press, 1984), 31.

36. As Solomon observes, it is significant that Bacon, in *New Atlantis*, describes scientists as 'Merchants of Light': the empirical backbone of the scientific venture is conceived of in terms of merchant journeying (520).

37. Lisa Jardine, 'Alien Intelligence: Mercantile Exchange and Knowledge Transactions in Marlowe's *The Jew of Malta*' in *Reading Shakespeare Historically* (London: Routledge, 1996), 102; hereafter cited in the text as RSH.

38. Fernand Braudel, *Civilisation and Capitalism 15th–18th Century*, vol.II (London: Collins, 1982), 410.

39. This is most evident in his engagement with cannibalism, HS, 390.

40. In this context, it is worth noting Brooke's reference to the 'general rule' for his Journal 'of never giving any native statements unless they go far to verify my own actual observations' (EB, I, 81).

41. P. J. Marshall notes how 'it was the duty of the Company's servants to keep copious records and to send copies of them home to their superiors in London' (*The Exotic in the Enlightenment*, 49). He also draws attention to the Company's practice of 'surveys', which involved more than just detailed mapping, but 'the collection of data of all sorts about geology, products and population' (50). Gullick notes how this practice of textual production continued a hundred years later: after the extension of British rule to the western Malay states in 1874, administrators were required to maintain journals of their daily working activities. See J. M. Gullick, *Malay Society in the late Nineteenth Century* (Singapore: Oxford University Press, 1987), 8.

42. Raffles, on the other hand, in his construction of 'original' cultures, is manifestly engaged in an ideological work.

43. The association of the inhabitants of the region with piracy – and the possibly uncertain boundary between 'trade' and 'piracy' – has already been discussed. See above p. 41.
44. This trope of 'the lazy native' is addressed by Syed Hussein Alatas in *The Myth of the Lazy Native* (London: Frank Cass, 1977).
45. See J. De V. Allen, 'Two Imperialists: A Study of Sir Frank Swettenham and Sir Hugh Clifford,' JMBRAS, xxxvii.1 (July 1964), 41–73. Robert Young quotes the following passage from Renan on 'regeneration', which shows clearly what 'regeneration' comes to imply: 'The regeneration of the inferior or degenerate races by the superior races is part of the providential order of things for humanity. ... Nature has made a race of workers, the Chinese race ... a race of tillers of the soil, the Negro ... a race of masters and soldiers, the European race'. *La réforme intellectuelle et morale de la France* (1871), quoted CD68–9.
46. Homi Bhabha, *The Location of Culture* (Routledge, 1994), 70.
47. Lady Sophia Raffles, *Memoir of the Life and Services of Sir Thomas Stamford Raffles, FRS etc.* (London: John Murray, 1830), 8; hereafter cited as *Memoir*. Lady Raffles was his second wife.
48. Raffles, Report to Lord Minto (10 June 1811), *Memoir*, 61.
49. Raffles could advise Minto on the characters of local rulers and the best ways to approach them.
50. Said notes that William Jones arrived in India to take up a post with the East India Company in 1783; in January 1784 he convened the inaugural meeting of the Asiatic Society of Bengal 'which was to be for India what the Royal Society was for England' (*Orientalism*, 78). The Batavian Society of Arts and Sciences was founded in 1778. At that time it was closely tied to the VOC: the Governor-General was automatically President; directorships were limited to members of the Governing Council. It had been moribund since 1792. Raffles revised the 1800 Rules of the Society to conform to the model of the Asiatic Society of Bengal. The Society lapsed back into inactivity again in 1816 with the return of Java to Dutch rule.
51. Marsden's *History of Sumatra* was presented as the model for their activities.
52. Thomas Stamford Raffles, *The History of Java* (1817). All references are to the reprint (Kuala Lumpur: Oxford University Press, 1965), cited as HJ.
53. See, for example, his footnote on the upas tree (HJ, 43).
54. Dirk van Hogendorp, *A Description of Java and its principal Productions ...* (1800); usually referred to by the shortened version of its Dutch title, *Bericht*.
55. Paul Wheatley, in his *Impressions of the Malay Peninsula in Ancient Times* (Singapore: Eastern University Press, 1964), provides a similar ideological distinction between 'savagery' and 'barbarism' in his account of the Neolithic people who migrated into Malaya from south-west China. They had 'attained to a barbarism which offered boundless opportunities for advancement', whereas their Palaeolithic predecessors lived 'in a state of stultifying savagery'. The mark of this advance was their farming, which meant 'they could discriminate between capital and income by consuming the increase of their animals while yet retaining in perpetuity their seed and stock' (17).
56. Anthony Forge, 'Raffles and Daniell: Making the Image Fit', in Andrew Gerstle and Anthony Milner (eds), *Recovering the Orient: Artists, Scholars,*

Appropriations (Chur, Switzerland: Harwood Academic Publishers, 1994), 109; hereafter cited as RO. I am heavily indebted to Forge in the following discussion of the illustrations.

57. Banks had taken Alexander Buchan along on the *Endeavour* to draw human figures, but Buchan died at Matavi Bay on 17 April 1769 early in the voyage.

58. Forge shows how these eighteenth-century traditions of representation relate to eighteenth-century artistic practices. Forge's argument is, however, somewhat undermined by the plates for Cook's *A Voyage Towards the South Pole* (1777), which include portraits of Polynesians which are neither Europeanised 'Noble Savages' nor 'depraved, fierce, subhuman'. Indeed, the plates include portaits of named individuals – for example, 'Otoo King of Otaheite', an engraving by J. Hall after William Hodge.

59. There were, in addition, two illustrations of weapons; two of landscapes; two of houses; and only a single human figure (the frontispiece).

60. *Malay Annals*, trans. John Leyden (London: Longman, Hurst, Rees, Orme & Brown, 1821).

61. Gullick suggests that the 1824 Anglo-Dutch Treaty and the 1826 Anglo-Siamese Treaty (which conceded to the East India Company what became the Straits Settlements) together with the lifting of restrictions on the emigration of Chinese from the south-east provinces of China (which provided a work-force) led to the transformation of peninsular Malaya. See J. M. Gullick, *Malay Society in the late Nineteenth Century: The Beginning of Change*, 2.

62. Tarling, PP, 18.

63. Tarling, 1957, 5.

64. D. J. M. Tate, *Rajah Brooke's Borneo* (Hong Kong: John Nicholson, 1988), 43; hereafter cited as RBB.

65. For a more detailed account of local politics, see Spenser St John, *The Life of Sir James Brooke, Rajah of Sarawak* (Edinburgh: William Blackwood, 1879). St John worked as Private Secretary to Brooke (in his capacity as Governor of Labuan) from 1845 to 1855, and then took over from Brooke as British Consul-General to the native states of Borneo until 1860.

66. In 1846, however, Raja Hassim and his family were murdered in a palace coup, and the Navy came in to support Brooke. As a result, in 1847, Brooke was confirmed in his tenure of Sarawak, and the island of Labuan was ceded to England. Brooke now 'set the pattern for "white raja" administration: a paternal informal government' (SH, 160).

67. As Gullick notes, the State Councils established in Selangor and Perak in 1877 as part of the Residency system had a precedent in the Sarawak Council of State established by Brooke in 1855. Hugh Low was a protégé of Brooke. J. M. Gullick, *Rulers and Residents: Influence and power in the Malay States 1870–1920* (Singapore: Oxford University Press, 1992), 39.

68. James Brooke, *Proposed Exploring Expedition to the Asiatic Archepelago.* Originally published in *Geographical Journal*, VIII.iii (1838), it appears as Appendix 1 in EB, II, i–xv.

69. He also compares the proposed expedition to African and Polar exploration.

70. Slavery in the archipelago did not, for example, have the racial dimension found in slavery in the United States and West Indies. Philip Holden notes

also (in a private communication) that anti-slavery was part of the construction of English liberal identity in the early nineteenth century. Thus Brooke was using a familiar political idiom, but the prevalent discourse of slavery encouraged a misperception of the Malay system.

71. Brooke had been collecting 'every known particular of the various islands of the Archipelago', G. L. Jacob, *The Raja of Sarawak* (London: 1876), I, 66.

72. Pratt, 25. Pratt derives the term from Daniel Boorstin, *The Discoverers* (New York: Random House, 1983), 16.

73. The importance and persistence of Raffles's views in the English colonisation of Malaya is suggested by W. H. Treacher's *Annual Report* (published in the *Pahang Government Gazette*, September 1901). Treacher raises a problem: 'The principal industry, that of mining, being practically controlled by Chinese and a few Europeans, it has been asked what has British Protection done for the Native peasantry, "the real Malay".' The answer could well have been written by Raffles: 'The reply is that it has given him security for life and property, unknown before to the common people, when wives, daughters, and orchards were at the mercy of the aristocracy; it has given him a perfect title to his land; ... it has abolished slavery and piracy; it has established the reign of law and equity throughout the land ... and it has freed him from arbitrary taxation and forced levies and the system of *kra* or compulsory labour'. In short, he concludes: 'The only complaint he can make is that the British advisers have not *forced* him to become industrious by making him work after the manner of the Dutch with their natives in the East Indies'.

74. As Marlow observes in *Lord Jim*: 'You know that sailor habit of referring to the weather in every connection' (LJ, 122). Marlow is being *faux naif*: the 'habit' was part of a sailor's training.

75. Brooke's experiences seem to lie behind Karain's meetings with the gunrunners in 'Karain: A Memory': 'He said himself that on such occasions he was only a private gentleman coming to see other gentlemen ... I fancy that to the last he believed us to be emissaries of Government, darkly official persons furthering by our illegal traffic some dark scheme of high statecraft. Our denials and protestations were unavailing' (TU12). They also obviously influence Lingard's involvement in Wajo politics in *The Rescue*. See Andrzej Braun, 'The Myth-Like Kingdom of Conrad', *Conradiana*, X.1 (1978), 3–16, for Conrad's other uses of Brooke's diaries.

3   The Inward Turn: Wallace and Clifford

1. Hugh Clifford was born in 1866 and died in 1941. I am indebted to Gladys Gaik-choo Saw's pioneering dissertation, 'The Works of Sir Hugh Clifford: A Literary and Biographical Approach', Unpublished MA Thesis, University of Malaya, 1969, for much of the biographical information that follows.

2. Clifford returned to Singapore as Governor and High Commissioner in 1927, after service in Trinidad, Ceylon, the Gold Coast and Nigeria. After two years as Governor, he resigned and retired to England.

3. In 1893 Reid had persuaded Swettenham to write a series of tales and sketches for the *Straits Times*. These had just been published in book-form as *The Real Malay*.

4. Clifford's reviews appeared under the pseudonym, 'The Worm'.
5. Joseph Conrad, 'An Observer in Malaya', NLL, 79–82.
6. NLL, 82. See also Letter to Clifford, 9 October 1899, CL2, 199–202.
7. Letter to William Blackwood, 13 December 1898, CL2, 129–130.
8. Richard Curle, 'Joseph Conrad: Ten Years Later', *Virginia Quarterly Review*, x (1934), 431; Richard Curle, *The Last Twelve Years of Joseph Conrad* (New York: Russell & Russell, 1968), 109.
9. Clemens, 305–15. Norman Sherry followed up Clemens's work in *Conrad's Eastern World*. Sherry argued, for example, that Wallace's assistant (Charles Allen), a German naturalist (Dr Bernstein), and William Lingard also contributed to the character and career of Stein.
10. Clemens, 309. Thus Wallace describes Delli as 'a most miserable place', with houses 'all of mud and thatch', surrounded by 'swamps and mud-flats' so that 'a single night often gives a fever to newcomers' (188–9); while Conrad refers to it as a 'miserable town of mud hovels' and Heyst expresses his fear that Morrison might be 'in for a bout of fever' (*Victory*, 13).
11. See A. R. Wallace, *A Narrative of Travels on the Amazon and Rio Negro* (London: Ward, Locke & Co., 1889).
12. James Marchant, Introduction to *Alfred Russel Wallace: Letters and Reminiscences* (London: Cassell & Co, 1916), xl; hereafter cited in the text as LR.
13. As Young points out, race theorists had similar problems with the population of Europe. See Robert Young, *Colonial Desire: Hybridity in Theory, Culture and Race* (London: Routledge, 1995), 75ff; hereafter cited as CD.
14. J. S. Mill, *Dissertations and Discussions*, I, 160.
15. Conrad to Cunninghame Graham, 7 October 1907, CL3, 491.
16. As Young observes, 'the possibility of enculturation means that everyone is at least potentially equal to everyone else' (CD, 33).
17. Thus, for example, Marsden follows the Enlightenment idea that each nation has a distinctive character, which has developed in relation to climate. See CD, 38.
18. This is perhaps most familiar through Pope's use of this model in *The Dunciad*.
19. The dominance of polygenism in this period meant that 'the modern style of anthropological analysis of different cultures in their own particular, discrete terms' (CD, 48) was not an option. This could only emerge at the end of the nineteenth century with the decline of polygenist thinking.
20. 100. He describes this group as 'being of a very deep brown colour, with broad nose, and thick hair' (100). Blumenbach gained possession of many of his skulls through his contact with Joseph Banks; the third edition was dedicated to Banks.
21. Knox, described by Young as 'a Saxon supremacist' (CD, 85), denied that either time or climate affected national character, and argued instead for 'the unalterable characters of races' (CD, 78).
22. The political orientation of the Ethnological Society is suggested by its history: the Aborigines' Protection Society, founded in 1837 to counteract the trend towards the extinction of indigenous peoples, became the Ethnological Society in 1843. Wallace had no time for the Anthropological Society. He referred to it, in a letter to Darwin (2 October 1865), as 'that

bête noire, the Anthropological Society' (LR, 165). In a later letter to Darwin (30 August [1868]), he referred scathingly to 'the anthropologists' who 'make the red man descend from the orang, the black man from the chimpanzee' (LR, 221).

23. As Young notes, the use of the term 'type' was a rhetorical strategy to sidestep the theoretical and terminological difficulties of 'species' and 'race' (CD, 13). The 'founding textbook' (CD, 66) of the new anthropology was Josiah C. Nott and George R. Gliddon, *Types of Mankind* (London: Trübner, 1854).

24. J. Buettner-Janusch, in his review of C. S. Coon's *The Living Races of Man*, spells out the implications of Mendel for a theory of race: 'A race of *Homo sapiens* is a Mendelian population, a reproductive community of individuals sharing a common gene pool.' See J. Buettner-Janusch, *American Journal of Physical Anthropology*, 25 (1966).

25. Hugh Clifford, *In Court and Kampong* (London: Grant Richards, 1897), viii; hereafter cited as ICK.

26. The 'Preface' supplies a clue when it compares its account of the 'local holy man' with 'his prototype in the *Naulakha*' (ICK, 21).

27. It is evident in *Soldiers Three* (1888) and *The Light That Failed* (1891).

28. Rod Edmond writes about the European use of the Pacific as an 'imaginary zone' (RSP, 131) onto which European concerns could be projected.

29. Hugh Clifford, *Studies in Brown Humanity* (London: Grant Richards, 1898), ix; hereafter cited as SBH. The sub-title, *Scrawls and Smudges in Sepia White and Yellow*, points to a more complex ethnic mix than a binary opposition can adequately control.Thus 'His Little Bill', for example, offers not a binary opposition but an evolutionary 'scale'.

30. See Alatas, *The Myth of the Lazy Native* (London: Frank Cass, 1977), for a full discussion of this stereotype.

31. See J. G. Frazer, *The Golden Bough*, 2 vols (London: Macmillan, 1890) for accounts of similar beliefs in other cultures and similar taboos relating to pregnancy.

32. Young notes the relevance to this story of the 'attraction/repulsion dialectic' ascribed to inter-racial sexuality (CD, 196).

33. Donna Harraway, *Primate Visions: Gender, Race, and Nature in the World of Modern Science* (London: Routledge, 1989), 5; hereafter cited in the text as PV.

34. As McClintock puts it: 'The primate body became a symbolic space for reordering and policing boundaries between humans and nature, women and men, family and politics, empire and metropolis' (IL, 216).

35. Consider, for example, the contrasting representations of the Malay lover and the European wife in *Since the Beginning*.

36. Stephen Greenblatt, *Renaissance Self-Fashioning: From More to Shakespeare* (University of Chicago Press, 1980), 224–5, 227–8; hereafter cited as RSF. Greenblatt is drawing on Daniel Lerner, *The Passing of Traditional Society: Modernising the Middle East* (New York: Free Press, 1958).

37. Edmund Spenser joined Lord Grey's administration in Ireland in 1580; Greenblatt analyses how Spenser's experience of colonial rule in Ireland pervades *The Faerie Queene* (RSF, 186).

38. Hugh Clifford, *Since the Beginning: a Tale of an Eastern Land* (London: Grant Richards, 1898), 33; hereafter cited as SB.

39. There are similarities between Frank Austin's situation in Pelesu and Hugh Clifford's in Pahang as described in his 1888 diary (now in the Arkib Negara, Kuala Lumpur).

40. Compare this with Willems after his first encounter with Aissa in *An Outcast of the Islands*, where an impulse to 'revolt' gives way to 'a depraved sense of pleasure' (OI, 72–3).

41. Compare with Aissa, who is of Arab and Iraqi extraction, or Jewel in *Lord Jim*, whose father and grandfather both seem to have been Dutch.

42. Clifford's story, 'A Daughter of Mohammedans', which he wrote in August 1898, should also be considered here. This story of Minah and her devotion to her husband, despite his development of leprosy, is also the story of the non-transmission of an 'unspeakable' disease. It can thus be read as a counter-version of *Since the Beginning*.

43. Hugh Clifford, *A Freelance of Today* (London: Methuen, 1903); hereafter cited as FT.

44. See Silva Kandiah, 'Hugh Clifford: His Malayan Novels as Studies in Denationalisation', Academic Exercise, University of Singapore, 1972.

45. The likely outcome of this process is suggested by the narrator's observation that he had turned 'from his own kind' to 'herd with natives' (FT, 9).

46. This 'unmapped country' perhaps stands in for the 'unmapped country' of Kelantan which Clifford entered during his pursuit of the 'Pahang rebels' in 1895.

47. It is significant that this implicit support for colonial rule is based on an explicit failure to understand the 'meaning structures' of the society he encounters: 'For the life of him he could not understand why the people, groaning and sweating under all manner of oppressions and spoliations, and possessing no rights of person or property, continued to fight for a system under which they suffered so much evil' (FT, 162). In Curzon's eyes (and perhaps also in Clifford's), the European's 'failure to understand' implies the unreasonableness of Malay behaviour. Curzon's 'failure to understand' is precisely a failure to understand the position of the raja in the Malay system.

48. I am grateful to Philip Holden for the observation that the missing finger clearly stands in for the missing penis.

49. Conrad was critical of this part of the novel. He noted a conflict between Maurice 'carefully shooting at the Dutch officers and then directly afterwards beside himself with horror at the mutilation of the dead bodies', which made him distrust 'both manifestations'. More generally, he described Curzon as 'too emotional to be quite convincing in his emotion'. See Letter to Hugh Clifford, 26 February 1903, CL3, 20–2.

50. Kim F. Hall, in *Things of Darkness: Economies of Race and gender in Early Modern England* (Ithaca: Cornell University Press, 1995), writes of the white male body as the constant referent in colonial writing, a referent which is simultaneously concealed, taken for granted, and projected as the norm. The mutilation – indeed, emasculation – of the white male body brings that concealed norm into consciousness. By making it the object of the gaze, the narrative expresses the anxieties that surround it – the threats and dangers from which its concealment is designed to protect it. McClintock has also noted 'a recurrent doubling in male imperial discourse', where 'imperial

megalomania' encounters fantasies of 'dismemberment and emasculation' (IL, 26–27). This 'crisis in male imperial identity' (IL, 27) issues in disavowal and displacement – in this case, through the demonising of the Malays. See also Julia Kristeva, *Powers of Horror: an Essay in Abjection*, trans. Leon S. Roudiez (New York: Columbia University Press, 1986) and Elizabeth Gross, 'The Body of Signification', in John Fletcher and Andrew Benjamin (eds), *Abjection, Melancholia and Love* (London: Routledge, 1990) for the 'clean and proper' body and the importance of its delimitation for the maintenance of the symbolic order.

51. Felicia Moorsom in 'The Planter of Malata' and Mrs Travers in *The Rescue* are Conrad's versions of this figure.
52. The conclusion, however, softens the criticism of this upper-class culture.
53. Compare this with Travers's class-based reading of Lingard in *The Rescue* (Re, 129ff).
54. The historical model for this hostage-taking was probably Tenhku Uma's capture of the SS *Hok Canton* in June 1886, where the captives included the wife of the Dutch captain. Saw notes also the capture of the crew of the *Nisero* in November 1883 when it ran aground of the west coast of Achin.

4 Cultural Diversity and Originary Identity: *Almayer's Folly* and *An Outcast of the Islands*

1. For an account of conspiracy in Conrad's fiction, see Teng Hong-Shu, 'Conrad and Conspiracy', Unpublished Ph.D. Thesis, University of London, 1999.
2. See Pappas.
3. Joseph Conrad, *Almayer's Folly*, 6–7.
4. The captain of the *Patna* is also 'a sort of renegade New South Wales German' (LJ, 14).
5. As Owen Knowles notes in his Introduction to the Everyman edition of *Almayer's Folly* (London: Everyman, 1995), 'the hero of adventure fiction conceived as a model of right conduct is, through Lingard, transformed into a new type of "hero" whose exploits derive from a dangerously ambiguous marriage of adventurous impulse, mercantilism and empire-building' (xxiv). The obvious model for such a hero is James Brooke (see Introduction). Similarly, as Andrea White suggests, young Almayer, 'strong in arithmetic; ready to conquer the world' (AF, 5), with his admiration for Lingard's smart business transactions (AF, 8), represents an embourge-oisification of the adventure hero: 'Others might have set out to "woo fortune" but not in traders' warehouses' (JCAT, 122).
6. Contrast, for example, John C. Hutcheson, *The Penang Pirate* (London: Blackie & Son, 1886), which, despite its title, actually features Chinese pirates.
7. The 'fight with the sea-robbers, when he rescued, as rumour had it, the yacht of some big wig from home, somewhere down Carimata way' (OI, 14) encapsulates what was to become *The Rescue*. 'Rumour', of course, hasn't quite captured the full picture. The historical William Lingard rescued a Dutch

man-of-war stranded on a reef in 1869 and destroyed a fleet of 'Lanun pirates' in 1875. (Hans van Marle, 'Jumble of Facts and Fiction: The First Singapore Reaction to *Almayer's Folly'*, *Conradiana* 10.2 [1978], 161–6, 165–6.) The fictional Tom Lingard was in alliance with the 'Lanun pirates'.

8. Dain Maroola actually takes his name from a Bugis who acted as the Bornean agent in Berau for Conrad's employer, Syed Mohsin Bin Salley Ali Jaffree (JCMN, 48). In the manuscript, he is described as coming from Lombok rather than Bali, and, as Gordan records, various elements in the published text show that 'Lombok remained in Conrad's imagination as the home of Maroola' (JCMN, 49).

9. *Almayer's Folly* is set in east Borneo in around 1887. After Brooke's intervention in Sarawak, the English were increasingly interested in west and north Borneo, while the Dutch renewed their interest in the remainder. *Almayer's Folly* and *An Outcast of the Islands* involve Bugis political ambitions in Sambir (as *Lord Jim* involves Bugis political ambitions in 'Patusan'); *The Rescue* focuses on the Wajo succession in Celebes.

10. In the same way, Dain Maroola's mission in Sambir is gradually disclosed after Almayer has presented the cover-story that Dain wanted 'to collect trepang and birds' nests', while Dain himself has made it clear that he 'did not want to buy gutta-percha or beeswax' (AF, 57).

11. The precise cultural coding of Almayer's meal of fish and rice is made clear in 'Falk'. Schomberg scornfully contrasts Falk's meal of 'rice and a little fish' with the 'meat' he provides 'all the year round' for his patrons; he hammers home the point by adding 'I am not catering for a dam' lot of coolies' (Ty, 174).

12. *An Outcast of the Islands*, 116.

13. The effect is similar to that which Andrew Michael Roberts has commented on, in relation to gender, in *Chance*. See 'Secret Agents and Secret Objects: Action, Passivity, and Gender in *Chance'*, *The Conradian*, 17.2, 89–104.

14. See Robert Hampson, '"The Genie out of the Bottle": Conrad, Wells, Joyce and *The Arabian Nights'* in Peter L. Caracciolo (ed.) *'The Arabian Nights' in English Literature* (London: Macmillan/New York: St Martin's Press, 1988), 218–43.

15. Sobhana Kumaran, 'The representation of the colonial subject in Rudyard Kipling's Indian fiction and Joseph Conrad's Malay novels', Unpublished Ph.D. Thesis, University of London, 2000. A similar appropriation – although it can hardly be seen as an act of resistance – is Mrs Willems's use of one of Almayer's books as a clothes-hook (OI, 301).

16. See Anne McClintock, *Imperial Leather: Race, Gender and Sexuality in the Colonial Contest* (London: Routledge, 1995), 181ff; hereafter cited as IL.

17. Young has noted the problematic nature of the post-colonial adoption of the term 'hybridity'. As he observes, the term is derived from biology and botany, where it signifies 'an animal or plant, produced from the mixture of two species' (*Webster's Dictionary*, 1828), but, once applied to humans, it brings with it the nineteenth-century race theory of different human species which was set against the earlier (and modern) idea of the unity and single origin of the human race (CD, 6ff). To add to the cultural mixing in this instance, Verdi's opera is probably being played on a German music-box (such as the Polyphon made in Leipzig around 1880).

18. Whereas the historical Olmeijer was Eurasian, it is implied that both of Almayer's parents were Dutch. William Thorn, in *The Conquest of Java* (London: 1812), noted that, in 1812 at least, 'with very few exceptions, that which is emphatically called the Mother Land, or Mother Country, is only known by name, and this is particularly the case with the Batavian women, few of whom are Europeans by birth'.

19. The 'chance visitor from Europe' mentioned at the end of *An Outcast* – 'a Roumanian, half naturalist, half orchid-hunter for commercial purposes' (OI, 360–1) – also describes to a 'surprised Almayer' the 'wonders of European capitals' (OI, 361). However, since this visit takes place during Nina's absence at school in Singapore, it cannot be seen as instrumental in Almayer's formation of his European dreams.

20. John Splinter Stavorinus, in *Voyages to the East Indies* (London: 1798), had commented on Dutch men with Asian or Eurasian wives, who, 'when they went back to Europe', often took the children with them, while leaving the wife behind.

21. K. S Maniam, *The Return* (1981; London: Skoob Pacifica, 1993).

22. According to Gordan, however, the Olmeijer family settled in Java in the eighteenth century (JCMN, 37).

23. See, for example, *Joseph Conrad: Betrayal and Identity*, 11–31. Gordan, however, suggests that Conrad's narrative 'completely disregarded the normal Dutch tolerance for Eurasians' (JCMN, 39). See also the letter to the *Straits Times*, 17 January 1896, quoted by van Marle in 'Jumble of Facts and Fiction' (164–5), which makes the same point.

24. *The Location of Culture*, 2. However, by 'performance', I would not want to suggest a voluntarist subject creating an identity through instrumental action. As Butler puts it, 'performativity must be understood not as a singular or deliberate "act", but, rather, as the reiterative and citational practice by which discourse produces the effects that it names' (*Bodies That Matter*, 2). It is 'a process of reiteration by which both "subjects" and "acts" come to appear' (*BTM*, 9). Similarly, when I refer to 'hybridity', I use it to mean not so much a mixing (as in the organic hybrid) as a contestation (as in Bakhtin's account of the novelistic hybrid). See M. M. Bakhtin, *The Dialogic Imagination* (Austin, Texas: University of Texas Press, 1981), 360.

25. In case this presents too unproblematic a picture of hybridity, comparison should be made with Mochtar Lubis's story 'Burnt to Ashes' in *The Outlaw and Other Stories* (Singapore: Oxford University Press, 1987), which also explores the situation of a part-Dutch, part-Indonesian woman: 'Her father, a Dutchman, was the administrator of a sugar plantation in East Java. Her mother was Javanese' (13). During the period of Japanese occupation, she 'lived among her mother's people and all of her father's Dutch cultural influence quickly faded' (14). Safira's problem ('am I Indonesian or am I Dutch' [15]) is dramatised when both her partner, a member of the Government of the Republic of Indonesia, and a member of the Dutch delegation approach her to work as a spy. As she says, 'life in this country is not easy' (15), but not just because of external pressures: 'often I feel a great passion arise in me to unite myself with Indonesians .... But at other times I feel a strange call, a feeling distant from them, and I think of Papa and I want to know his people' (16).

26. *Nomadic Subjects*, 15, 14.
27. In a letter to Marguerite Poradowska (18 August 1894), Conrad outlined the new novel he had just started writing: 'I am calling it "Two Vagabonds", and I want to describe in broad strokes … two human outcasts such as one finds in the lost corners of the world. A white man and a Malay' (CL1, 171). But, in a later letter to her, he had to report that 'Mrs M. Wood has stolen my title' (CL1, 182–5).
28. Joseph Conrad, *An Outcast of the Islands* (Oxford: Oxford University Press, 1992), edited by J. H. Stape and Hans van Marle, Introduction by J. H. Stape, xxiv; hereafter cited as Stape.
29. Stape reads this as an allusion to Omar, but the situation in which Omar, as the disabled father, is being carried from the catastrophe would seem to rule him out as the referent. He is more clearly equivalent to Aeneas's father, whom Aeneas carries out of Troy, and Babalatchi is the 'piratical and sonless Aeneas'.
30. Cf. 'Karain', where there is the same double-take in relation to Karain as statesman. It raises the question whether the statesmen mentioned by Tennyson's Ulysses are any more significant than Karain.
31. For the rhizome, see Gilles Deleuze and Félix Guattari, *A Thousand Plateaus: Capitalism and Schizophrenia* (London: Athlone, 1988), 3–25.
32. See Cedric Watts, *The Deceptive Text: an Introduction to Covert Plots* (Sussex: Harvester, 1984), 47.
33. Jean-Luc Godard and Jean-Pierre Gorin, *Letter to Jane*, 1972.
34. As Lingard suspects, Hudig had exactly the same objectives (OI, 18). Hudig's attempt to use Willems to learn the navigation secrets of Lingard's river anticipates Abdulla's actions.
35. See *Negara*, 89–91, 204–5; A. K. Nielsen, *Leven en Avonturen van een Oostinjevaarder op Bali* (Amsterdam, 1928), cited in *Negara*, 206.
36. Alice Meynell, 'Decivilised', *National Observer* (24 January 1891), reprinted in *The Rhythm of Life* (1893) and as Appendix to *Almayer's Folly* (Everyman, 1995), 190–2, to which all references are made.
37. From an additional paragraph to the 'Author's Note' written by Conrad for the Heinemann Collected edition (1921).
38. He goes on: 'For, their land – like ours – lies under the inscrutable eyes of the Most High'. There is an obvious (but, at the time, covert) instability about that phrase 'like ours': it equivocates between the reader's 'land' and the novelist's; it thus marks a cultural division between the reader and the novelist at the very moment of using an appeal to this shared 'land' as the basis for affirming a common humanity. Ironically, there is more similarity between Poland and Malaysia than between either and England: where Malaysia was an area of contention between Dutch and English imperialists, Poland was divided between Austria, Prussia, and Russia.
39. Clifford Geertz, *The Interpretation of Cultures* (New York: Basic Books, 1973), 35; hereafter cited as IC.
40. This should be contextualised by reference to the problematic nature of the humanist attempt to 'take no account of race or colour' (TU, 26). As GoGwilt observes: 'The impulse to take an impartial view of the world's inhabitants is compromised by the very indifference to racial or ethnic difference upon which such a view is predicated' (IW, 45).

41. However, the novel also notes 'the sense of superior virtue that leaves us deaf, blind, contemptuous and stupid before anything which is not like ourselves' (OI, 254). There is clearly a certain instability in the narratorial position.

5 Encountering the Other: 'Race' and Gender in 'The Lagoon' and 'Karain'

1. Roland Barthes, *S/Z* (Paris: Editions du Seuil, 1970), trans. Richard Miller (New York: Hill and Wang, 1974), 18.
2. Private communication.
3. I have discussed *Almayer's Folly* in relation to Schopenhauer and Victorian erotophobia in *Joseph Conrad: Betrayal and Identity*. See also J.D. Patterson, 'The Representation of Love in the Novels of Joseph Conrad: 1895–1915', D.Phil. Thesis, Oxford University (1984). In addition, I am grateful to Dr Zawiah Yahya for drawing my attention to the way in which the representation of Nina draws on and repeats conventional European representations of Malay women. As she argued in her paper, 'Of White Man and Brown Woman in Colonialist Discourse', given at the 34th International Congress of Asian and North African Studies, Hong Kong 1993: 'Western discourse has constructed the oriental woman as a relentless and perversely sexual animal'.
4. For the *femme fatale*, see Elaine Showalter, *Sexual Anarchy: Gender and Culture at the 'Fin de Siècle'* (London: Bloomsbury, 1991), 144–68, and Rebecca Stott, *The Fabrication of the Late Victorian 'Femme Fatale'* (London: Macmillan, 1992); for the figuring of the colonial space as female and the situating of women and non-Europeans as part of nature not culture, see Helen Carr, 'Woman/Indian: "The American" and His Others', in Francis Barker *et al.*, *Europe and Its Others* (Colchester: University of Essex Press, 1985), 14–27; for an exploration of such figuring in Conrad's work, see Padmini Mongia, 'Empire, Narrative, and the Feminine in *Lord Jim* and "Heart of Darkness"', in Keith Carabine, Owen Knowles, and Wieslaw Krajka (eds), *Contexts for Conrad* (Boulder: East European Monographs, 1993), 135–50. See also Susan Jones, *Conrad and Women* (Oxford: Clarendon Press, 2000), 10, for Aissa as *femme fatale*.
5. Joanna de Groot, '"Sex" and "Race": The Construction of Language and Image in the Nineteenth Century', in Susan Mendus and Jane Rendall (eds), *Sexuality and Subordination* (London: Routledge and Kegan Paul, 1989).
6. This reality had already been glimpsed in *An Outcast*. Babalatchi observed to Lingard: 'We Malays hear many sounds near the places where men are buried' (OI, 231–2), and asked him 'do you white people ever hear the voices of the invisible ones?' (OI, 231).
7. Compare with Clifford in *Studies in Brown Humanity*, cited p. 85 above.
8. Conrad wrote to Cunninghame Graham (8 February 1899) that 'Fraternity means nothing unless the Cain-Abel business' (CL2, 159). Kristeva has observed that 'the assertion "all men are brothers" has to include "that portion of conflict, hatred, violence and destructiveness" that is part of the reality of "fratricidal closeness"' (J. Kristeva, *Nations Without Nationalism* [New York: Columbia University Press, 1993], 27).

9. 'Ghost-writing (in) "Karain"'. I am indebted to Conroy's paper for certain points in my discussion of 'Karain'. For other recent work on 'Karain', see Erdinast Vulcan and Andrew Michael Roberts. See also Mark A. Wollaeger, *Conrad and the Fictions of Skepticism* (Stanford: Stanford University Press, 1990), 42–51.

10. Richard Ambrosini, *Conrad's Fiction as Critical Discourse* (Cambridge: Cambridge University Press, 1991), 75. Ambrosini here fuses two distinct issues: (1) the narrator's use of theatrical references; (2) the theatrical quality of Karain's power. The former is obviously revealing about the narrator; the latter relates to the nature of leadership in Malay culture.

11. GoGwilt provides an analysis of this thread motif (IW, 48–9).

12. Both Karain's curiosity about Queen Victoria and the gun-runners' inventiveness have a proleptic function (like many other details in this second section).

13. Consider the implications of 'words are spoken that take no account of race or colour' (TU, 26).

14. Karain's story about a Dutchman and a Malay woman told to an English audience is a story about cultural displacement that involves a further cultural displacement in its telling.

15. As GoGwilt observes, the European narrator's 'nostalgia for a lost era of adventure ... crucially distorts the historical and political backdrop to the story. The inner tale describes a series of disruptions mapped out across all of Southeast Asia and obscurely alluding to a whole history of "native risings". The narrator, fixated on the immobility of Karain's "conquered foothold", fails to grasp that it is only a launching ground for some (unnamed) military offensive – though he himself is the one providing guns for such an offensive' (IW, 56). Karain's home is in South Celebes; his 'conquered foothold' is in Mindanao.

16. A fifth kingdom was under European domination; Si Dendring, formerly dependent on Boni, had also recently become an independent kingdom (NEBC, 61).

17. Brooke mentions a 'rajah Karain' whom he met in Celebes (NEBC, 111). In March 1840, Karain visited Brooke on board the *Royalist* (NEBC, 122).

18. The scene of reading, after all, involved a newspaper account relating to 'the intelligence of various native risings in the Eastern Archipelago' (TU, 3). Curiously, although Karain has been involved in anti-colonial struggles against both the Dutch and the Spanish, he seems to have a blind spot towards the English. The narrator suggests that he seems to identify Victoria with memories of his dead mother (TU, 13). His acceptance of the charm with its Jubilee sixpence again might suggest that Karain identifies with English colonised subjecthood even as he buys weapons to resist the Dutch. (In the same way, Karain might be read as rejecting the 'oriental' *femme fatale* but subjecting himself to an idealised image of woman, in the shape of Queen Victoria.) See Linda Dryden, *Joseph Conrad and the Imperial Romance* (London: Macmillan, 2000).

19. First published in *The Week's News*, 28 April 1888; collected in *In Black and White* (Allahabad: A. H. Wheeler & Co, 1888; London: Sampson Low, 1890).

20. Wollaeger observes: 'he cannot allow the perception of irrational forces to invade the refuge of rational civilisation represented by Greenwich standard

time.The felt presence of absent causes must be categorized and dismissed as superstition in order to preserve the sheltered retreat afforded by the spatialized regularity of time' (48).

21. Compare with the juxtaposition of Umbopa and Quatermain in *King Solomon's Mines*.

22. Bongie, for example, reads this episode as revealing 'a condescending attitude towards native superstition'. See Chris Bongie, *Exotic Memories: Literature, Colonialism, and the Fin de Siècle* (Stanford: Standford University Press, 1991), 160; hereafter cited as EM.

23. Conroy describes this direct address to the reader as a 'slippage' which foregrounds the narrator's own moment of narration (9).

24. For an analysis of the description of the Strand, see Robert Hampson, '"Topographical Mysteries": Conrad and London', in Gene M. Moore (ed.), *Conrad's Cities: Essays for Hans van Marle* (Amsterdam/Atlanta GA: Rodopi, 1992), 159–74, esp.161–3; also Wollaeger, 42–5. Wollaeger is particularly good on the narrator as a man 'consistently unwilling to pursue the implications of his own words' (47) and resistent to 'unsettling redefinitions of the real' (48).

25. GoGwilt expresses this in different terms. For him, the tale's framework raises the question 'whether the outer narrative ... uses Karain's experience to fit an imperial idea, or whether the inner tale subverts that narrative frame' (IW, 46).

26. Paul Ricoeur, 'Civilisation and National Cultures', in *History and Truth*, trans. Charles A. Kelbley (Evanston, Illinois: Northwestern University Press, 1965), 278.

6   Speech and Writing in *Lord Jim*

1. See Robert Hampson, 'The Affair of the Purloined Brother', *The Conradian*, VI.2 (June, 1981), 5–16, and *Joseph Conrad: Betrayal and Identity*, 116–136. More recently see White, JCAT, 65, 171, and Dryden.

2. As Edmond notes, Kingston and Ballantyne 'translated the Pacific archive into the emergent form of boys' adventure fiction' (RSP, 146). These works also tended to register their own intertextual relation to the archive: in *Coral Island*, for example, Jack is a great reader of books of travel, while Ralph finds a volume of Cook's *Voyages*. Thus Jim's reading of adventure books places him in relation to a tradition of boy's adventure, and his own entry into that tradition is facilitated because those adventures are already textualised not only in the authors' use of the archive but also in their heroes' awareness of the same textual tradition.

3. EM,175.

4. EM, 176. Or, as Henricksen puts it, 'the Patusan episode exists as an evocation and critique of the romantic, self-congratulatory myths produced by early capitalism in its narrating of its own encounter with other cultures' (Bruce Henricksen, *Nomadic Voices: Conrad and the Subject of Narrative* [Urbana & Chicago: University of Illinois Press, 1992] 98).

5. The pioneering work on Conrad and gossip is Michael Greaney's Ph.D. thesis, which will be published as *Conrad's Storytellers* (Cambridge:

Cambridge University Press, forthcoming). Interestingly, Gordan described Conrad's sources for the first part of the novel as 'hearsay', while he shows how Conrad draws on his reading of material relating to Brooke for Patusan (JCMN, 64).

6. Thus Brown's challenge to Jim, 'Have we met to tell each other the story of our lives?' (LJ, 383), represents a refusal of communality. Cf. Mr Jones's abrupt response to Heyst: 'We haven't met to talk about the weather' (V, 376).

7. This picture of a community of expatriates constituting itself through gossip should be related to Jan B. Gordon's description of gossip as 'a virtual icon of dispossession and discursive homelessness'. See: *Gossip and Subversion in Nineteenth-Century British Fiction* (London: Macmillan, 1996), 352; hereafter cited in the text as GS.

8. Patricia Meyer Spacks, *Gossip* (New York: Alfred A. Knopf, 1985); hereafter cited in the text as *Gossip*. Spacks defines 'idle talk' in terms of situations in which 'gossipers bandy words and anecdotes about other people, thus protecting themselves from serious engagement with one another' (*Gossip*, 7).

9. On the issue of the gendered narrative, see Nina Pelikan Strauss, 'The Exclusion of the Intended from Secret Sharing in Conrad's *Heart of Darkness*', Novel 20 (1987), 123–37 and Andrew Michael Roberts, *Conrad and Masculinity* (London: Macmillan, 2000)

10. 'One of us' is a problematic term. See, for example, the note by Cedric Watts to his 1986 Penguin edition, which ends by suggesting that the phrase means variously: 'a fellow-gentleman', 'a white gentleman', 'a white man', 'a good sea-man', 'an outwardly-honest Englishman', 'an ordinary person', and 'a fellow human being' (354). Whatever the meaning, the phrase operates by a process of inclusion and exclusion. The uncertainty of reference – the shifting senses of 'one of us' – is appropriate for a narrative concerned with the uncertainties of Jim's identity and status.

11. Compare Mrs Brookenham's role in Henry James's *The Awkward Age*, where gossip is similarly disguised as professional consultation.

12. Schomberg re-appeared in 'Falk' as both a hotel-keeper and 'an awful gossip' (Ty, 155). As Falk complains: 'this fellow is always making out something wrong, and can never rest till he gets somebody to believe him' (Ty, 198).

13. Padmini Mongia, '"Ghosts of the Gothic": Spectral Women and Colonized Spaces in *Lord Jim*', in Andrew Michael Roberts (ed.), *Conrad and Gender* (Amsterdam: Rodopi, 1993), 1–16, 1; hereafter cited in the text as GG. Mongia reads this story as a Gothic narrative competing with the adventure narrative in Patusan; at the heart of this narrative is 'the confusion between mothers and daughters … and the daughter's struggle to create for herself an identity separate from her mother's' (GG, 9).

14. Ranajit Guha, *Elementary Aspects of Peasant Insurgency in Colonial India* (New Delhi: Oxford University Press, 1983), 17. As GoGwilt puts it: 'A story of women's experience, it disrupts the masculine codes of Marlow's story of Jim's claim to heroic fame. Indeed, the story becomes something of an allegory of the exclusion of women's experience in the narrative' (IW, 103).

15. Gordan sees the source for this as Brooke's formal handing over of Sarawak to his nephew (JCMN, 69ff).

16. This narrative of male succession might be seen as a fantasy of patrilineality effected through a denial of the female role in reproduction.

17. Ironically, what differentiates it is the absence of any sense of desire or passion. As Mongia notes, 'the maternal bodies twin secrets of procreation and sexuality are signified only by Jewel's mother', while Jewel herself 'remains curiously asexual' (GG, 10). Sexual knowledge and sexual transgression are located in the missing narrative of Jewel's mother. The story also differs in its conclusion: usually, the man leaves and the woman dies; this time the man dies and the woman leaves. See Pratt, 97.

18. Conrad, of course, had read Clifford's *Since the Beginning*, where Frank Austin makes financial arrangements for his Malay lover, when he returns to England, but makes no allowance for the strength of her emotional attachment to him.

19. Arnold van Gennep, *La Formation des légendes*, (Paris: Ernest Flammarion, 1910), 160.('Fantasy and error are normal, even with us, and ... the tendency to distortion ... comes into play from the moment of observation. It comes into play particularly when transmission is by means of oral narration.')

20. Van Gennep, 1–2.

21. Francis M. Cornford, *Thucydides Mythistoricus* (London: Edward Arnold, 1907), 130.

22. Cornford, 131.

23. Wallace wrote to his mother (25 December 1855), after spending Christmas with Brooke in Sarawak: 'Many of the distant tribes think the Rajah cannot be a man ... and I have no doubt for many years after his death he will be looked upon as a deity and expected to come back again' (LR, 59).

24. In the Fort Cornwallis Museum, Penang, there is the Sri Rambai Cannon, which was submerged in front of the Esplanade in 1871 and raised from the sea in 1880. The cannon 'refused to leave the seabed until Tunku Kudin tied a rope to it and ordered it to rise'. Cf. the firestone in Babalatchi's flintlock. He tells Lingard: 'I had it from a man wise and pious that lives in Menang Kabau. ... He spoke words over that stone that make its sparks good' (OI, 233).

25. Sura's belief in the 'soul of things' and his attendance at 'rice sowings and reapings' (LJ, 266) bears some similarity to J.G. Frazer's account of 'The Rice Mother in the East Indies', which describes practices based on 'the simple conception of the rice as animated by a soul like that which these people attribute to mankind'.See Sir James Frazer, *The Golden Bough: a Study in Magic and Religion* (Abridged Edition) (London: Macmillan & Co., 1963), 544. For an account of Conrad's possible knowledge of Frazer's work, see my essay 'Frazer, Conrad and the "truth of primitive passion"', in Robert Fraser (ed.), *Sir James Frazer and the Literary Imagination* (London: Macmillan, 1990), 172–91.

26. Cornford, 132. *Almayer's Folly* offers an alternative (or supplementary) explanation: 'The coast population of Borneo believes implicitly in diamonds of fabulous value, in gold mines of enormous richness in the interior. And all those imaginings are heightened by the difficulty of penetrating far inland,

especially on the north-east coast, where the Malays and the river tribes of Dyaks or Headhunters are eternally quarrelling' (AF, 39). Raffles noted how the ruler of Succadana 'still possesses the large diamond which has been for eight generations in his family' (*Memoir*, 142).

27. Conrad began work on 'The Rescuer' in March 1896; he finished Part I in June 1896 and Part II by March 1898; he put it aside in early 1899 and didn't finish it until 1919. See Owen Knowles, *A Conrad Chronology* (London: Macmillan, 1989), 23, 24, 30–32.

28. W. J. Ong, *Orality and Literacy: The Technologising of the Word* (London: Routledge, 1982), 23.

29. Allan Simmons, 'Ambiguity as Meaning in Joseph Conrad's Fiction', Unpublished Ph.D. Thesis, University of London, 1991, 125.

30. A version of this reputation is also current in the archipelago through his 'famous gardens' in which 'you can find every plant and tree of tropical lowlands' (LJ, 349).

31. This scientific project has left its trace in other parts of Conrad's Malay fiction: in Almayer's father, who worked at the Botanical Gardens in Buitenzorg; in the Roumanian, 'half naturalist, half orchid-hunter for commercial purposes' who visits Almayer in Sambir (OI, 361); even in 'Amy Foster', where the narrator (like Stein) has worked in his youth as the assistant to a naturalist in the archipelago.

32. Stein's activities as the 'correspondent of learned societies' (LJ, 217) is given a further twist, when Marlow playfully describes the discourse of astronomers (about the 'irregularities' of planetary movements and the 'aberrations' of planetary light) as 'scientific scandal-mongering' (LJ, 218). His subsequent playful reference to the 'irregularities and aberrations' of Patusan being known in 'government circles in Batavia' (LJ, 218) neatly ties together the scientific project, gossip, and the information gathering of colonial powers.

33. 'Geography and Some Explorers' was written in November 1923.

34. There is also attention, as in *Almayer's Folly*, to the nature of archipelago slavery: '... her daughters, her servants, her slave-girls. You know how it is in these households: it's generally impossible to tell the difference' (LJ, 256).

35. Compare the position in Berau, where the indigenous inhabitants had been subdued by Malay Muslims. After a civil war in 1844, part of the region became the Sultanate of Sambaliung (under Rajah Allam or Allang); the remainder became the Sultanate of Gunung Tabur.

36. See F. McNair, *Perak and the Malays*, 130–1, where the Bugis are described as 'intelligent, courageous, and enterprising' but also vengeful.

37. Brooke is echoing Raffles, who advocated 'continuing to the peasant the protection of laws made for his benefit, by allowing full scope to his industry, and encouraging his natural propensity to accumulate' (HS, 161). As Chapter 2 showed, both men think in terms of *homo economicus* and enterprise.

38. As Henricksen puts it, there is the strong possibility that each re-telling will carry 'its own pragmatic spin' (NV, 87).

39. Thus, on 17 September 1895, Conrad wrote to Garnett announcing the completion of *An Outcast of the Islands*. As with the completion of *Almayer's*

Folly, the announcement was given the form of a death notice ('the sad death of Mr Peter Willems'), followed by an account of the funeral: 'As soon as I recovered from the shock I busied myself in arranging the affairs of the two inconsolable widows of our late lamented friend ...' and so on through an account of the behaviour of Lingard, Almayer and Mrs Willems at the funeral (CL1, 245).

40. On the other hand, Milner has noted that there is no evidence of a developed sense of interiority in Malay writings of the pre-colonial period (IPCM, 22). The emphasis on formal codes and ceremonies in *kerajaan* ideology means that 'personal individuality' as conceived of in modern Europe is a problematical category. The concept of 'personal individuality' through which a post-colonial criticism might operate is thus itself an ethnocentric category. To the same effect, Henricksen notes MacIntyre's observation that, in heroic societies, 'values were given and one's place was predetermined, as were one's privileges and duties: "A man in heroic society is what he does;" a person and his actions are identical, and one "has no hidden depths"' (NV, 94). See Alasdair MacIntyre, *After Virtue: a Study in Moral Theory* Notre Dame, Ind.: University of Notre Dame Press, 1981), 26.

41. 'The Other exists only as empty sign, a cipher' (Stephen Greenblatt, *Marvellous Possessions: the Wonder of the New World* [Oxford: Clarendon Press], 60).

42. Bongie suggests an alternative approach: if Patusan is self-consciously a romance world, occupying an impossible 'exotic space', then Doramin and his circle are not representations of Malays (or Bugis), but self-conscious recourse to the static characterisation of romance (EM, 176). This sits uneasily, however, with Sherry's presentation of Nakhoda Trong as a real-life source (CEW, 161).

43. As Henricksen notes, 'There are Brown-legends as there are Jim-legends' (NV,101). Indeed, Brown's history is 'a dark version of Jim's story': 'Jim and Brown are two sides of the same historical phenomenon, the white man's impact on other races and cultures' (NV,100).

44. In 1875, the Spanish destroyed the town of Jolo and the settlements of Maimbung and Parang; they then established a garrison and several forts on the island of Jolo.

45. These were laid 1870–71.

46. It is interesting that Brown regards his attack on Dain not as a 'massacre' but as 'a lesson' (LJ, 404) – the same language used of Brooke's attack on Beting Marau.

47. Later, after the news of Brown's attack on Dain reaches Patusan, again 'rumours flew': 'The robbers were coming back, bringing many others with them, in a great ship, and there would be no refuge in the land for anyone' (LJ, 410). Again, the politics of rumour testify to the 'sense of utter insecurity' (LJ, 410) that now affects Patusan, while also reflecting the Malay awareness of European power.

48. Compare with Clifford's *A Freelance of Today*, where the English hero experiences frustration at the Achinese reluctance to engage in fighting – and their preference for either symbolic display or ambush.

49. Marshall Sahlins, *Islands of History* (Chicago: Chicago University Press, 1985). Sahlins interposes a third term between the terms 'structure' and

'event': 'the situational synthesis of the two in a "structure of the conjuncture"' (xiv). An event is 'not simply a phenomenal happening' but is always 'appropriated in and through the cultural scheme' (xiv). For 'event', 'structure', and 'conjuncture' in a different sense, see F. Braudel, *The Mediterranean and the Mediterranean World in the Age of Philip II*, 2 vols (London: Fontana/Collins, 1975). Sahlins's 'structure of the conjuncture' allows more for 'the structuration of the situation': it is a 'situational set of relations, crystallised from the operative cultural categories and actors' interests' (125).

50. Sahlins makes the point that this is not simply an intercultural collision. He argues that the Hawaiian priests and the Hawaiian King conceived different relations in the same event, 'whence their own conflict in the structure of the conjuncture' (xvii). Edmond discusses Sahlins's account of the death of Cook and criticisms of it (RSP, 58–61).

51. Stephen Greenblatt, *New World Encounters* (Berkeley: University Of California Press, 1993), x; hereafter cited as NWE.

52. In the same way, in Sahlins's account, with the unexpected return of Cook, 'the tensions and ambivalences in the social organisation' of Hawaii (particularly between the priests and the king) were now revealed (127).

7 Absence and Presence in *Victory*

1. Edward Said, 'Conrad: the Presentation of Narrative', in *The World, The Text and The Critic* (1984; London: Vintage, 1991), 90–110; 95; hereafter cited as WTC.

2. As Robert Eaglestone puts it, 'the text's very existence is based on absence': 'representation comes into existence in order to represent what is absent' (*Ethical Criticism: Reading After Levinas* [Edinburgh: Edinburgh University Press, 1997], 46).

3. The incident hinges on the treatment of country traders by the colonial powers. In this case, the Portuguese authorities in Delli had 'inflicted a fine' (V, 12) and arrested Morrison's brig with the intention of taking the ship from him. 'Freya of the Seven Isles' similarly shows a Dutch gunboat captain using his powers to arrest (and wreck) the ship of his rival in love, an English country-trader.

4. The Suez Canal, the replacement of sailing ships by steam, and the laying of telegraph cables are the late-nineteenth-century technological developments that radically re-shape the archipelago. In 'Falk', the narrator, the young captain of a sailing ship, who is waiting for Falk to tow his ship down-river to the sea, observes: 'I never realised so well before that this is an age of steam. The exclusive possession of a marine boiler had given Falk the whip hand of us all' (Ty, 181).

5. See J. B. Hartley, 'Maps, knowledge, and power', in D. Cosgrove and S. Daniels (eds), *The Iconography of Landscape: Essays on the symbolic representation, design and use of past environments* (Cambridge: Cambridge University Press, 1988), 277–312.

6. The image of radiating lines centred on Samburan also resonates with the earlier name given to Heyst by the island gossip: 'the Spider'.

7. As Spacks puts it, 'At one extreme, gossip manifests itself as distilled malice. It plays with reputations, circulating truths and half-truths and falsehoods' (*Gossip*, 6).

8. Earlier gossip by Schomberg has brought Jones and Ricardo down on him. They tell him of someone they met in Manila who gave them his name: 'He said you set a lot of scandal going about him once' (V, 101). As Spacks observes: 'rarely can one locate with precision the damage gossip causes, yet the chance of damage always remains' (*Gossip*, 51). In this case, the damage Schomberg caused by circulating gossip about another has been repaid by the circulation of gossip about him to Jones and Ricardo.

9. Earlier in the day, Davidson had been told by one of Schomberg's customers that Zangiacomo 'ran amuck' (V, 48), a formula that turns Zangiacomo into a Malay.

10. Barbara Herrnstein Smith, *On the margins of discourse: the Relation of Literature to Language* (Chicago: University of Chicago Press, 1978), 85.

11. GoGwilt, for example, reads Marlow's written report to the 'privileged man' in terms of 'a contest for readership between the "Little Englanders" ... and the promoters of a "Greater Britain"' (IW, 89). Henricksen's approach through pragmatics proposes a reading of the Gentleman Brown episode as 'a dialogic response to this particular narratee', whose belief in his own ethnic group 'is darkly mirrored in Brown's "blind belief in the rightness of his will against all mankind' (NV, 101).

12. The obvious addressee is Marlow. Bongie suggest that Jim's letter is, in effect, an answer to the 'gossipy letters' Marlow wrote in Chapter 15, while Jim came to to terms with the collapse of his old world: 'Perhaps remembering that distant night, Jim himself, when his new world has been folded back into the old, tries to write' (EM, 178).

13. Consider also, on a more trivial level, the ambiguity of whether the 'wonderful presence' refers to the portrait of the father or to the 'heavy frame'.

14. Roland Barthes, *Image Music Text* (London: Fontana, 1977), 141–8, hereafter cited as IMT.

15. J. Derrida, *Dissemination* (Chicago: Chicago University Press, 1981), 146

16. See Hampson, Introduction to the Penguin edition of *Victory* (1989), 17–19.

17. Jerry Brotton, '"This Tunis, sir, was Carthage": Contesting colonialism in *The Tempest* 'in Ania Loomba and Martin Orkin (eds), *Postcolonial Shakespeares* (Routledge, 1998), 23–42; hereafter cited in the text as TT.

18. See Leslie Heywood, 'The Unreadable Text: Conrad and "The Enigma of Woman" in *Victory*', *Conradiana*, 26.1 (Spring 1994), 3–19, for an interpretation of this motif that contests the idea of absolute difference.

19. Paul Brown, '"This thing of darkness I acknowledge mine"': *The Tempest* and the discourse of colonialism', in Jonathan Dollimore and Alan Sinfield (eds), *Political Shakespeare: New essays in cultural materialism* (Manchester: Manchester University Press, 1985), 48–71.

20. Peter Hulme *Colonial Encounters: Europe and the Native Caribbean 1492–1797* (1986; Routledge, 1992), 88–134. Brotton notes how *The Tempest* 'carries resonances of different geographical trajectories' (TT31). Where (post)colonial criticism of the play has emphasised the 'New World' encounter, Brotton attends to the Mediterranean and 'Old World' aspects of the play, the neglected 'eastern frontier' of maritime expansion, to situate the play

precisely at the 'geopolitical bifurcation between the Old World and the New'.

21. The Alfuros were originally from the northern provinces of Celebes.

22. Indeed, Peter Bagnall has convincingly connected Ricardo with the Ripper murders. See Peter Bagnall, 'Joseph Conrad and Jack the Ripper', Unpublished D.Phil. Thesis, University of Oxford, 1998.

23. This is the shift that takes place between Conrad's early and late Malay novels. See Chapter 8 on *The Rescue*.

24. Consider, for example, Mrs Norris (in *Mansfield Park*) who also 'lives alone'.

25. Women also fall into this category. Note Davidson's surprise when he engages Mrs Schomberg in conversation: 'one was inclined to think of her as an It – an automaton, a very plain dummy, with an arrangement for bowing the head at times and smiling stupidly now and then' (V, 40). Silenced by her husband, she nevertheless shows that she has a voice. She also acts: she helps Lena to escape (and perhaps also tries to kill Jones and company by giving them salt water for their voyage).

26. I am following McClintock's use of 'fetishism' to denote practices in which mundane objects become invested with power. McClintock records how Binet brought 'fetish' into the discourse of sexuality in 1880 to signify 'the sexual adoration of inanimate objects' (IL, 189). His major work in this area, 'Le Fétichisme dans l'amour', published in *La Revue Philosophique* in 1887, suggested that all people are fetishists to some extent.

27. Betty Vanderweilen, 'Gender Performance in *Victory'*, *Conradiana* 26.2/3 (Autumn 1994), 201–10, interestingly reads this incident in terms of Lena attempting to invest Heyst 'with what she conceives as his proper patriarchal attitudes' (207).

28. It also registers the material culture of the region. Thus, in Part IV, Chapter 2, she appears in 'the brown and yellow figured Celebes sarong' (V, 293), traditional Bugis cloth.

8 Dialogue and Cross-Dressing in *The Rescue*

1. This strategy of ignorance might be compared to Conrad's use of the covert plot in *Almayer's Folly*: the overt plot is presented through Almayer's consciousness; the covert plot is what Almayer does not see. See Cedric Watts, *The Deceptive Text: an Introduction to Covert Plots* (Brighton: Harvester Press, 1984), 47–53.

2. 'The Rescuer', 570. See, generally, Lingard's account to Mrs Travers, 'The Rescuer', 566 ff.

3. Lingard tries to ignore this dimension of his activities, but Jörgensen insists on making the political implications explicit (Re, 101). In 'The Rescuer', the 'agent for a Dutch crockery house', who is outed by Jörgensen as a Dutch spy, is described as reporting on Lingard's activities.

4 Geoffrey Galt Harpham, *One of Us: the Mastery of Joseph Conrad* (Chicago: University of Chicago Press, 1996), 108; hereafter cited as OU.

5. In this respect, *The Rescue* should be compared with 'The Planter of Malata', which focuses on a similar hopeless passion for an upper-class English woman. Clifford had already approached this territory in *A Freelance of Today*.

6. In 'The Rescuer', this incident leads to Lingard being remembered by the Malays as the European 'who showed respect to our dead as though all had been his brothers' (134).
7. Gun-powder is a scarce (and controlled) commodity.
8. For the significance of New Guinea, see the discussion of Raffles in Chapter 2.
9. See Mundy, NECB, I, 50 ff., 61–5.
10. Tengga similarly exposes European double standards when he questions the injunction not to attack the yacht people: 'We must not touch them because their skin is like yours and to kill them would be wrong, but at the bidding of you whites we may go and fight with people of our own skin and our own faith – and that is good' (Re, 173).
11. Hassim's questions are directly comparable to those faced by Brooke, see pages 69–70 above, and NECB, I, 50ff.
12. For the staging of languages, see Robert Hampson, '"Heart of Darkness" and "The Speech That Cannot Be Silenced",' *English*, 39.163 (Spring 1990), 15–32.
13. Stape, xxiii.
14. Stape, xxiii.
15. 'Dialogue' is a misleading term, since this 'dialogue' between Lingard and Shaw is rather a competition: neither really listens to the other; each wants the other as audience for their own utterance. See Chapter 7, 146–7.
16. Clemens, 310.
17. A. R. Wallace, *The Malay Archipelago*, 3rd edition (London: Macmillan, 1872), 173.
18. See Hampson, 'Frazer, Conrad and the "Truth of Primitive Passion".'
19. Bongie, 174. As Krenn puts it, 'they represent two successive eras in the development of European imperialism (LT, 109). In a letter to Blackwood (CL1, 381), Conrad described Lingard as 'the simple, masterful, imaginative adventurer'. The opening of the novel presents him in relation to an idealised image of Brooke.
20. See LT, 132.
21. Hampson, 'The Speech That Cannot Be Silenced', 18.
22. Juliet McLauchlan, 'A Reconsideration of *The Rescue*', in Mario Curreli (ed.), *The Ugo Mursia Memorial Lectures* (Milan: Mursia International, 1987), 216. Krenn also comments on this element in the novel (LT, 130ff).
23. Reina Lewis, *Gendering Orientalism* (London: Routledge, 1996), 117.
24. Iain Sinclair, *Lights out for the Territory* (London: Granta, 1997), 13.
25. Another context is Immada's sexual cross-dressing in male clothes. Brooke had noted a custom of cross-dressing among the Bugis: 'some men dress like women, and some women like men; not occasionally, but all their lives, devoting themselves to the occupations and pursuits of their adopted sex' (NEBC, 83). Immada's dressing in male clothes is perhaps an understated reference to this practice. In this case, the sarong Lingard intends for Immada is both a misreading of her and an attempt to impose a gender identity upon her.
26. Simon During, 'Rousseau's Patrimony: primitivism, romance and becoming other', in Francis Barker, Peter Hulme, Margaret Iverson (eds), *Colonial Discourse/Postcolonial Theory* (Manchester: Manchester University Press, 1994), 47–71; 60.

27. Brooke responded similarly. After watching an Ilanun 'war-dance', he observed that it 'might have elicited the applause of the opera-house' (EB, I, 198).

9 Homecoming

1. James Clifford, 'On Ethnographic Self-Fashioning: Conrad and Malinowski', in *The Predicament of Culture: Twentieth Century Ethnography, Literature, and Art* (Cambridge, Mass.: Harvard University Press, 1988), 92–113, 100.
2. This 'death in exile' is one of the elements of the plot anticipated by the novel's epigraph: 'Qui de nous n'a eu sa terre promise, son jour d'extase et sa fin en exil?. As Knowles observes, in the notes to his edition, Amiel was referring here to the fate of Moses (165).
3. Mr Siegers, in 'Falk', should be added to this gallery: he 'retired from business on a fortune and got buried at sea going home' (Ty, 179).
4. Serialised in the *Illustrated London News*, 14, 21, 28 December 1901; collected in *Typhoon, and Other Stories*.
5. Julia Kristeva, *Strangers to Ourselves*, includes 'incomprehensible speech, inappropriate behaviour' among the 'difficulties the foreigner will necessarily encounter'(6). She goes on: 'A lost origin, the impossibility to take root, a rummaging memory, the present in abeyance. The space of the foreigner is a moving train. ... As to landmarks, there are none' (7–8).
6. Myrtle Hooper, in '"Oh, I hope he won't talk": Narrative and Silence in "Amy Foster"', *The Conradian*, 21.2 (Autumn, 1996), 51–64, argues that Yanko puts Amy into an impossible position, where she has to choose between her roles as mother and wife: 'by speaking to her child in a strange language, Yanko is, in Amy's eyes, trying to turn the child into a stranger, to replicate in the child his own alienness and difference' (60).
7. Like Kennedy, he seems to have a maritime background. Consider the evidence supplied in the opening paragraph. After refering to a 'dilapidated windmill' and a Martello tower, he comments 'These are the official seamarks for the patch of trustworthy bottom represented on the Admiralty charts by an irregular oval of dots enclosing several figures six, with a tiny anchor engraved among them, and the legend "mud and shells" over all' (Ty, 105).
8. Julia Kristeva, *Nations Without Nationalism*, trans. Leon S. Roudiez (New York: Columbia University Press, 1993), 29. This reading would be contested by Hooper. Hooper attends to Amy Foster's silence in order to challenge Kennedy's narration. She notes the doctor's scientific background, but also how he uses the distance of scientific observation to protect himself from encountering Yanko's Otherness. Kennedy's narrative also involves an Othering of Amy. Hooper, subsequently, reads Amy's silence – not as dullness (the gloss Kennedy provides) – but as Amy's refusal to confirm the doctor's narrative. In the end, instead of offering the multiple voices of the modern ethnographic account, Kennedy's story reveals the relations of power that serve to silence Amy.
9. Cf. GoGwilt's account of Conrad's 'splitting and crossing of European cultural origins', and the question he poses: 'Does Conrad's sense of affiliation to Poland encode a cryptic lost European presence in his work, or does it mark an absence of European political identity?' (IW, 111ff.).

10. See Homi Bhabha, *The Location of Culture*, (London: Routledge, 1994), 57.
11. Frederick Karl, *Joseph Conrad: the Three Lives* (London: Faber, 1979); Bernard Meyer, *Joseph Conrad: a Psychoanalytic Biography* (Princeton: Princeton University Press, 1967), 3.
12 Emmanuel Levinas, *En découvrant l'existence avec Husserl et Heidegger* (Paris: Vrin, 1949; 2nd ed., 1967, 1974), 191. Cited by Colin Davies, *Levinas: an Introduction* (Cambridge: Polity Press, 1996), 33.
13. Levinas, 'The Trace of the Other', 348
14. Andrew Gibson, *Towards a postmodern theory of narrative* (Edinburgh: Edinburgh University Press, 1996), 165. This is taken from Gibson's description of 'the principle of the Creole'.
15. C. Kaplan, 'Deterritorializations: the Rewriting of Home and Exile in Western Feminist Discourse', *Cultural Critique* 6 (Spring 1987), 187–98, 197.

Bibliography

Joseph Acosta, *The Naturall and Morall Historie of the East and West Indies* (London: Edward Blount & William Aspley, 1604).

W. H. Davenport Adams, *'In Perils Oft': Romantic Biographies Illustrative of the Romantic Life* (London: John Hogg, 1885).

Aijaz Ahmad, *In Theory: Classes, Nations, Literatures* (London: Verso, 1992).

Syed Hussein Alatas, *Thomas Stamford Raffles 1781–1826: Schemer or Reformer* (Sydney: Angus and Robertson, 1971).

Syed Hussein Alatas, *The Myth of the Lazy Native* (London: Frank Cass, 1977).

J. De V. Allen, 'Two Imperialists: a Study of Sir Frank Swettenham and Sir Hugh Clifford,' JMBRAS, xxxvii.1 (July 1964), 41–73.

Jerry Allen, *The Thunder and the Sunshine: a Biography of Joseph Conrad* (New York: G. P. Putnam's Sons, 1958).

Jerry Allen, *The Sea Years of Joseph Conrad* (London: Methuen, 1967).

Richard Ambrosini, *Conrad's Fiction as Critical Discourse* (Cambridge: Cambridge University Press, 1991).

Kenneth R. Andrews, *Trade, Plunder and Settlement: Maritime Enterprise and the Genesis of the British Empire, 1480–1630* (Cambridge University Press, 1984).

Benedict Anderson, *Imagined Communities* (London: Verso, 1996).

Talal Asad (ed.), *Anthropology and the Colonial Encounter* (London: Ithaca Press, 1975).

Talal Asad, 'The Concept of Cultural Translation in British Social Anthropology', in James Clifford and George E. Marcus (eds), *Writing Culture: the Poetics and Politics of Ethnography* (Berkeley: University of California Press, 1986), 156–64.

Bill Ashcroft, Gareth Griffiths, and Helen Tiffin, *The Empire Writes Back: Theory and Practice in Post-Colonial Literatures* (London: Routledge, 1989).

Francis Bacon, *The Advancement of Learning and New Atlantis* (London: Oxford University Press, 1966).

John R. Baker, *Race* (Oxford: Oxford University Press, 1974).

Peter Bagnall, 'Joseph Conrad and Jack the Ripper', Unpublished D.Phil. Thesis, University of Oxford, 1998.

M. M. Bakhtin, *The Dialogic Imagination* (Austin, Texas: University of Texas Press, 1981).

Nigel Barley, *The Duke of Puddle Dock: Travels in the Footsteps of Stamford Raffles* (London: Viking, 1991).

Nigel Barley, *The Golden Sword: Stamford Raffles and the East* (London: British Museum Press, 1999).

Roland Barthes, *S/Z* (Paris: Editions du Seuil, 1970), trans. Richard Miller (New York: Hill and Wang, 1974).

Roland Barthes, *Image Music Text* (London: Fontana, 1977)

D. K. Bassett, 'British Commercial and Strategic Interests in the Malay Peninsula During the late Eighteenth Century', in J. Bastin and R. Roolvink (eds), *Malayan and Indonesian Studies* (Oxford: Clarendon, 1964).

J. Bastin, 'Raffles and British Policy in the Indian Archipelago, 1811–1816', *JMBRAS* xxvii.1 (May 1954), 100–3.

J. Bastin and R. Roolvink (eds), *Malayan and Indonesian Studies* (Oxford: Clarendon, 1964).

J. C. Beaglehole (ed.), *The Endeavour Journal of Joseph Banks 1768–1771*, 2 vols (Sydney: Angus & Robertson, 1962).

Peter Bellwood, *Prehistory of the IndoMalaysian Archipelago* (North Ryde, NSW: Academic Press Australia, 1985).

Homi Bhabha, *The Location of Culture* (London: Routledge, 1994).

Marialuisa Bignami, 'Joseph Conrad, the Malay Archipelago, and the Decadent Hero', *Review of English Studies*, XXXVIII.150 (1987), 199–210.

Johann Friedrich Blumenbach, *De Generis Humani Varietate Nativa* (1775; third edition, 1795).

Johann Friedrich Blumenbach, *The Anthropological Treatises of Blumenbach and Hunter*, trans. Thomas Bendyshe (London: Longman, Green, Longman, Roberts and Green, 1865).

Chris Bongie, *Exotic Memories: Literature, Colonialism, and the Fin de Siècle* (Stanford: Stanford University Press, 1991).

W. W. Bonney, *Thorns & Arabesques: Contexts for Conrad's Fiction* (Baltimore: The Johns Hopkins University Press, 1980).

Daniel Boorstin, *The Discoverers* (New York: Random House, 1983).

Rosi Braidotti, *Patterns of Dissonance* (Cambridge: Polity Press, 1981).

Rosi Braidotti, *Nomadic Subjects* (New York: Columbia University Press, 1994).

Fernand Braudel, *The Mediterranean and the Mediterranean World in the Age of Philip II*, 2 vols, trans. Sian Reynolds (London: Fontana/Collins, 1975).

Fernand Braudel, *Afterthoughts on Material Civilization and Capitalism*, trans. Patricia M. Ranum (Baltimore: Johns Hopkins University Press, 1977).

Fernand Braudel, *On History*, trans. Sarah Matthews (London: Weidenfield & Nicolson, 1980).

Fernand Braudel, *Civilisation and Capitalism 15th–18th Century*, 2 vols, trans. Sian Reynolds (London: Collins, 1981, 1982).

Andrzej Braun, 'The Myth-Like Kingdom of Conrad', *Conradiana*, X.1 (1978), 3–16.

I. Brockway, *Science and Colonial Expansion: the Role of the British Royal Botanic Gardens* (New York: Academic Press, 1979).

James Brooke, 'Proposed Exploring Expedition to the Asiatic Archipelago', *Geographical Journal*, VIII.iii (1838).

Margaret Brooke, *My Life in Sarawak* (London: Methuen, 1913).

Jerry Brotton, *Trading Territories* (London: Reaktion Books, 1997)

Jerry Brotton, '"This Tunis, sir, was Carthage": Contesting Colonialism in *The Tempest*', in Ania Loomba and Martin Orkin (eds), *Postcolonial Shakespeares* (London: Routledge, 1998), 23–42.

Paul Brown, '"This thing of darkness I acknowledge mine": The Tempest and the Discourse of Colonialism', in Jonathan Dollimore and Alan Sinfield (eds), *Political Shakespeare: New Essays in Cultural Materialism* (Manchester: Manchester University Press, 1985), 48–71.

Charles Buckley, *An Anecdotal History of Old Times in Singapore* (Singapore: Fraser and Neave, 1902).

Judith Butler, *Gender Trouble: Feminism and the Subversion of Identity* (London: Routledge, 1990).

Judith Butler, *Bodies that Matter: On the Discursive Limits of 'Sex'* (London: Routledge, 1990).

Laura Chrisman, 'The Imperial Unconscious? Representations of Imperial Discourse', *Critical Quarterly*, 32, 3 (1990).

Florence Clemens, 'Conrad's Favorite Bedside Book', *South Atlantic Quarterly* XXXVII (1939), 305–15.

Hugh Clifford and Frank Swettenham, *A Dictionary of the Malay Language*, Part 1: A–G (Taiping, Perak: Government Printing Office, 1894–1902).

Hugh Clifford, Personal Diary for 1888, Arkib Negara, Kuala Lumpur.

Hugh Clifford, Personal Diary for 1893, Arkib Negara, Kuala Lumpur.

Hugh Clifford, *In Court and Kampong* (London: Grant Richards, 1897).

Hugh Clifford, *Since the Beginning: a Tale of an Eastern Land* (London: Grant Richards, 1898).

Hugh Clifford, *Studies in Brown Humanity: Scrawls and Smudges in Sepia White and Yellow* (London: Grant Richards, 1898).

Hugh Clifford, 'The Genius of Mr. Joseph Conrad', *North American Review*, 178 (June 1904), 842–52.

Hugh Clifford, *A Freelance of Today* (London: Methuen, 1903).

Hugh Clifford, *Further India* (London: Lawrence & Bullen, 1904).

James Clifford and George E. Marcus (eds), *Writing Culture: the Poetics and Politics of Ethnography* (Berkeley: University of California Press, 1986).

James Clifford, 'On Ethnographic Self-Fashioning: Conrad and Malinowski', in *The Predicament of Culture: Twentieth Century Ethnography, Literature, and Art* (Cambridge, Mass.: Harvard University Press, 1988), 92–113.

H. P. Clodd, *Malaya's First British Pioneer: the Life of Francis Light*, London, 1948.

Mark Conroy, 'Ghostwriting (in) "Karain"', *The Conradian*, 18.2 (Autumn, 1994), 1–16.

James Cook, *A Voyage Towards the South Pole* (1777).

Francis M. Cornford, *Thucydides Mythistoricus* (London: Edward Arnold, 1907).

Richard Curle, *Into the East: Notes on Burma and Malaya* (1923).

Richard Curle, 'Joseph Conrad: Ten Years Later', *Virginia Quarterly Review*, x (1934).

Richard Curle, *The Last Twelve Years of Joseph Conrad* (New York: Russell & Russell, 1968).

Colin Davis, *Levinas: an Introduction* (Cambridge: Polity Press, 1996).

Joanna de Groot, '"Sex" and "Race": the Construction of Language and Image in the Nineteenth Century', in Susan Mendus and Jane Rendall (eds), *Sexuality and Subordination* (London: Routledge and Kegan Paul, 1989).

Gilles Deleuze and Félix Guattari, *A Thousand Plateaus: Capitalism and Schizophrenia* (London: Athlone, 1988).

Jacques Derrida, *Writing and Difference*, trans. Alan Bass (Chicago: University of Chicago Press, 1978).

Jacques Derrida, *Dissemination*, trans. Barbara Johnson (Chicago: Chicago University Press, 1981).

C. Dobbin, *Islamic Revivalism in a Changing Peasant Economy: Central Sumatra 1784–1847* (London & Malmo: Scandinavian Institute of Asian Studies, 1983).

Simon During, 'Rousseau's Patrimony: Primitivism, Romance and Becoming Other', in Francis Barker, Peter Hulme, Margaret Iverson (eds), *Colonial Discourse/Postcolonial Theory* (Manchester: Manchester University Press, 1994), 47–71.

Linda Dryden, '"Karain": Constructing the Romantic Subject', *L'Epoque Conradienne* (1997), 29–50.

Linda Dryden, 'Conrad and Hugh Clifford: an "Irreproachable Player on the Flute and A Ruler of Men"', *The Conradian*, 23.1 (Spring 1998), 51–73.

Linda Dryden, *Joseph Conrad and the Imperial Romance* (London: Macmillan, 2000).

Robert Eaglestone, *Ethical Criticism: Reading after Levinas* (Edinburgh: Edinburgh University Press, 1997).

Rod Edmond, *Representing the South Pacific: Colonial Discourse from Cook to Gauguin* (Cambridge: Cambridge University Press, 1997).

Daphna Erdinast Vulcan, *Joseph Conrad and the Modern Temper* (Oxford: Oxford University Press, 1991).

Lloyd Fernando, 'Conrad's Eastern Expatriates', PMLA 91 (1976), 278–90; reprinted in Keith Carabine (ed.), *Joseph Conrad: Critical Assessments* (Helm Information, 1992), II, 51–70.

Lloyd Fernando, *Scorpion Orchid* (Singapore/Kuala Lumpur: Times Books International, 1992).

Gail Fincham and Myrtle Hooper (eds), *Under Postcolonial Eyes: Joseph Conrad after Empire* (Cape Town: University of Cape Town Press, 1996).

Anthony Forge, 'Raffles and Daniell: Making the Image Fit', in Andrew Gerstle and Anthony Milner (eds), *Recovering the Orient: Artists, Scholars, Appropriations* (Chur, Switzerland: Harwood Academic Publishers, 1994).

J. P. de Fonseka, 'The Muses in Malaya: the Literary Work of Sir Hugh Clifford and Lady Clifford', *British Malaya* (August 1928), 101–3, 108).

Johann Reinhold Forster, *Observations Made during a Voyage round the World* (1778; reprinted Honolulu: University of Hawi'i Press, 1996).

Michel Foucault, *The Order of Things: an Archaeology of the Human Sciences* (1966), (New York: Vintage Books, 1973).

Michel Foucault, *The Archeology of Knowledge* (1969), trans. A. M. Sheridan Smith (London: Routledge, 1997).

Michel Foucault, *Language, Counter-Memory, Practice: Selected Essays and Interviews*, ed. Donald F. Bouchard (Oxford: Basil Blackwell, 1977).

Michel Foucault, *Power/Knowledge: Selected Interviews and Other Writings* (Sussex: Harvester Press, 1980).

R. W. Frantz, *The English Traveller and the Movement of Ideas 1660–1732* (Lincoln, Nebraska: University Studies of the University of Nebraska, 1934).

J. G. Frazer, *The Golden Bough*, 2 vols (London: Macmillan, 1890).

Howard Fry, *Alexander Dalrymple and the Expansion of British Trade* (London: Cass, 1970).

Harry A. Gailey, *Clifford: Imperial Proconsul* (London: Collings, 1982).

Marjorie Garber, *Vested Interests: Cross-Dressing and Cultural Authority* (London: Routledge, 1992).

John Gascoigne, *Joseph Banks and the English Enlightenment: Useful Knowledge and Polite Culture* (Cambridge: Cambridge University Press, 1994).

John Gascoigne, *Science in the Service of Empire: Joseph Banks, the British State and the Uses of Science in the Age of Revolution* (Cambridge: Cambridge University Press, 1998).

Henry Louis Gates (ed.), *'Race', Writing, and Difference* (Chicago: University of Chicago Press, 1986).

Hildred Geertz and Clifford Geertz, *Kinship in Bali* (Chicago: University of Chicago Press, 1975).

Clifford Geertz, *The Interpretation of Cultures* (New York: Basic Books, 1973).

Clifford Geertz, *Negara: the Theatre State in Nineteenth-Century Bali* (Princeton: Princeton University Press, 1980).

Clifford Geertz, *Works and Lives: the Anthropologist as Author* (Cambridge: Polity, 1988).

Clifford Geertz, *After the Fact: Two Countries, Four Decades, One Anthropologist* (Cambridge, MA.: Harvard University Press, 1995).

Andrew Gerstle and Anthony Milner (eds), *Recovering the Orient: Artists, Scholars, Appropriations* (Chur, Switzerland: Harwood Academic Publishers, 1994).

Andrew Gibson, *Towards a Postmodern Theory of Narrative* (Edinburgh: Edinburgh University Press, 1996).

Andrew Gibson, *Postmodernity, Ethics and the Novel* (London: Routledge, 1999).

Christopher GoGwilt, *The Invention of the West: Joseph Conrad and the Double-Mapping of Europe and Empire* (Stanford: Stanford University Press, 1995).

John Gordan, *Joseph Conrad: the Making of a Novelist* (Cambridge, MA: Harvard University Press, 1940).

Jan B. Gordon, *Gossip and Subversion in Nineteenth-Century British Fiction* (London: Macmillan, 1996).

Rupert T. Gould, *John Harrison and his Timekeepers* (London: National Maritime Museum, 1987).

Michael Greaney, 'Conrad's Storytellers', Unpublished Ph.D. thesis, University of Lancaster, 1998.

Derek Gregory, *Geographical Imaginations* (Oxford: Blackwell, 1994).

Stephen Greenblatt, *Renaissance Self-Fashioning: From More to Shakespeare* (University of Chicago Press, 1980).

Stephen Greenblatt, *Marvellous Possessions: the Wonder of the New World* (Oxford: Clarendon, 1988).

Stephen Greenblatt, *New World Encounters* (Berkeley: University of California Press, 1993).

James Greenwood, *The Adventures of Reuben Davidger; Seventeen Years and Four Months Captive Among the Dyaks of Borneo* (London: S. O. Beeton, 1865).

James Greenwood, *The Wild Man at Home, or, Pictures of Life in Savage Lands* (London: Ward, Locke & Co., 1879).

Elizabeth Gross, 'The Body of Signification', in John Fletcher and Andrew Benjamin (eds), *Abjection, Melancholia and Love* (London: Routledge, 1990).

Ranajit Guha, *Elementary Aspects of Peasant Insurgency in Colonial India* (New Delhi: Oxford University Press, 1983).

J. M. Gullick, *Malay Society in the Late Nineteenth Century: the Beginning of Change* (Singapore: Oxford University Press, 1987).

J. M. Gullick, *Rulers and Residents: Influence and Power in the Malay States 1870–1920* (Singapore: Oxford University Press, 1992).

Emily Hahn, *Raffles of Singapore: a Biography* (Singapore: University of Malaya Press, 1968).

D. G. E. Hall, *A History of South-East Asia* (London: Macmillan, 1955).

Kim F. Hall, *Things of Darkness: Economies of Race and Gender in Early Modern England* (Ithaca: Cornell University Press, 1995).

Robert Hampson, 'The Affair of the Purloined Brother', *The Conradian*, VI.2 (June, 1981), 5–16.

Robert Hampson, '"The Genie out of the Bottle: Conrad, Wells, Joyce and *The Arabian Nights*', in Peter L. Caracciolo (ed.), *'The Arabian Nights' in English Literature* (London: Macmillan/New York: St Martin's Press, 1988), 218–43.

Robert Hampson, '"Heart of Darkness" and "The Speech That Cannot Be Silenced",' *English*, 39.163 (Spring 1990), 15–32.

Robert Hampson, 'Frazer, Conrad and the "truth of primitive passion"', in Robert Fraser (ed.), *Sir James Frazer and the Literary Imagination* (London: Macmillan, 1990), 172–91.

Robert Hampson, '"Topographical Mysteries": Conrad and London', in Gene M. Moore (ed.), *Conrad's Cities: Essays for Hans van Marle* (Amsterdam/Atlanta GA: Rodopi, 1992), 159–74.

Robert Hampson, *Joseph Conrad: Betrayal and Identity* (London: Macmillan, 1993).

Geoffrey Galt Harpham, *One of Us: the Mastery of Joseph Conrad* (Chicago: University of Chicago Press, 1996).

Donna Harraway, *Primate Visions: Gender, Race, and Nature in the World of Modern Science* (London: Routledge, 1989).

J. B. Hartley, 'Maps, Knowledge, and Power' in D. Cosgrove and S. Daniels (eds), *The Iconography of Landscape: Essays on the Symbolic Representation, Design and Use of Past Environments* (Cambridge: Cambridge University Press, 1988).

Jeremy Hawthorn, *Cunning Passages: New Historicism, Cultural Materialism and Marxism in the Contemporary Literary Debate* (London: Arnold, 1996).

L. V. Helms, *Pioneering in the Far East* (London: 1882).

Bruce Henricksen, *Nomadic Voices: Conrad and the Subject of Narrative* (Urbana & Chicago: University of Illinois Press, 1992).

G. A. Henty, *In the Hands of the Malays* (London: Blackie & Sons, 1905).

Leslie Heywood, 'The Unreadable Text: Conrad and "The Enigma of Woman" in *Victory*', *Conradiana*, 26.1 (Spring 1994), 3–19.

D. L. Higdon, 'Conrad's Clocks', *The Conradian* 16.1 (September 1991), 1–18.

Diana and Geoffrey Hindley, *Advertising in Victorian England, 1837–1901* (London: Wayland, 1972).

Philip Holden, *Orienting Masculinity, Orienting Nation: W. Somerset Maugham's Exotic Fiction* (Westport, CT.: Greenwood Press, 1996).

Myrtle Hooper, '"Oh, I hope he won't talk": Narrative and Silence in "Amy Foster"', *The Conradian*, 21.2 (Autumn, 1996), 51–64.

Derek Howse, *Greenwich Time and the Discovery of the Longitude* (Oxford: Oxford University Press, 1980).

Peter Hulme and Ludmilla Jordanova (eds), *The Enlightenment and Its Shadows* (London: Routledge & Kegan Paul, 1990).

Peter Hulme, *Colonial Encounters: Europe and the Native Caribbean 1492–1797* (1986; London: Routledge, 1992).

Jefferson Hunter, *Edwardian Fiction* (Cambridge MA.: Harvard University Press, 1982).

John Hunter, *Disputatio Inauguralis Quaedam de Hominum Varietatibus et harum Causis Exponens* (Edinburgh: Balfour & Smellie, 1875).

Michael Hunter, *Science and Society in Restoration England* (Cambridge University Press, 1981).

Michael Hunter, *The Royal Society and Its Fellows 1660–1700: the morphology of an early scientific institution* (Oxford: BSHS Monographs, 1982).

John C. Hutcheson, *The Penang Pirate* (London: Blackie & Son, 1886).

G. L. Jacob, *The Raja of Sarawak* (London: 1876).

Lisa Jardine, 'Alien Intelligence: Mercantile Exchange and Knowledge Transactions in Marlowe's *The Jew of Malta*' in *Reading Shakespeare Historically* (London: Routledge, 1996).

Lisa Jardine, *Worldly Goods* (London: Macmillan, 1996).

Lisa Jardine, 'A Cogitative Courtier', THES (9 October 1998), 27.

Martin Jay, *Downcast Eyes: the Denigration of Vision in Twentieth Century French Thought* (Berkeley: University of California Press, 1993).

Susan Jones, *Conrad and Women* (Oxford: Clarendon Press, 1999).

Sut Jhally, *The Codes of Advertising: Fetishism and the Political Economy of Meaning in the Consumer Society* (London: Frances Pinter, 1987).

Silva Kandiah, 'Hugh Clifford: His Malayan Novels as Studies in Denationalisation', Unpublished Academic Exercise, University of Singapore, 1972.

C. Kaplan, 'Deterritorializations: the Rewriting of Home and Exile in Western Feminist Discourse', *Cultural Critique* 6, (Spring 1987), 187–198.

Frederick Karl, *Joseph Conrad: the Three Lives* (London: Faber, 1979).

Henry Keppel, *The Expedition to Borneo of H.M.S. Dido for the Suppression of Piracy*, 2 vols (London: Chapman & Hall, 1846).

Douglas Kerr, 'Crowds, Colonialism and *Lord Jim*', *The Conradian*, 18.2 (Autumn, 1994), 49–64.

Rudyard Kipling, *In Black and White* (Allahabad: A. H. Wheeler & Co., 1888; London: Sampson Low, 1890).

Rudyard Kipling, *Soldiers Three* (Allahabad: A. H. Wheeler & Co., 1888).

Rudyard Kipling, *The Light That Failed* (1891).

Owen Knowles, *A Conrad Chronology* (London: Macmillan, 1989).

Robert Knox, *The Races of Men* (London: Henry Renshaw, 1850).

Boo Eng Koh, 'Contradictions in Colonial History in *Lord Jim*', *Conradiana*, 28.3 (Autumn 1996), 163–81.

Heliéna Krenn, *Conrad's Lingard Trilogy: Empire, Race, and Women in the Malay Novels* (New York: Garland Publishing, 1990).

Julia Kristeva, *Powers of Horror: an Essay in Abjection*, trans. Leon S. Roudiez (New York: Columbia University Press, 1986).

Julia Kristeva, *Strangers to Ourselves*, trans. Leon S. Roudiez (London: Harvester Wheatsheaf, 1991).

Julia Kristeva, *Nations without Nationalism*, trans. Leon S. Roudiez (New York: Columbia University Press, 1993).

Sobhana Kumaran, 'The Representation of the Colonial Subject in Rudyard Kipling's Indian fiction and Joseph Conrad's Malay novels', Unpublished Ph.D. Thesis, University of London, 2000.

J.D. Legge, 'The Writing of South-East Asian History', in N. Tarling (ed.), *The Cambridge History of Southeast Asia*, vol. I (Cambridge University Press, 1992).

Daniel Lerner, *The Passing of Traditional Society: Modernising the Middle East* (New York: Free Press, 1958).

Emmanuel Levinas, *En découvrant l'existence avec Husserl et Heidegger* (Paris: Vrin, 1949; 2nd ed., 1967, 1974).

Emmanual Levinas, 'The Trace of the Other', in Mark C. Taylor (ed.), *Deconstruction in Context* (Chicago: Chicago University Press, 1986).

Emmanuel Levinas, *Ethics and Infinity* (1982), trans. Richard A. Cohen (Pittsburgh, PA.: Duquesne University Press, 1985).

Emmanuel Levinas, *Time and the Other*, trans. Richard A. Cohen (Pittsburgh, PA.: Duquesne University Press, 1987).

Reina Lewis, *Gendering Orientalism* (London: Routledge, 1996).

J. Leyden (trans.), *Malay Annals* (London: Longman, Hurst, Rees, Orme and Brown, 1821).

Carl Linné, *The System of Nature* (1735).

Mochtar Lubis, *The Outlaw and Other Stories* (Singapore: Oxford University Press, 1987).

Anne McClintock, *Imperial Leather: Race, Gender and Sexuality in the Colonial Contest* (London: Routledge, 1995).

Alasdair MacIntyre, *After Virtue: a Study in Moral Theory* (Notre Dame, Ind.: University of Notre Dame Press, 1981).

Juliet McLauchlan, 'A Reconsideration of *The Rescue*', in Mario Curreli (ed.), *The Ugo Mursia Memorial Lectures* (Milan: Mursia International, 1987),

F. McNair, *Perak and the Malays* (London, 1878).

Mahathir bin Mohamad, *The Malay Dilemma* (Kuala Lumpur: Times Books International, 1970).

C. A. Majul,'Political and Historical Notes on the old Sulu Sultanate', *Journal of the Malaysian Branch Royal Asiatic Society*, XXXVIII, 1 (July 1965).

K. S Maniam, *The Return* (1981; London: Skoob Pacifica, 1993).

James Marchant, *Alfred Russel Wallace: Letters and Reminiscences*, 2 vols (London: Cassell & Co, 1916).

F. S Marryat, *Borneo and the Indian Archipelago* (London: Longman & Co., 1848).

William Marsden, *The History of Sumatra* (1783; reprint of third edition [1811] Kuala Lumpur: Oxford University Press, 1966).

William Marsden (trans.), *The Travels of Marco Polo* (London: Longman, Hurst, Rees, Orme & Brown, 1818).

William Marsden (trans.), *Memoirs of a Malayan Family* (London: J. Murray, 1830).

William Marsden, *A Brief Memoir* (London: Private Circulation, 1838).

P. J. Marshall, *The Exotic in the Enlightenment*.

Fadillah Merican et al., *A View of Our Own: Ethnocentric Perspectives in Literature* (Kuala Lumpur: Universiti Kebangsaan Malaysia, 1996).

Bernard Meyer, *Joseph Conrad: a Psychoanalytic Biography* (Princeton: Princeton University Press, 1967).

Alice Meynell, 'Decivilised', *National Observer* (24 January 1891), reprinted in *The Rhythm of Life* (1893).

J. Hillis Miller, *Fiction and Repetition: Seven English Novels* (Cambridge, MA.: Harvard University Press, 1982).

Anthony Milner, *Kerajaan: Malay Political Culture on the Eve of Colonial Rule* (Tucson: University of Arizona Press, 1982)

A. Milner, *The Invention of Politics in Colonial Malaya* (Cambridge: Cambridge University Press, 1995.

Padmini Mongia, '"Ghosts of the Gothic": Spectral Women and Colonized Spaces in *Lord Jim*', in Andrew Michael Roberts (ed.), *Conrad and Gender* (Amsterdam: Rodopi, 1993), 1–16.

J. H. Moor (ed.), *Notices of the Indian Archipelago and Adjacent Countries* (1837; London: Frank Cass, 1968).

Bart Moore-Gilbert (ed.), *Writing India 1757–1990: the Literature of British India* (Manchester: Manchester University Press, 1996).

Michael Valdez Moses, *The Novel and the Globalization of Culture* (New York: Oxford University Press, 1995).

Rodney Mundy, *Narrative of Events in Borneo and Celebes,* 2 vols (London: John Murray, 1848).

Josiah C. Nott and George R. Gliddon, *Types of Mankind* (London: Trübner, 1854).

W. J. Ong, *Orality and Literacy: the Technologising of the Word* (London: Routledge, 1982).

P. A. Pappas, 'The Hallucination of the Malay Archipelago: Critical Contexts for Joseph Conrad's Asian Fiction', Unpublished Ph.D. Thesis, University of Essex, 1997.

Mungo Park, *Travels in the Interior of Africa* (Edinburgh: Adam & Charles Black, 1860).

Benita Parry, *Conrad and Imperialism: Ideological Boundaries and Visionary Frontiers* (London: Macmillan, 1983).

J.D. Patterson, 'The Representation of Love in the Novels of Joseph Conrad: 1895–1915', Unpublished D.Phil. Thesis, Oxford University (1984).

Markku Pettonen (ed.), *The Cambridge Companion to Bacon* (Cambridge: Cambridge University Press, 1996).

M. J. Pintado, *Portuguese Documents on Malacca*, vol. 1, 1509–11 (Kuala Lumpur: National Archives of Malaysia, 1993).

Mary Louise Pratt, 'Field Work in Common Places' in James Clifford and George Marcus (eds), *Writing Culture* (Berkeley: California University Press, 1987).

Mary Louise Pratt, *Imperial Eyes: Travel Writing and Transculturation* (London: Routledge, 1992).

Richard Price, *First-Time: the Historical Vision of an Afro-American People* (Baltimore: Johns Hopkins University Press, 1980).

Lady Sophia Raffles, *Memoir of the Life and Public Services of Sir Thomas Stamford Raffles FRS etc.* (London: John Murray, 1830).

Thomas Stamford Raffles, *The History of Java* (1817; reprinted Kuala Lumpur: Oxford University Press, 1965).

Neil Rennie, *Far-Fetched Facts: the Literature of Travel and the Idea of the South Seas* (Oxford: Clarendon Press, 1995).

G. J. Resink, 'The Eastern Archipelago under Joseph Conrad's Western Eyes', *Indonesia's History Between the Myths* (The Hague: W. van Hoeve, 1968), 307–87.

Thomas Richards, *The Commodity Culture of Victorian Britain: Advertising and Spectacle, 1851–1914* (London: Verso, 1990).

Thomas Richards, *The Imperial Archive: Knowledge and the Fantasy of Empire* (London: Verso, 1993).

Paul Ricoeur, 'Civilisation and National Cultures', in *History and Truth*, trans. Charles A. Kelbley (Evanston, Illinois: Northwestern University Press, 1965).

Andrew Michael Roberts, 'Secret Agents and Secret Objects: Action, Passivity, and Gender in *Chance*', *The Conradian*, 17.2, 89–104.

Andrew Michael Roberts, *Conrad and Masculinity* (London: Macmillan, 2000).

William R. Roff, *The Origins of Malay Nationalism* (New Haven: Yale University Press, 1967).

G. S. Rousseau and Roy Porter (eds), *Exoticism and the Enlightenment* (Manchester: Manchester University Press, 1990).

Richard Ruppell, '"Heart of Darkness" and the Popular Exotic Stories of the 1890s', *Conradiana*, 21 (1989), 3–14.

Richard Ruppell, 'Yanko Goorall in The Heart of Darkness: "Amy Foster" as Colonialist Text', *Conradiana* 28.2 (Summer 1996), 126–32.

Kiernan Ryan (ed.), *New Historicism and Cultural Materialism: a Reader* (London: Arnold, 1996).

Marshall Sahlins, *Islands of History* (Chicago: Chicago University Press, 1985).

Edward Said, *Orientalism* (1978; New York: Vintage Books, 1979).

Edward Said, 'Conrad: the Presentation of Narrative', in *The World, The Text and The Critic* (1984; London: Vintage, 1991).

Edward Said, *Culture and Imperialism* (London: Chatto & Windus, 1993).

Spenser St. John, *The Life of Sir James Brooke, Rajah of Sarawak* (Edinburgh: William Blackwood, 1879).

Gladys Gaik-choo Saw, 'The Works of Sir Hugh Clifford: a Literary and Biographical Approach', Unpublished MA Thesis, University of Malaya, 1969.

Norman Sherry, *Conrad's Eastern World* (Cambridge: Cambridge University Press, 1966).

Norman Sherry, *Conrad: The Critical Heritage* (London: Routledge & Kegan Paul, 1973).

Linda M. Shires, 'The "Privileged" Reader and Narrative Methodology in *Lord Jim*', *Conradiana*, 17.1 (1985), 19–30.

Allan Simmons, 'Ambiguity as Meaning in Joseph Conrad's Fiction', Unpublished Ph.D. Thesis, University of London, 1991.

David Simpson, *Fetishism and Imagination: Dickens, Melville, Conrad* (Baltimore: The Johns Hopkins University Press, 1982).

David Simpson (ed.), *Subject to History: Ideology, Class, Gender* (Ithaca: Cornell University Press, 1991).

Iain Sinclair, *Lights out for the Territory* (London: Granta, 1997).

Maureen Sioh, 'Authorizing the Malaysian Rainforest: Configuring Space, Contesting Claims and Conquering Imaginaries', *Ecumene*, 5.2 (1998), 144–67.

Barbara Herrnstein Smith, *On the Margins of Discourse: the Relation of Literature to Language* (Chicago: University of Chicago Press, 1978).

Julie R. Solomon, '"To Know, To Fly, To Conjure": Situating Baconian Science at the Juncture of Early Modern Modes of Reading', *Renaissance Quarterly*, vol. 44 (1991), 513–58.

David E. Sopher, *The Sea-Nomads: a Study of the Maritime Boat People of Southeast Asia* (Singapore: National Museum, 1977).

Patricia Meyer Spacks, *Gossip* (New York: Alfred A. Knopf, 1985).

Thomas Sprat, *History of the Royal Society* (1667; reprinted London: Routledge and Kegan Paul, 1959).

J. H. Stape and Owen Knowles (eds), *A Portrait in Letters: Correspondence to and About Conrad* (Amsterdam: Rodopi, 1996).

John Splinter Stavorinus, *Voyages to the East Indies* (London: 1798).

Niels Steengaard, *The Asian Trade Revolution of the Seventeenth Century: the East India Company and the Decline of the Caravan Trade* (Chicago: University of Chicago Press, 1973).

A. J. Stockwell, 'Sir Hugh Clifford's Early Career (1863–1903)', JMBRAS 49.1 (1976), 89–112.

A. J. Stockwell, 'The White Man's Burden and Brown Humanity: Colonialism and Ethnicity in British Malaya', *Southeast Asian Journal of Social Science*, 10.1 (1982), 44–68.

Nina Pelikan Strauss, 'The Exclusion of the Intended from Secret Sharing in Conrad's *Heart of Darkness*, *Novel*, 20 (1987), 123–37.

Frank Swettenham, *Malay Sketches* (1895).

Anne Tagge, 'The Butterfly Hunters', *Conradiana*, 28.3 (Autumn 1996), 182–89.

Anne Tagge, '"A Glimpse of Paradise": Feminine Impulse and Ego in Conrad's Malay World', *Conradiana*, 29.2 (Summer 1997), 101–12.

Nicholas Tarling, 'British Policy in the Malay Peninsula and Archipelago 1824–1871', *Journal of the Malayan Branch of the Royal Asiatic Society*, vol. xxx, pt.1 (October 1957),

Nicholas Tarling, *Anglo-Dutch Rivalry in the Malay World, 1780–1824* (Sydney, 1962).

Nicholas Tarling, *Piracy and Politics in the Malay World: a Study of British Imperialism in Nineteenth-Century South-East Asia*, (Melbourne: F. W. Cheshire, 1963).

Nicholas Tarling, *A Concise History of Southeast Asia* (New York/London: Frederick A. Praeger, 1966).

Nicholas Tarling, *Britain, the Brookes and Brunei* (Oxford: Oxford University Press, 1971).

Nicholas Tarling, *Sulu and Sabah: a Study of British Policy towards the Philippines and North Borneo from the Late Eighteenth Century* (Kuala Lumpur: Oxford University Press, 1978).

Nicholas Tarling (ed.), *The Cambridge History of Southeast Asia*, vols I and II (Cambridge: Cambridge University Press, 1992).

D. J. M. Tate, *Rajah Brooke's Borneo* (Hong Kong: John Nicholson, 1988).

G. M. Tate, *Rajah Brooke's Borneo* (Hong Kong: John Nicholson, 1988).

Teng Hong-Shu, 'Conrad and Conspiracy', Unpublished Ph.D. Thesis, University of London, 1999.

William Thorn, *The Conquest of Java* (London, 1812).

K. G. Tregonning (ed.), *Papers in Malayan History* (Singapore: University of Malaya Press, 1962).

Carl Trocki, *Prince of Pirates: The Temenggongs and the Development of Johor and Singapore, 1784–1885* (Singapore: Singapore University Press, 1979).

David Trotter, 'Colonial Subjects', *Critical Quarterly*, 32.3 (1990).

C. Mary Turnbull, *A Short History of Malaysia, Singapore and Brunei* (Singapore: Graham Brash, 1981).

Dirk van Hogendorp, *A Description of Java and its Principal Productions ...* (1800).

Betty Vanderweilen, 'Gender Performance in *Victory*', *Conradiana*, 26.2/3 (Autumn 1994), 201–10.

Arnold van Gennep, *La formation des légendes* (Paris: Ernest Flammarion, 1910).

J. C. van Leur, *Indonesian Trade and Society* (The Hague: Van Hoeve, 1955)

Hans van Marle, 'Jumble of Facts and Fiction: the First Singapore Reaction to *Almayer's Folly'*, *Conradiana* 10.2 (1978), 161–6.

Brian Vickers (ed.), *Francis Bacon* (Oxford: Oxford University Press, 1996).

A. R. Wallace, *A Narrative of Travels on the Amazon and Rio Negro* (London: Ward, Locke, & Co., 1889).

A. R. Wallace, *The Malay Archipelago* (1869; 3rd ed. London: Macmillan, 1872).

A. R. Wallace, *My Life: a Record of Events and Opinions*, 2 vols (London: Chapman & Hall, 1905).

Wang Gungwu, 'The Opening of Relations Between China and Malacca, 1403–5' in J. Bastin (ed.), *Malayan and Indonesian Studies* (Oxford: Clarendon, 1964), 87–104.

James Francis Warren, *The Sulu Zone 1768–1898: the Dynamics of External Trade, Slavery and Ethnicity in the Transformation of a Southeast Asian Maritime State* (Singapore: Singapore University Press, 1981).

James Francis Warren, 'Joseph Conrad's Fiction as Southeast Asian History: Trade and Politics in East Borneo in the Late Nineteenth Century', *The Brunei Museum Journal* (1977), 21–34

C. T. Watts (ed.), *Joseph Conrad's Letters to Cunninghame Graham* (Cambridge: Cambridge University Press, 1969).

Cedric Watts, *The Deceptive Text: an Introduction to Covert Plots* (Brighton: Harvester Press, 1984).

Russell West, 'Travel and the failure(s) of Masculinity in *Almayer's Folly* and *An Outcast of the Islands'*, *L'Epoque Conradienne* (1997), 11–28.

Paul Wheatley, *Impressions of the Malay Peninsula in Ancient Times* (Singapore: Eastern University Press, 1964).

Andrea White, *Joseph Conrad and the Adventure Tradition: Constructing and Deconstructing the Imperial Subject* Cambridge: Cambridge University Press, 1993).

Patrick Williams and Laura Chrisman (eds), *Colonial Discourse and Post-Colonial Theory: A Reader* (Sussex: Harvester, 1993).

R. O. Winstedt (ed.), *The Malay Annals or Sejarah Melayu*, JMBRAS, XVI.iii (1938).

R. O. Winstedt, *a History of Malaya* (Kuala Lumpur: Marican, 1988).

Mark A. Wollaeger, *Conrad and the Fictions of Skepticism* (Stanford: Stanford University Press, 1990).

R. S. Woolhouse, *The Empiricists* (Oxford: Oxford University Press, 1988).

C. E. Wurtzburg, *Raffles of the Eastern Isles* (London: Hodder & Stoughton, 1954).

Zawiah Yahya, *Resisting Colonialist Discourse* (Kuala Lumpur: Universiti Kebangsaan Malaysia, 1994).

Robert Young, *White Mythologies: Writing History and the West* (London: Routledge, 1990).

Robert Young, *Colonial Desire: Hybridity in Theory, Culture and Race* (London: Routledge, 1995).

Index